THE ACT OF LIVING

MW00352418

THE ACT OF LIVING

Street Life, Marginality, and
Development in Urban Ethiopia

Marco Di Nunzio

CORNELL UNIVERSITY PRESS **ITHACA AND LONDON**

Copyright © 2019 by Cornell University

All rights reserved. Except for brief quotations in a review, this book, or parts thereof, must not be reproduced in any form without permission in writing from the publisher. For information, address Cornell University Press, Sage House, 512 East State Street, Ithaca, New York 14850. Visit our website at cornellpress.cornell.edu.

First published 2019 by Cornell University Press

Library of Congress Cataloging-in-Publication Data
Names: Di Nunzio, Marco, 1984– author.
Title: The act of living : street life, marginality, and development in urban Ethiopia / by Marco Di Nunzio.
Description: Ithaca : Cornell University Press, 2019. | Includes bibliographical references and index.
Identifiers: LCCN 2018050332 (print) | LCCN 2018051959 (ebook) | ISBN 9781501735134 (e-book pdf) | ISBN 9781501735530 (e-book epub/mobi) | ISBN 9781501735127 | ISBN 9781501735127 (hardcover) | ISBN 9781501736261 (pbk.)
Subjects: LCSH: Marginality, Social—Ethiopia—Addis Ababa. | Street life—Ethiopia—Addis Ababa. | Poor—Ethiopia—Addis Ababa. | Informal sector (Economics)—Ethiopia—Addis Ababa. | Addis Ababa (Ethiopia)—Social conditions. | Addis Ababa (Ethiopia)—Economic conditions. | Ethnology—Ethiopia—Addis Ababa.
Classification: LCC HN789.A93 (ebook) | LCC HN789.A93 D56 2019 (print) | DDC 307.1/41209633—dc23
LC record available at https://lccn.loc.gov/2018050332

Contents

Illustrations

Acknowledgments

This book is the product of a long journey to which many people have contributed. First of all, I thank the Wenner Gren Foundation, the Institute of Social and Cultural Anthropology, Wolfson College and All Souls College at the University of Oxford, the British Institute in Eastern Africa in Nairobi, and the Fondation Wiener Anspach and Fond National de la Recherche Scientifique in Brussels for their support of the different stages of my research in Addis.

In Addis Ababa, I was affiliated with the Institute of Ethiopian Studies and the Department of Sociology at Addis Ababa University and the Centre Française d'Etudes Ethiopiennes. I am deeply grateful to Aklilu Yilma, Zelalem Teferra, Ezana Amdework, Selam Esayas, and David Ambrosetti for their support and understanding. Wondwosen Admassu, Seble Ayalew, and Nolawit Teshome helped me with my archival research on crime and urban life in Addis Ababa. Without their help, I never would have been able to write a history of street life. The care and companionship of Marco Pittalis, Alessia Villannuci Mattia Grandi, Elisa Barracu, Marianella Lippi, Graziano Savà, and Kate Fayers Kerr made my life in Addis Ababa more joyful, especially when my ethnographic restlessness became overwhelming. I owe my knowledge of Amharic to the kindness and devotion of the teachers of the Joint Language School in Addis Ababa. Among them, Yenesaw Wasihun assisted me and supported me as both a friend and an attentive mentor.

The generosity of my neighbors and friends in Arada, their willingness to help me in my research, and their patience in listening to and answering my insistent and naive questions allowed me to learn much more than I had anticipated during the initial stages of my research. My friends Tadious Genebera and Wasihun Gebre and my research assistant Zelalem Yilma made me feel at home and welcome. The people in the book I name Fasil, Teshome, Wondimu, Gizachew, Fatima, Sara, and Netsanet were always ready and open to talk to me about their lives and experiences. The men I call Ibrahim, Mikias, and Haile deserve a special mention. They were my source of inspiration in Addis Ababa and continue to inspire me in life more broadly. This book is a testament to your search for open-endedness, living, and hope. Your friendship and trust are humbling and precious to me.

Over the years I received mountains of generous comments and suggestions. Laura Camfield, always prompt with comments and suggestions, supported and advised me at the early stages of my research. I am deeply grateful to Shiferaw

Bekele, Bahru Zewde, Yeraswork Admassie, Andreas Samuel Admassie, Julian Taddesse, Semeneh Ayelew, Simeneh Betreyohannes, Shimelis Bonsa, Dagmawi Yimer, Fasil Giorghis, Elias Yitbarek, Zegeyye Chernet, Bisrat Kifle, Rahel Shawl, Alula Pankhurst, Sarah Vaughan, Catherine Dom, Lovise Aalen, René Lefort, and Kjetil Tronvoll for insightful discussions on Ethiopia, its present, past, and future. Michelle Osborn, Abby Hardgrove, Neil Carrier, Jacob Wiebel, Ewa Majczak, and Marlene Schafers read early versions of the chapters of the book and offered precise and inspiring comments.

I am indebted to Jim Lance at Cornell University Press for believing in my book when it was a draft manuscript and for always being ready with helpful and joyful advice. The two anonymous reviewers provided insightful comments and advice that helped me tease out more effectively the complexities and tensions of the act of living. Henrik Vigh and Jonny Steinberg read an early version of this manuscript and provided helpful feedback and encouragement. You have both been of such great inspiration. Special thanks go to Fatima Raja, who helped me find the words when I did not have them.

An early version of chapter 8 was published as "Embracing Uncertainty: Young People on the Move in Addis Ababa's Inner City" in the volume *Ethnographies of Uncertainty in Africa*, edited by Elizabeth Cooper and David Pratten and published in 2015 by Palgrave Macmillan. The comments I received in the process of writing and rewriting that chapter, in particular by Elizabeth Cooper, helped me shape my understanding of open-endedness and uncertainty. Extracts from chapter 1 appeared in "Marginality as a Politics of Limited Entitlements: Street Life and the Dilemma of Inclusion in Urban Ethiopia," *American Ethnologist* 44, no. 1 (2017): 91–103. Parts of chapter 4 were published in "Thugs, Spies and Vigilantes: Community Policing and Street Politics in Inner City Addis Ababa," *Africa* 84, no. 3 (2015): 444–465. Extracts from chapters 4 and 7 were originally written for a piece called "'Do Not Cross the Red Line': The 2010 General Election, Dissent and Political Mobilization in Urban Ethiopia," *African Affairs* 113, no. 452 (2014): 409–430. I wish to thank the editors and anonymous reviewers of these journals for their advice.

I owe a lot to the institutions where I have been based over the years. At the Università di Napoli "L'Orientale," Andrea Manzo, Alessandro Triulzi, Cristina Ercolessi, and the late Rodolfo Fattovich inspired me as a young student and taught me about the importance of combining passion and commitment in the study of history and politics. At the Università degli Studi di Torino, I owe to Pier Paolo Viazzo my commitment to ethnography. At the University of Oxford, I was fortunate to mold my anthropology and thinking on Ethiopia at the Institute of Social and Cultural Anthropology and the African Studies Centre. David Anderson, Marcus Banks, Wendy James, and David Turton gave me invaluable advice and guidance. I was blessed to be part of the discussions and debates at the Horn of Africa Seminar and to share that forum with Toni Weis, Julianne Parker Weis, Jason Mosley, and Iginio Gagliardone. At the Laboratoire d'Anthropologie des Mondes Contemporains at the Université libre de Bruxelles, I was honored and fortunate to have the support of my colleagues Joel Noret and Pierre Petit and my friend Hannah Hoechner, and the comradeship of the ABBA gang, in particular Denis Regnier and Laurent Legrain. At LSE Cities at the London School of Economics, I am deeply grateful to Ricky Burdett, who ensured I was able to write the final revisions of this book. I am thankful for the support and encouragement of Philipp Rode, Nuno Ferreira Da Cruz, Suzi Hall, Claire Mercer, Sue Parnell, and Eyob Balcha Gebremariam as well as Deborah James, who provided me with the encouragement to ask for what I needed to complete the book. Finally, I want to thank Insa Nolte, Keith Shear, Kate Skinner, Benedetta Rossi, Juliet Gilbert, Leslie Fesenmyer, Reginald Cline-Cole, and Max Bolt at the Department of African Studies and Anthropology at the University of Birmingham for their encouragement. I look forward to many discussions to come.

Friendship has been my keystone during the process of writing this book. I owe a lot to my partners in crime Sara Marzagora, Davide Chinigò, Diego Maria Malara, and Alessandro Jedlowski; to my mates Olly Owen and Insa Koch; and to my brother from another mother, Simone Montella. Without the support, the encouragement, and the example of my mentors, I would have been lost and this book unfinished. I owe much to David Pratten, who attentively guided me throughout this journey, showing me ways of dealing with the challenges I encountered and teaching me how to write the complexities of what I witnessed during my ethnography. Dinah Rajak has been a model of scholarship and engagement and a thoughtful, concerned, and supportive friend and mentor. David Berliner helped me navigate the hard years of writing. His wit, unconditional support, and belief in shaping anthropology so as to make sense of the multifaceted nature of the human have guided my scholarship, kept me sane, and inspired many of this book's reflections on the act of living. A special mention goes to the late Mathieu Hilgers, a friend and mentor whose brilliance and advice I deeply miss.

I dedicate this book to those people who mean the most to me. To my father, Arcangelo, and my mother, Mariacira, who taught me the sense of justice and love for humankind. To my sister Adelaide, with whom I shared dreams and beautiful experiences of growing up. And to Emma as always, who inspired me to keep writing this book and whose love, imagination, and care make me every day happier.

Glossary

Amharic words in the text appear in their singular form.

abbat: father

adegegna bozene: dangerous vagrants

ammet bal: holiday

Arada: name of the inner city

Arada: a smart person

arakie: strong local brandy

bale-wuqabe: person with a relationship with a spirit (*wuqabe*)

bammilo: thug realism

bergo: cheap hotel

birr: Ethiopia's currency

čaqquli: hurry

čebeta: squeezed

čebu: stealing after hitting the victim on the back of the neck

chewa: good, genuine guy

č'iggir: problem

č'inqet: stress, worry

čista: broke

COOPI: Cooperazione Internazionale I (nongovernmental organization)

debtera: religious expert

Derg: "the committee"; the military junta that ruled Ethiopia between 1974 and 1991

duriye: thug

EC: Ethiopian calendar

EPRDF: Ethiopian People's Revolutionary Democratic Front

EPRP: Ethiopian People's Revolutionary Party

faranjii: foreigner

farra: country bumpkin

ganja: cannabis

gashe: term of address to an elderly man

geta: lord

GTZ: German Technical Cooperation (now GIZ)

gujbet: broke

habesha: Ethiopian

hardegna: hard man / gangster

hilinna: conscience

idil: chance

joffe: a hustler

IMF: International Monetary Fund

injera: Ethiopian pancake

inqisiqase: move around

khat: plant with a mild narcotic effect chewed across East Africa and the Middle East

khat bet: *khat* chewing house

kibur: respect

krar: Ethiopian lyre

listro: shoeshine boy

manfas: spirit

Meison: Amharic acronym of All Ethiopia Socialist Movement (AESM)

mella: a way of getting by

mirča: choice

NEBE: National Electoral Board of Ethiopia

NGO: nongovernmental organization

ruffiano: sycophant

ṣäṣät: repentance

sefer: neighborhood

taj bet: honeywine drinking house

tanqway: sorcerer / fortune teller / medium

tara askabari: queue keepers, minibus touts

tigab: arrogance

TPLF: Tigray People's Liberation Front

video bet: video house / video parlor

yeArada kwankwa: Arada's slang

yemot midib: "those who are destined to die"; a gang in Arada

THE ACT OF LIVING

INTRODUCTION

Men make their own history, but they do not make it as they please.

—Karl Marx, *The Eighteen Brumaire of Louis Bonaparte*

Each man is unique, so that with each birth something uniquely new comes into the world.

—Hannah Arendt, *The Human Condition*

The Act of Living

This book is about the tension between becoming and history, action and contingency, under enduring conditions of marginality and subjugation. The title of this book, *The Act of Living*, situates that tension in the experience of living, meant not as merely surviving but as an act caught between the predicament of being defined by contingency and the quest to transcend the circumstances of one's place in history (Das 2007; Rorty 1989). By narrating marginality through the tension of living, this book does not intend to celebrate the inherent capacity of the weak to resist (De Certeau 1984). Nor does it describe how the marginalized and excluded reproduce their condition of marginality by trying to transcend it (cf. Bourdieu 1977; Bourgois 2003; Willis 1977). Rather, it documents how action and living are made up of attempts to be something other than one's constraints while remaining firmly embedded within experiences of subjugation and exclusion (Jackson 1989, 2005). This is a tension that remains fundamentally unresolved. Yet, as it endures unresolved, this tension is a fertile terrain for the elaboration of existential and moral concerns about open-endedness, respect, chance, the self, and the future.

These moral and existential concerns that pervade the act of living go beyond the self. They trigger the proliferation of claims and demands about development, marginality, the political, and the future (Das 2007). Living, however, is not inherently "political" in the sense of being an expression of disagreement or the imagination of the open-endedness of collective futures (Arendt 1958). Rather, it is the circumstances in which living occurs, and the unfolding of that tension between becoming and history, action and contingency, that make existence

1

potentially political. Thus, this book is about the tensions of living, as well as the specific circumstances in which the experiences of living documented in these pages are situated. It considers how, despite apparently favorable circumstances of change and transformation, economic growth and development continue to fail the urban poor and their hopes of improvement, empowerment, and emancipation. *The Act of Living* documents the ordinary dimension of existence under the effects of this failed promise of growth. It also investigates whether the existential and moral concerns that enable people to live within marginality can help us imagine development alternatives and a more just future.

I embark on this journey by following two men, aged forty-nine and thirty-nine, whom I call, respectively, "Haile" and "Ibrahim," as they seek to navigate their condition of marginality. Born in Arada, Addis Ababa's inner city, between the 1960s and the 1970s, Haile and Ibrahim witnessed their country, Ethiopia, lift itself from being the global symbol of famine, poverty, and crisis in the 1980s and early 1990s to become the paradigmatic African success story by the early 2010s. Amid this transformation Haile and Ibrahim also experienced changes, not in their individual destinies but in their relation with the fortunes of Ethiopia. Growing up during a period of economic stagnation—the 1970s and 1980s—the two men had learned to recognize their own condition of poverty and marginality as the effect of widely shared experiences of exclusion and scarcity. As their country seemed to flourish and high-rise steel-and-glass buildings began popping up in Addis Ababa's wealthier neighborhoods, however, Haile's and Ibrahim's condition of marginality persisted. For them and many of their peers in inner city Addis, marginality was no longer an experience of a widely shared condition of scarcity but a sense of being out of tune with history.

The Act of Living explores why people like Haile and Ibrahim were not empowered by economic growth and how they understood and acted on the endurance of their condition of marginality in a time of promise. I show how marginality is not simply an arbitrary side effect or an unintentional consequence (cf. Gupta 2012; Ferguson 1994) of economic growth and development. It is, rather, a political product and a historical outcome contingent on the ways policies, interventions, and other acts of government have made marginality the terms of the integration of the poor into economic growth and development. I show how practices of street smartness and existential moves to embrace uncertainty constituted the paradigms, or the genres (Berlant 2011), for living within a tight nexus of marginality and political subjugation. These modes of existence and practice represented an attempt to live meaningfully through enduring subjugation while maintaining a sense of promise and open-endedness that economic growth had denied them.

Haile and Ibrahim shared their cultivation of smartness and their search for open-endedness not only with each other but also with a wide range of others who dotted their existence and affected the unfolding of their act of living. Growing up in a condition of enduring poverty, Haile and Ibrahim by their midteens had taken their first steps into the street economy of hustling and getting by. In doing so, they did not just find means of surviving or even a certain form of economic independence. They joined a wider community of shared practices within which they built networks of friends and peers and developed a deep sense of self-worth by embodying a notion of inner city smartness. This smartness was embodied in the concept of *being Arada*, after the historical inner city area where my informants lived. This was not just a matter of homonymy; it expressed the inherent connection that my informants felt existed between the urban history of poverty and scarcity in the inner city and the ideas of smartness and sophistication they cultivated. Rather than merely signaling their allegiance to the urban (cf. Ferguson 1999), *being Arada* voiced the deep fascination they felt with the ability of the hustler to make do and, importantly, with his or her capacity to live smartly and toughly through a condition of marginality and exclusion.

Cultivating street smartness enabled Haile, Ibrahim, and their peers to navigate their condition of subjugation and oppression but not to transcend it. Smartness operated *within* the limits of marginality and exclusion. Their lives, however, did not exclusively revolve around hustling. Haile and Ibrahim were proud to see themselves as *Arada*, yet, since their early twenties, they had been looking for a change, often away from the streets of the inner city. In their respective quests for change, Haile and Ibrahim learned to combine smartness with an appreciation of the potentialities of the unexpected, the uncertain, and the unknown. When I met the two for the first time in January 2010, I observed that smartness and the search for open-endedness coexisted in their everyday lives, setting a double tempo to the pace of their existence (cf. Vigh 2006). Smartness gave them the skills to get by and to navigate the known coordinates of their condition of marginality. Appreciating—or even embracing—the unknown and uncertain enabled them to cultivate the possibility that their present existence of subjugation and exclusion could have an open end.

The search for open-endedness is inspired by an appreciation of the future as indeterminate and unknown, yet it is a practice and a mode of existence that is particularly grounded in the present—namely, in the experience of being *present* (De Martino 2002) and alive in the here and now. Talking about the challenges he had encountered getting by on the streets and trying to become something other than what had been assigned to him by birth, Ibrahim told me: "Marco, living is the most important thing. We have this life, we live it." For Ibrahim and many others whose stories I tell in the book, living was important because staying alive was the ultimate condition for being able to turn the unexpected and the uncertain into possibility. The experience of being alive gave them the sense they still had time to pursue trajectories that were different from the destiny of poverty toward which they felt their lives might be heading. Living contained the seeds of open-endedness, possibility, and reversibility, because while we live, no final judgment can be made of who we are and what our lives have been about. Only death is final and irreversible (Glover 1990).

With this analysis, this book joins an existing ethnographic critique of the anthropological and philosophical temptation to operationalize Aristotle's distinction between a life of just living (*zoë*) and a life of actions (*bios*) to understand the predicaments of the marginalized (Das 2007; Holston 2008; cf. Fassin 2009). Philosophers such as Agamben have argued that the desire to be and to persist is easily exploited and exploitable. This is because the subject's attachment to life contains a fundamental predicament. As Hegel argued a long time ago, the lives of the marginalized, the subjugated, and the excluded are made possible through the very relations of power that constrain them. When life assumes an intrinsic value and survival becomes the main concern of the subject, the individual is caught in the mechanisms governing the reproduction of regimes of political subjugation and the cycle of capitalist production (Arendt 1958; Agamben 1998). This is a "life," philosophers and anthropologists alike (Piot 2010; Appadurai 2013) have argued, of "just living" that strips human beings of the exclusive human capacity to act beyond expectations and "perform what is infinitely improbable" (Arendt 1958, 178).

By narrating the life trajectories of my informants over the three to four decades of their existence, I argue there is not much to gain in making a distinction between a life of "just living" and a life of action. Getting by and surviving are not mere experiences of letting oneself live and breathe. They are what ultimately enables the actualization of existence as a site of possibility and reversibility. The attempts and trajectories of people keeping themselves alive and trying to be something other than their constraints are important and often unaccounted components of the making of history—the ultimate domain of human action.

In arguing this, however, I seek to expand what we mean by history. I contend that our understanding of history and the ways life trajectories of the marginalized intertwine with it cannot be exclusively about searching for and examining those conjunctures when young and marginalized people come into the light, take the stage of history, and drive moments of political unrest. Studies on youth and the marginalized in Africa have contended that young people's attempts to deal with the pain and anxiety emerging from their inability to fulfill their aspirations have triggered new paradigms, identities, and subjectivities that shape not only the lives of the marginalized but also, potentially, the making of history (Honwana and de Boeck 2005; Abbink and van Kessel 2005). In Madagascar, the *jeunes* (the wide range of identities young people have adopted in urban contexts) were believed to be behind regime change in 2009 (Cole 2010). In Côte d'Ivoire, *nouchi* urban culture shaped the paradigms of *Ivorianité* that framed the 2002 conflict (Newell 2012). In Ethiopia, the predicaments of unemployed youth were highlighted as the engine of riots in 2005 (Mains 2012a, 2012b). More recently, activism and protests by rural and urban youth in the southern region of Oromia between 2014 and 2016[1] have been seen as the main trigger behind a moment of reform in Ethiopia, beginning with the appointment of Abiy Ahmed as Prime Minister in March 2018.[2] My ethnography does not question the validity of these assessments. At the same time, I contend that our understanding of how life and history intertwine depends also on our ability to appreciate the historicity of the ordinary and the everyday, as both situated in history and affecting the unfolding of history (Das 2007).

In an interview with Antonio Negri, Gilles Deleuze distinguished between history and becoming (Deleuze 1990). "History" amounts to a succession of before and after. "Becoming" runs together with history, and it is made of actions and experiences that have not produced regime changes, shifts in the systems of production, or a reconfiguration in the distribution of resources. Yet they are *historical facts* that proliferate under the surface and constitute the connective tissue between the everyday life, the ordinary, the "political," and the unfolding of long-term social and economic processes (Das 2007).

I take this distinction as a useful starting point to examine how wider political, social, and economic processes shaped my informants' personal experiences of becoming, as well as to point out the impacts that poor people's attempts to be something else than their constraints have on history. History, I will show, pervaded my informants' experiences of living, shaping the terrains and the circumstances of their actions as well as the conceptual boundaries of their imaginations. Becoming affects history cumulatively (Johnson-Hanks 2006; Cole 2010; Sewell 2005). Individual experiences of becoming, individual searches for open-endedness, and individual attempts to live meaningfully through marginality and exclusion unevenly affect history. However, cumulatively and over time, these experiences of becoming have amounted to a long and undocumented history of endurance that has populated politics and remains incommensurable with the ways living and action have been governed. As a result, projects of domination, control, and development are rarely final and fully successful, but need to be constantly reiterated, reworked, recrafted, improved, expanded, and—as the history of Ethiopia shows—violently enforced.

---

1. "'Freedom!': The Mysterious Movement That Brought Ethiopia to a Standstill," *Guardian*, March 13, 2018, https://www.theguardian.com/global-development/2018/mar/13/freedom-oromo-activists-qeerroo-ethiopia-standstill.
2. "Ethiopia Seeks Calm with a New Leader," *New York Times*, March 28, 2018, https://www.nytimes.com/2018/03/28/world/africa/ethiopia-prime-minister-oromo.html.

Living in an African Success Story

The conjuncture of economic growth and development that Haile and Ibrahim witnessed, especially from the mid-2000s, was seen by commentators as a sort of miracle. In the early 1990s, business reports and media accounts, including the *Economist*, portrayed Africa's poverty as a threat to rich countries (Ferguson 1999; Jerven 2015). Twenty years later, they described Africa's economic growth as bringing the promise of an ongoing expansion of opportunities for investment and wealth creation around the globe (McKinsey Global Institute 2012; Accenture 2011; Knight Frank 2017). While the rest of the world was in recession, Africa was rising. Figures of annual gross domestic product (GDP) growth provided the grounds for this paradigm shift in representations of the continent and of some countries in particular that were seen to rise from the ashes of famine, civil war, and stagnation toward economic growth and political stability. Ethiopia was one of those countries. In the words of the *Time* business correspondent Michael Schuman, Ethiopia belonged to a new generation of emerging economies, PINE (Philippines, Indonesia, Nigeria, and Ethiopia), which would take the place of BRICS (Brazil, Russia, India, China, and South Africa) in the future. Ethiopia, with its steady economic growth, Schuman wrote, was a particularly exciting case: "Once synonymous with poverty, peace and strong management have turned the nation around."[3]

Because of its success, Ethiopia began to be described as a model in development circles and in parts of the academic community. A growing number of studies on developmental patrimonialism (Kelsall 2013) and poverty reduction (Devereux and Whyte 2010) cited Ethiopia and other African success stories, such as Rwanda and to some extent Uganda and Angola, as constituting a political and developmental laboratory for ideas and formulas for growth in the continent. For these scholars and development practitioners, the central role of the state in these economies was a key factor in their remarkable success and a sign of the emergence of an alternative to neoliberal orthodoxies of the market.

The persistence of Haile's and Ibrahim's condition of marginality and their sense of being out of tune can appear to contradict the sense of promise and hope pervading narratives of Africa rising. Liberal understandings of marginality and exclusion could even suggest that Haile and Ibrahim should share the blame if they were not able to profit from their country's favorable circumstances. However, growth, including state-led economic growth, and the existence of "alternatives" to the neoliberal orthodoxy of the market are not necessarily guarantees

---

3. Michael Schuman, "Forget the BRICs; Meet the PINEs," *Time*, March 13, 2014, accessed March 2, 2018, http://time.com/22779/forget-the-brics-meet-the-pines/.

of a more just society (cf. Ong 2006). Over the last twenty years in Ethiopia, inequality has deepened (UN-Habitat 2008a, 2010, 2017). Real incomes in urban areas have increased, but only for the wealthiest households have they risen significantly. The incomes of poorer households have actually declined (Bigsten and Negatu Makonnen 1999). As a result, while poor households have witnessed increased availability of goods and services in an expanded market, their ability to access them has actually decreased (Solomon Mulugeta 2006).

Moreover, the central role of the state—in particular, the Ethiopian People's Revolutionary Democratic Front (EPRDF), the party that has been in power since 1991—in managing the country's economy has not resulted in greater empowerment for the poor. Political stability and the ability of the ruling party to influence the economy have historically been grounded in a pervasive form of authoritarian politics, which constrained the emergence of competitors (Vaughan and Tronvoll 2003; Aalen and Tronvoll 2009; Abbink 2006; Tronvoll 2011) and the ability of ordinary citizens to express dissent and affect policy. Large-scale development programs that target the urban poor through the promotion of entrepreneurship programs, for instance, have not succeeded in reducing social inequality or opening spaces for political emancipation (Di Nunzio 2015a). However, over the years they increased the number of people directly and indirectly dependent on the EPRDF for their survival, fostering the expansion of the ruling party's apparatus of political mobilization, control, and surveillance (Chinigò 2014; Di Nunzio 2014a, 2014b; Emmenegger, Keno, and Hagmann 2011; Human Rights Watch 2010a, 2010b; Lefort 2010, 2012).

Ethiopia is going through a process of political reform and opening, led by the new Prime Minister Abiy Ahmed. Members of opposition parties have been released from prison and restrictions on media and civil society lifted, resulting in a wave of optimism and hope across the country. Whether these reforms will entail a radical rethinking of Ethiopia's developmental model and whether the greater enjoyment of political rights will result in an increased ability of people at the bottom of urban and rural societies to affect policy is unclear. While opposition politicians, journalists and media activists have seen their room for maneuvering increase, the apparatus of political control and mobilization that the ruling party has built over the past twenty-five years to ground itself at the bottom of urban and rural societies in the country remains largely in place. The effectiveness of this conjuncture of reform will depend on whether the new EPRDF administration will be able to address the shortcomings of the previous ones and implement policies and interventions that result in greater political liberties and opportunities of social mobility for those at the bottom of urban and rural societies. As a reminder of the challenges ahead, this book focuses on the "recent past" of Ethiopia's success story. It examines how the pervasiveness of forms of political authoritarianism, the deepening of patterns of social differentiation, and the failure of development programs to deliver opportunities of social improvement have hindered desires and expectations for a better life at the bottom of urban society.

Even in the midst of political authoritarianism, narratives on growth and success were resilient to critique. There are many reasons for the resilience of this narrative of success, whether expressed by critically minded development practitioners, the national government, or institutions such as the International Monetary Fund (IMF) and the World Bank. One was of Ethiopia as both an "alternative" and an "African success story" (World Bank 2011). The other was the simplistic representation of neoliberalism as fundamentally opposed to the activism and interventionism of the state. This interpretation has had particular leverage in progressive scholarship and the debate on African success stories, with serious implications for the ways the debate on "alternative" visions of development have amounted to an endorsement of authoritarian regimes.

Anthropologists and scholars of governmentality have provided important correctives to the understanding of neoliberalism as antistate ideology. Neoliberalism is a political project about, and not against, crafting the state (Foucault 2008; Hilgers 2012; Wacquant 2010). Besides, and perhaps more importantly, this is not a monolithic political project that is simply to be adopted or refused. Neoliberalism is best understood as a set of ideological moves, policies, and assumptions that are employed and instrumentally evoked, often in combination with government practices and rationalities embedded in different and sometimes opposing political visions (Rose, O'Malley, and Valverde 2006; Ong 2006; Ferguson 2009; Collier 2012). From this perspective, Ethiopia's developmental experiment has not resulted in the emergence of an "alternative" to neoliberalism. Conversely, it demonstrates how national political elites elaborate visions of potential economic growth by combining their political and ideological concerns with ideas drawn from the international development agenda.

Notably, informed by Marxist-Leninist ideas of political centralism, the EPRDF (2006, 54) historically opposed liberalism. Yet its political documents and the writings of the late Meles Zenawi (2006), the longtime prime minister, party chair, and main ideologue, suggest that the party leadership has long appreciated the significance of combining opposing ideological principles, such as the idea of development as a political process, the dream of making Ethiopia a collectivist society, and the acceptance of the free market (Bach 2011; Vaughan 2011). The willingness of the new Prime Minister Abiy Ahmed to pursue a more thorough liberalization of the economy suggests that the current moment of change and reform might result in a more open embrace of the free market agenda. However, it remains to be seen how this new moment of reform will qualitatively transform Ethiopia's developmental experiment. The new course might result in a kinder assessment of liberalism, but probably not a complete rejection of EPRDF's previous attempts to provide a developmentalist synthesis of opposing political views.

From the 1990s onward, economic success, the spectacular transformation of the capital Addis Ababa, and, notably, the EPRDF's political and ideological synthesis increased Ethiopia's appeal for the international development community. Long before the recent moment of political opening and despite EPRDF's repressive and authoritarian politics, Ethiopia was a significant recipient of development aid. While the ruling party in Ethiopia pursued a politics of state building based on the strengthening of state bureaucracy and the expansion of the apparatus of political mobilization and control (cf. Aalen and Tronvoll 2009), aid rose from nearly US$1.6 billion in 2001 to US$3.5 billion in 2011. After decades-long narratives of crisis, state failure, and dysfunctionality, the trajectories of African countries like Ethiopia and the commitment of its leadership to development, including the adoption of World Bank and IMF-style policies, enabled international development institutions to claim a progressive role in Africa and in the developing world. Earlier discourses on crisis had forced development organizations and donors either to adopt pessimistic narratives regarding the future of the African continent or else to radically question the assumptions regarding the state, markets, and society on which these institutions operate. A "successful" Ethiopia gave the World Bank, IMF, and donors the sense that their formulas and policy directives were, ultimately, the right ones.

Having said that, this convergence between donors' prescriptions on growth and the EPRDF's developmental politics would not have been effective if, in spite of their specific ideological differences, the EPRDF, international donors, and external commentators did not also share similar normative and teleological understandings of development and change (Dereje Feyissa 2011; cf. Englund 2006). Business reports, media accounts, and some developmental literature have shown a tendency to regard political authoritarianism and growing social inequality as transitional phases and to argue that time is needed for economic growth to fully realize its potential.

With this perspective, informed commentators such as Alex De Waal (2013) invited scholars to give a fair hearing to the development vision of the late Meles Zenawi and to wait for it to be realized. That these selective representations of African political economies were widely shared is revealing. It bore witness to the extent of the wider consensus in development discourse on Africa and signalled the return of modernization theory to Africa after three decades of economic decline (cf. Ferguson 1999; Van De Walle 2016). Modernization theory, as Appadurai (2013) pointed out, relies on a "hidden ontology of trajectorism" (223)—that there is a succession of necessary steps a society should go through to achieve modernity, development, and prosperity. Political stability, economic growth, social equity, and the fair distribution of political and civil rights are prioritized in a sequence leading to the inevitable realization of a democratic, developed, and affluent society. Such exhortations to wait for modernity to be realized are rooted in a politics of time that, directly or indirectly, comes to justify whatever happens in the present as an inevitable step toward the future. The logic of these narratives is the logic of the trade-off. As "success stories" are made, praised, and celebrated, political authoritarianism and growing social inequalities are pushed into the background, while the benefits of economic growth are enumerated and emphasized. Authoritarianism in the present is thus endorsed as an inevitable step toward democracy in the future, just as growing social inequality is described as an inevitable effect of economic growth.

This argument has a long history in the ways development has been imagined on the African continent and beyond. During the financial crisis, for instance, the politics of austerity around the world, especially in southern Europe, argued for necessary sacrifices in the present to guarantee a future of growth, while actively rejecting more grounded and far-reaching measures to improve the living conditions of people experiencing social exclusion in the here and now. By focusing on the paradigmatic Ethiopian case, this book shows how this politics of time, which justified authoritarianism and social inequality as necessary steps toward development, was not only a matter of narratives and discourses. This policy materialized in the ways development programs carved out a social and political space at the bottom of urban society within which the urban poor were envisioned to live their lives and contribute to the making of an African success story.

This book is an assessment of the effects of this politics of space and a critique of the politics of time that informed it. Development's teleological politics of time have helped conceal and justify elite accumulation of power and wealth, while the politics of space have produced that complex nexus between marginality and political subjugation that failed Haile and Ibrahim's search for a better life in a moment of promise and development. In unpacking how economic growth produces subjugation, I document my informants' investment in open-endedness as their attempt to act on the endurance of their condition of oppression. I embrace this open-endedness as the paradigm of this book's ethnographic critique of teleological and normative understandings of development and change. As a form of radical empiricism, open-endedness is grounded in an appreciation of the fact that the future is indeterminate. It focuses on the lived experience in the present to assess and evaluate while suspending judgment on the future because of its fundamental indeterminacy. This stand is productive not only in the ways it enabled this book's protagonists to establish grounds for action but also in the ways it voiced an unequivocal call for reinstating social justice as a fundamental and indispensable criterion for critically assessing and imagining "development alternatives."

The Act of Living documents my informants' search for open-endedness by looking at ordinary and everyday experiences of becoming that proliferate under the surface. I document how a large number of people who had been excluded from enjoying the benefits of economic growth and had experienced decades of political authoritarianism elaborated a way of living through their condition of subjugation and marginality, while reinstating the possibility of being something other than their constraints. As Ethiopia is witnessing an unprecedented conjuncture of reform and promise, these stories still rarely surface in debates on the prospects of Ethiopia transitioning to an era of greater political and civil rights. Just as in the heyday of political authoritarianism, these stories of ordinary experiences of exclusion and marginality are essential. They remind us that the imagined future, whatever it is, can hardly be the term of reference for our evaluation of the present and that the promise of a better future is inherent in the arrangements that shape our present.

Regimes of Interconnectedness

Haile's and Ibrahim's condition of oppression and subjugation cannot be described as a straightforward experience of abandonment, as scholars like to describe marginality and exclusion (Agamben 1998; Appadurai 2013; Piot 2010). This does not mean, however, denying this condition of exclusion and marginality. Emphasizing abandonment and rejection can make us miss the "normalized" and "relational" dimensions of marginality. Besides, all the marginalized poor are exposed to humanitarian crisis or risk. For many, marginality is just part of the everyday, an ordinary experience of subjugation and oppression. Haile and Ibrahim were marginalized, but not in the sense that they lived at the margins of, or outside, society. The marginalized are part of the society in which they are marginalized: they are placed in this condition by a range of power relationships that define the terms of being inside society.

At first glance, conceptualizing marginality as lying inside might seem oxymoronic. However, marginality's apparent antonyms—integration, inclusion, and participation—are not straightforward guarantees of emancipation from oppression and subjugation. Inclusion can be instrumental in producing marginality and enforcing forms of subjugation and oppression (Henkle and Stirrat 2001; Levitas 1996). As well, abjection itself is not synonymous with rejection. As the anthropologist James Ferguson famously put it, disconnection implies a "relation and not the absence of relation" (1999, 238).

For Haile and Ibrahim, marginality was the double product of both the un-equal distribution of access to resources and the ways relationships of force, power relations, and the implementation of development programs have connected and integrated the urban poor, through forms of oppression and subjugation, to wider society (cf. Levitas 1996; Perlman 1976, 2004). I argue that my informants' experiences of marginality and exclusion are best understood as embedded in the production of forms and regimes of interconnectedness: the ways these urban poor are connected and integrated into wider society frames and defines their experiences and forms of marginality.

The production of interconnectedness is embedded in history. Social oppression and political subjugation have a long history. This book explores how Haile and Ibrahim were acted upon by a history of relations and policy interventions that firmly positioned them at the bottom of urban society. However, the fact that marginality endures does not mean that its persistence is due to structural inertia, continuity, and lack of change (cf. Bourdieu 1977). Continuity is itself a historical product. Likewise, marginality is a historical product that endures because it is in the constant "process of being produced" (Butler 1997, 93). As such, while there is nothing seemingly new about the existence of marginality and exclusion on the streets of inner city Addis Ababa, there is, however, something time-specific in experiences of marginality. This specificity, I argue, lies in the *forms* of interconnectedness being created.

The first form of interconnectedness concerns exclusion from access to resources and opportunities for social improvement. For most of their lives, the protagonists of this book occupied the lower tiers of the street economy and, at times, engaged in low-wage labor. Only occasionally were they able to access a higher level of street business, including fencing stolen goods and brokering, and the world of legit business was often too far in the horizon of their possibilities. Focusing on the experiences of my informants in the inner city, I show that their condition of social exclusion is a result of the cleavages within the city and its economies, which, in the eyes of my informants, determine who gets what, how he gets it, and through whom. This is an economy of relations where the volume and kinds of social and symbolic capital that people hold significantly affect how far they can go. In my informants' reckonings, the economy of opportunities and resources was dominated by the logic of "relatives with relatives, donkeys with ashes" (*zemed ka zemdu, aya ka amdu*); that is to say, people who are connected are likely to help each other, while those who are outside their networks are left with nothing but "ashes."

The second form results from the arrangements emerging from the implementation of development programs, especially those concerning entrepreneurship for the poor. These development schemes followed a moment of intense political conflict and disorder on the streets of Addis Ababa. In 2005, for the first time, opposition parties registered significant electoral success, particularly in the capital. The day after the election, the ruling party recognized the success of the opposition in Addis Ababa but declared it had won the election with support from the rural areas. This statement, which was followed by a ban on public demonstrations and a delay in the official declaration of the electoral results, triggered street protests in support of the opposition in June and again in November that year. The ruling party labeled the protesters as "dangerous vagrants" (*adegegna bozene*) and "unemployed youth" and responded with heavy-handed repression: more than two hundred people were killed in Addis Ababa and thirty thousand were detained in the capital and other major towns. Police repression and the criminalization of dissent were not the ruling party's only responses, however. In the years that followed, the implementation of development programs targeted what the government believed to be the main reason for political and social unrest among young people: their lack of employment. Through these programs, the ruling party sought to tackle the predicaments of Addis Ababa's marginalized youth and, by doing so, co-opt them.

Ibrahim and Haile were among the many who joined government entrepreneurship programs in the years after the 2005 riots, either out of fear of imprisonment or to make ends meet, or both. Ibrahim and, later, Haile joined one of the many cooperatives of car attendants—or as people say in Addis, "parking guys"—that the government established to give jobs to the city's "unemployed youth." Their jobs consisted of issuing parking tickets every half hour to cars parked on the streets assigned to them by the local government office (the *kebelle*, now called *woreda*) and collecting payments from drivers. By joining these programs, Haile and Ibrahim gained a regular monthly income but also became dependent on the government and the ruling party for their survival. Even though they were not supporters of the EPRDF, they understood that if they wanted to keep their jobs, they were expected—indeed, required—to act as supporters and to show up at meetings and rallies.

The implementation of development programs enabled the ruling party to expand its reach into the population, mobilizing a significant number of people and triggering a process of formalization that reconfigured the street economy as a terrain of economic practice and political action. At the same time, these programs did not necessarily affect the cleavages that limited Ibrahim's, Haile's, and their peers' access to business networks. As parking guys in government-supported cooperatives, Haile and Ibrahim still could not embark on trajectories of social mobility. They continued to be marginal actors of the city's and inner city's economies while experiencing the increased pervasiveness of the ruling party's apparatus of political control in their lives.

This combination of growing social inequality, persistent social exclusion, and enforced mobilization as part of the ruling party's developmental and political machine constituted the particular "regime of interconnectedness" that integrated Haile and Ibrahim into wider society. It is clear this was a particular kind of integration. Haile and Ibrahim had been integrated but could not fully negotiate the terms and conditions of their integration. Social inequality and failing development programs had carved a place at the bottom of urban society within which they, as part of the large constituency of the urban poor, were expected to live their lives and contribute to the overall development of the country. With their low wages and unskilled labor, Haile and Ibrahim became part of the ruling party's growing developmental service economy. With their compliance, the protagonists of the book, and many others, wittingly or unwittingly strengthened the ruling party, granted political elites overwhelming electoral victories, and enabled the political stability that commentators and donors lauded as the key factor underpinning economic growth in Ethiopia and its fellow African success stories.

Incommensurability and the Tension of the Subject

The story that this book tells does not begin and end with the moment when Haile, Ibrahim, and the street economy they have long inhabited with their hustling were incorporated into the political structures of the ruling party. The close interaction between my informants' everyday lives, the politics of the ruling party, and the broader transformation of the city's economy were part of the political and social arrangements on which the making of Ethiopia as an African success story was grounded. Yet, the lives of Ibrahim and Haile, like those of many others in Ethiopia, cannot be not fully understood if examined and narrated as a direct consequence of policies and development interventions. Their life trajectories are not stories of internalization and domestication. My informants were busy trying to find their own ways of navigating the society they lived in.

Ibrahim's and Haile's biographies cannot be confined to the five years between 2010 and 2015 when I knew them as parking guys in a government-supported cooperative. Before this, Ibrahim had been a promising student, a street fighter, a skillful hustler and thief, a manager of video houses, a specialized construction worker, a guard, an assistant carpenter, a stoneworker, and, for a short time, a successful shoe seller. The plurality and heterogeneity of the potential trajectories Ibrahim had engaged with over the years had made his life, as he himself reckoned it, long and intense.

Haile could also claim to have lived a long and intense life. He had been a student until fourteen years of age, then a pickpocket, a burglar, and a daily laborer at construction sites. With the collapse of the Derg, Ethiopia's socialist military junta from 1974 to 1991, he, like many other young people, tried to make his way out of the country. At the age of twenty-two he spent nine months as a refugee in Kenya. As soon as he realized that he was not going to be able to leave the continent, he returned to Addis Ababa. A new succession of possible lives followed. He worked as a manager of video houses, then enlisted as a soldier in the 1998–2000 Ethiopian-Eritrean war. After the war ended, Haile returned to Addis. His veteran status did not open up any particular social opportunities, and he found himself relying on his own means to get by. After a few years hustling on the street, he was invited to join a government-supported cooperative producing precast concrete blocks for construction sites. This work lasted as long as the government provided Haile's enterprise with contracts. When the enterprise eventually closed down, Haile joined Ibrahim in the cooperative of parking guys.

The multiplicity of experiences and engagements that composed the trajectories of their lives offers a picture that is significantly different from the common representation of youth and marginality as a condition of "crisis" (Cruise O'Brien 1996), "being stuck" (Hansen 2005), and "waiting" (M. Ralph 2008; Mains 2007, 2012a; Jeffrey 2010; Honwana 2012). The reason why these interpretations do not apply to the lives of the protagonists of this book is a particular sociological dimension of people's acts of "waiting" that often goes unaccounted for: those who wait are often those who *can* wait. In other words, waiting is viable for those who have access to an economy of exchanges, networks, and transactions that enable them to wait for what might be better social opportunities (Mains 2012a) and to "time" the unfolding of their existence toward the pursuit of desired social goals (Bledsoe 2002). For Haile and Ibrahim and many others in this book, waiting was simply not an option. When you do not have much, my informants taught me, it does not make much sense to spend time wondering about the future you wish for and then wait for it to come. Haile and Ibrahim did dream, but visions of a prefigured future of achieved aspirations were rarely imagined as actual plans to pursue. They were just dreams. What you can realistically hope for, my informants believed, is not an idealized idea of a "good life" (cf. Appadurai 2004, 2013) but simply a "better life." And if you want to get that "better life," they reckoned, you cannot stay still, waiting for it to appear. You must act or, as they put it, "move around" (*inqisiqase*).

Haile and Ibrahim had certainly had a life of moving around. Unfortunately, their "movement" has been "without motion" (Vigh 2006); it had not resulted in durable trajectories of social mobility. Scholars such as Arjun Appadurai

(2004, 2013) have argued that this lack of motion is due to the unequal distribution of the "capacity to aspire"—that is, the enacted capacity that poor people lack to map, plan, and then act toward the achievement of a desired social goal (Appadurai 2004, 2013). Before Appadurai, Bourdieu (1977) understood the persistence of conditions of marginality and exclusion as the product of the apparent coincidence between people's sense of the possible and their position in wider society. In other words, Bourdieu would argue, as Haile and Ibrahim moved around, the choices they made and the trajectories they embarked on to pursue their quests for social mobility "wittingly or unwittingly, willy-nilly" contributed to the reproduction of their condition of marginality and exclusion. Bourdieu argued that this happens because these practices and choices are a product of a modus operandi—the habitus—of which Haile and Ibrahim are not producers (1977, 79). For Bourdieu, such a modus operandi is naturalized and internalized through practice—that is, in the very moments when agents try to act on the circumstances of their lives.

Inspired by Bourdieu, Willis (1977) and Bourgois (2003) pointed out in their seminal ethnographies of young working-class men in Britain and Puerto Rican crack dealers in New York, respectively, that in contexts of oppression and exclusion the personal search for dignity and grounds for action often come to reproduce conditions of marginality. The attempts of young working-class men in Britain to resist and oppose the educational system that denied them recognition and respect, for instance, also cut them off from opportunities for social mobility through schooling. Likewise, among crack dealers in New York, engaging in the drug economy was an attempt to gain respect and an income but also reinforced the harsh conditions of social segregation, criminalization, and oppression that encompassed the lives of young Puerto Rican men in inner city New York.

In inner city Addis Ababa, my informants' engagement with the street economy and notions of street smartness emerged in opposition to their experiences of exclusion and categories of social differentiation. Like the crack dealers in New York and the working-class men in Britain, street hustlers in Arada were faced with the fact that their engagement with hustling and cheating, smartness, and toughness had not taken them anywhere other than the poor neighborhoods of inner city Addis Ababa. This ethnography, however, does not assume that my informants' sense of the possible coincides with their social position or that this coincidence is the independent variable in the reproduction of their condition of marginality and exclusion. I argue that the positions people occupy do not necessarily and fully determine their understandings of society and the self. Or rather, while the sense of what people can and cannot do is elaborated through their experience of power relations, this does not mean that the constraints imposed on them are internalized as given and natural.

The lack of "motion" is a product of the landscapes of relationships of power, patterns of social differentiation and regimes of political control, and the ways they constrained how far my informants could go with their "movement." However, the protagonists of this book kept moving in spite of their lack of motion. They did so because they could not do otherwise. Moving around was their key strategy for making ends meet, combining different incomes at the same time, and jumping from one activity to another as new opportunities for getting by arose. They kept moving for another important reason. When you have nothing to expect but continued exclusion and subjugation, the chance (*idil*) that can make your life better is fundamentally a stroke of luck. As such, this chance is indeterminate and unknown; it is hard to know what it might be, when it will come, and where it will take you. By moving around, my informants were trying to take advantage of this indeterminacy, keeping things open, and exposing themselves to the possibility of getting that chance.

Moving around has not challenged the long-term experiences of marginality and exclusion that encompassed my informants' existence. Yet the fact that the protagonists of this book kept moving bears witness to a tension in poor people's actions that studies on internalization and habitus have often left unaccounted. This is the realization and the experience of the tension that is at the center of this book's exploration of the act of living: trying to be and become something other than their constraints while living an existence that is firmly embedded in experiences of subjugation and exclusion (Jackson 1989, 2005). In philosophical terms, this is a tension that emerges from the fact that the subject is "*neither* fully determined by power nor *fully* determining of power" (Butler 1997, 18). Such incommensurability of power dynamics and the subject does not necessarily produce gaps, cracks, and interstices in which the agency of the marginalized can "trick" the broader landscape of power relations framing his or her existence (cf. de Certeau 1984). To fully make sense of the complex and ambivalent relations between power and the subject, Judith Butler (1997) suggests that we go beyond "politically sanctimonious forms of fatalism" or "naïve forms of political optimism" that conceptualize agency as always and only opposed to power (17) (see also Ortner 1995). The subject exceeds the logic of his or her making. However, "exceeding is not escaping, and the subject exceeds precisely that to which it is bound" (18). Caught in between, the subject is the site of a fundamental ambivalence: the subject is both "the *effect* of a prior power" and "the *condition of possibility* for a radically conditioned form of agency" (14).

As this ethnography shows, this tension and ambivalence remain fundamentally unresolved, making the experience of trying to be something other than one's constraints a painful one (Fanon [1952] 2008; Weiss 2005, 2009) and a cause of stress, anxiety, suffering, and strain. Yet, as this tension endures unresolved because of people's stubborn acts of moving around, it is fertile terrain for elaborating a repertoire of practices for living, assessing, criticizing, hiding, and bypassing. It was through this repertoire that my informants grounded their act of living in an ironic and cruel sense of realism (Berlant 2011; Weiss 2002), externalized "power" as something other than the self, and distanced themselves from what they identified as the sources of their predicaments—namely, the authoritarian politics of the ruling party and the inexplicable riches of the wealthy. These acts of realism, externalization, critique, and even "distancing" and disengagement are ways of relating to the broader political economy and therefore are neither forms of resistance (Scott 1985; de Certeau 1984) nor the internalization of structural constraints and technologies of control (Foucault 1979; Bourdieu 1977). Instead, they are acts embedded in an everyday exercise of reflexivity through which people position themselves in society, seek to act morally, live meaningfully (Das 2007; Lambek 2010; Fassin 2010, 2012; Jackson 2005; Biehl, Good, and Kleinman 2007), and ultimately cultivate a sense of incommensurability with notions of development that are supposed to govern and control their action and their lives.

Narrating incommensurability as the product of my informants' *act of living*, the terrain of a search for open-endedness, and the premises for an imagination of alternative visions of development is the ethnographic and political challenge that this book poses to dominant understandings of development and marginality. Incommensurability has theoretical implications for studies of exclusion and oppression, as it questions the assumption that marginality endures because poor people internalize the structures of power that oppress them. Incommensurability reveals that while economic growth triggers visions of abundance and wealth among the urban poor, political authoritarianism and pervasive forms of control and surveillance have a limited capacity to shape people's subjectivities and their understanding of society. Authoritarian regimes can be successful in enforcing compliance, but have been less so in making their ideas of society, order, and progress coincide with the desires of the general population (cf. Burawoy 2012). Ultimately, incommensurability shows how the marginalized are seeking to reinstate the sense of promise that economic growth has ultimately denied to them. This has direct effects on contemporary history and in particular on the current trajectories of economic growth and development in Africa. It reminds us that the making of African success stories has hardly addressed the range of desires, claims, and demands made by the urban poor and the marginalized. Witnessing and documenting such a disjuncture is not just a matter of enriching the investigation of historical processes with a "conscientious" representation of poor people's everyday lives (cf. Spivak 1999, 191; Roy 2011, 229). Making sense of the tensions and predicaments faced by ordinary citizens is key to imagining feasible, sustainable, and inclusive trajectories of development and change for the present and the future.

Two Lives, Three Men, and the Streets

When I began my fieldwork in late 2009, I knew I was interested in examining young people's experience of politics, protest, and repression in the years after the 2005 riots and demonstrations. In the first months of my fieldwork, I had to learn to recognize how the ruling party's politics had reinvented itself and was infiltrating everyday lives in Addis Ababa's poor neighborhoods. I had to understand that the social, economic, and cultural reality I had thought to be populated by "dangerous vagrants," "young people," and "unemployment"—concepts borrowed from government discourses on unrest and disorder—had a complexity and history that I would miss if I did not change my assumptions and terminology. In government discourse, "youth" and "unemployment" acted as signifiers (Durham 2000, 2004; Vigh 2006) of the governmental concern with controlling a large urban constituency that the ruling party had not only failed to understand or capture but also actively criminalized for its involvement in opposition politics.

People who populated the streets were not generic "young people." Some were young, or rather (as in Haile and Ibrahim's case) defined themselves as young, but what made them "dangerous" in the eyes of government officials was not their "youthful" dispositions or their lack of employment. My interlocuters had little in common with the educated youth who used family resources to stay unemployed while waiting for higher prestige office jobs (see chapter 1; Krishnan, Tesfaye Gebre Selassie, and Dercon 1998; Mains 2012a).[4] Instead, what made the protagonists of this book agents of disruption in the eyes of government officials was their enduring and highly visible presence in the urban space and involvement in street life.

---

4. Economists and anthropologists have pointed out that the unemployed are often very similar to public sector workers (Krishnan 1996, 174) in that many unemployed youth appear to be relatively highly educated (Krishnan, Tesfaye Gebre Selassie, and Dercon 1998; Mains 2012a). Such links between education and unemployment have suggested that unemployment is not only a matter of absence of work. The rise in education has corresponded to an increase in social expectations. Educated young people, in this regard, seek public sector jobs rather than taking employment in the informal private sector or becoming self-employed. However, the reduction in employment available in the public sector under the impact of neoliberal policies has resulted in a decrease in the opportunities that educated young people have to fulfill those expectations. In this context, aspiring for a public sector job has, in fact, a significant effect on the probability of being unemployed.

The street is a place populated by many: individuals pass by, busy with their errands; street vendors sell their wares; street children shine shoes or sell tissues and chewing gum; old men and women beg for food; sex workers wait for their customers; hustlers look for ways of making do. This diversity of individuals and livelihoods sharing a common location and potentially becoming agents of unrest has both concerned politicians and government officials and inspired ethnographers of the political and the ordinary. For Asef Bayat, it is the "unplanned, unstructured, and instantaneous possibility" of collective action grounded in the experiences of people sharing the same location and confronted by a similar threat (such as an eviction) that makes the streets politically dangerous (Bayat 1997, 17–19). However, my own experience in inner city Addis Ababa taught me that, without a shared sense of place, meaning, and history, the streets do not have an intrinsic ability to become a common site of practice and action. In other words, while a street vendor might carry out his or her activities on the streets, it does not mean she or he sees herself or himself sharing lives, experiences, and actions with others (such as hustlers and sex workers) who also occupy the streets. What makes the difference is the extent to which people inhabiting the streets recognize themselves as part of that wider repertoire of memories, practices, and collaborations as well as past and present antagonisms that I describe as *street life*.

Street life, in this regard, does not have the consistency to create a street "culture" or a "sub-culture" (cf. Hall and Jefferson 2006; Bourgois 2003, 8) characterized by certain markers of belonging, attachments, and consumption, speaking to a particular predicament, desire, or demand. Instead, in Arada, street life was a community of shared practices, meaning not purposeful actions as in the case of Wenger's (1998) definition of a community of practice, but the experience of sharing and recognizing others' actions as similar or at least comparable. As I learned to read and detect the various constituencies inhabiting the streets, my research became an examination of a particular experience of street life, fundamentally revolving around hustling and street smartness. My conversations and explorations gradually became more focused so as to document being on the streets as embedded in notions and ideals of street smartness, the sociality of hustling, and memories about hustling and street life in the past. The initial concern with studying the street as a generic site of the politics of unrest and dissent at a given moment in Ethiopia's history was replaced by a wider interest in situating street life and the biographies of my interlocutors into the examination of a long history of marginality and exclusion. This shift in my research was a result of the ways the street, as a site of city politics, had changed since the ruling party's campaigns of repression and mobilization after the 2005 riots and demonstrations. By the time I began my research in 2009, the events of 2005 were remembered by my interlocutors as history, often evoked nostalgically when wondering how the present could have been had things gone differently. Politics continued to pervade the streets, but as the experience of the expansion of the ruling party's politics of mobilization, surveillance, and control. The dissent that had moved people to take to the streets did not disappear. It transformed into a wider sense of frustration that grew deeper as the ruling party's entrepreneurship programs specifically, and the making of a landscape of abundance and growth in Addis Ababa more generally, failed to open avenues of social mobility for the poor. To capture this wider sense of frustration, I felt I had to stretch the time frame of my examination across my interlocutors' biographies so as to include their memories of the past, experiences of marginality in the present, and hopes for the future.

My involvement with Arada was fortuitous. In the very first days of my fieldwork, I had to simply find a place where I could carry out my research. Being relatively new to the city, I reckoned that the only way I could find my field site was by taking long walks. The flow of people passing by, sitting and chatting on the streets of Arada drew me to the inner city. This was not because I enjoyed the flow of people aesthetically, as a *flâneur* passing through without interacting with the stories and singularities within that flow. Instead, I was drawn in as random strangers— shop owners, residents, young people lounging with their friends on street corners, hustlers looking for a fee—invited me to join them for coffee, tea, or a chat.

Identifying a field site did not mean being able to immediately unearth stories that spoke to that entanglement of history, becoming, and politics this book seeks to document and discuss. I had to build my knowledge of how the wider history of the country played out on the streets of Arada. This meant befriending street hustlers but also carrying out in-depth interviews with government officials, members of the inner city business community, and residents, including those who ended up becoming my neighbors during the two years I lived there. I also went back to the library at Addis Ababa University to consult—with the help of two research assistants—old and new newspapers and magazines, in English and Amharic, to build a more accurate time line for my analysis of the social history of the inner city.

I did not see Haile and Ibrahim as the protagonists of my book at the very beginning of my work. I met them only in January 2010, four months after I had started my fieldwork. This meeting was, to some extent, the culmination, or even the prize, after months of trying to establish myself in inner city Addis Ababa. Haile and Ibrahim are exceptional individuals whose richness in experience, memories, eloquence, and generosity enabled me to better navigate and understand the streets and, ultimately, write this book. At the same time, they were also part of a wider community of memories, practices, and identities with whom they shared modes of living, understanding, and navigating the persistence of their condition of marginality.

I met Haile and Ibrahim at a meeting organized by the government for the local "youth," and they and their networks of friends, colleagues, and contemporaries soon became my key and privileged interlocutors. Their stories and experiences constitute the foreground of my investigation. At the same time, I continued to befriend a large number of people to whom I frequently returned for information, ideas, suggestions, and advice, as well as to triangulate information, stories, and memories of street life and the community history of Arada. Such individuals, both men and women, are the coprotagonists of this book and constituted the broader network of interlocutors on which I relied to build up a detailed and diversified understanding of the background of my examination of living, marginality, development, and street life.

Hence, while centered on the experiences of Haile and Ibrahim and their immediate social circle, my research concomitantly moved along a complex and entangled web of networks, relations, and interactions that often provisionally and situationally came to link together people who often spent time on the streets, whether working, looking for means of getting by, or chilling with friends. These included a loose network of "street guides" hustling foreigners or, alternatively, showing tourists around for a fee; female *players* looking for customers or lovers to make some money at night; a group of fences who operated on the main roads in cahoots with local jewelers' shops; groups of touts who controlled minibus stops in the area and who had been formally recognized as "private investors" within the frame of the politics of mobilization of the ruling party; and, finally, a considerable number of occasional or full-time hustlers who spent their days finding ways of getting by—running errands for a few bucks, brokering petty transactions for a fee, helping friends, neighbors, and acquaintances in exchange for a meal or a couple of drinks.

While embedded in a variety of insights and heterogeneity of experiences, this book is also a result of a particular gendered experience of street life, marginality, and research. Negotiating my presence in the streets across gender lines turned out to be the hardest challenge I encountered in the field, as male and female spaces of sociality and the everyday remained fundamentally separate. Over the years I had the opportunity to carry out lengthy and in-depth interviews with sex workers as well as younger and older women in the neighborhood. However, I feel I have never been able to gain a detailed knowledge of these women's trajectories that was comparable to the ones I had gained for Haile and Ibrahim and a few others among my male interlocutors.

Moreover, as a man—the third man in the ethnographic equation of *The Act of Living*—and in particular as a white man, I was viewed in relation to other white men populating the streets of the inner city. Often these were white men cruising for sex. My ability to do research was thus contingent on the extent to which I was able to show that my behavior and conduct significantly differed from theirs. Therefore, I needed to be careful that my presence on the street was perceived to be free of any suspicion that I was a white john who used "research" as a random excuse to approach sex workers and bargain for a better deal for a quick sexual encounter. This resulted in me being shy in seeing women, and in particular sex workers, as key interlocutors. Without a doubt, I could have been bolder. Mine was a methodological choice, imposing a limit to my final analysis of living, marginality, and street life. Nevertheless, being recognized unequivocally as a good and genuine guy, a *chewa*, not only helped me carry out my research but allowed me to build, gradually and slowly, meaningful relations of trust with those few sex workers and players who appear in the text (see chapters 5 and 8).

This gender positioning reflects a central dimension of my interlocutors' *act of living* under conditions of subjugation and exclusion: marginality is both produced and lived as fundamentally a gendered experience. Street life had historically provided men and young men with ways of living through marginality and exclusion through paradigms of smartness and toughness, which, in their turn, came to shape gendered understandings of living, the ordinary, and the everyday (Cornwall, Karioris, and Lindisfarne 2016; Cornwall and Lindisfarne 1994; Miescher and Lindsay 2003). The country's politics periodically reinforced this logic. Government discourses on "dangerous vagrants" and "the unemployed youth," as well as the measures that followed the 2005 riots and demonstrations to integrate the marginalized into the ruling party's structure of political mobilization, were mainly focused on regulating and controlling men's behaviors in the city's and country's political space.

In exploring this intertwining of politics, the everyday, and street life, my ethnography and this book are inevitably an exploration of marginality *within* the gendered coordinates of that nexus between subjugation and subjectivities (Butler 1997; Werbner 2002). However, exploring the gendered ontology of my informants' experiences of marginality and living is regrettably not the immediate focus of the book. I narrate how within the contours of this gendered existence the protagonists and coprotagonists of this book sought to navigate their condition of marginality, made sense of their experience of living with others, and crafted their act of living as a site of reflexivity, mediation, and possibility.

Outline of the Book

This book's ethnographic appreciation of the act of living is contingent to a particular place (Addis Ababa, the capital of Ethiopia) and time (the decade of Africa rising), and it is specific to the stories of two lives, with their particularities of gender, location, and upbringing. These specificities characterize the book's examination of living, not as the description of undifferentiated and generic features of human existence, but as the narration of one of many particular ways of experiencing the tension between becoming and history, action and contingency. The particularity of a given realization, however, does not limit its relevance. The uniqueness of a story, as Hannah Arendt (1958) puts it, tells about the infinite potentialities of living and existence. At the same time, even while unique, existence unfolds in places, times, and modes of being in the world that are shared and resonate with the experience of a wider range of others.

By following the life trajectories of Haile and Ibrahim, this book aims to tease out the cumulative effects of experiences of "becoming" on history and to spell out the paradigms of my informants' attempts to be something other than their constraints: smartness, respect, morality, age and time, open-endedness, and indeterminacy. As we will see, these notions and categories did not just shape my informants' individual lives but were embedded in the collective urban history they were trying to navigate and which they, directly or indirectly, voiced wider political and moral concerns about living conditions and poverty, political authoritarianism and exclusion, the patronizing attitudes of government officials and development practitioners toward poor people's predicaments, and the limited ability that poor people had to decide and affect how development policies were imagined, defined, and implemented.

The ethnography situates these concerns into my informants' experiences of exclusion by pointing out their ambivalent and contradictory nature, especially when justifying actions like hustling and cheating, of which I myself hardly approved. At the same time, however, echoing Philippe Bourgois's (2003, 18) response to Laura Nader's (1972) remarks about the dangers of studying exclusion ("don't study the poor and powerless because everything you say about them will be used against them"), I engage with an ethnographic politics of witnessing as a peculiar modality of writing about marginality. Witnessing is about both documenting the different facets of urban marginality and questioning the assumptions that justify regimes of exclusion and oppression.

I believe that the realization of open, more democratic, and more developed societies in the present does not depend on the perceived efficacy of our predictions and forecasts of the future. It is ultimately embedded in whether stories about and from marginalized subjects are included in the narration and the imagination of the collective past, present, and future. And regrettably, the concerns that my informants, as part of the large constituency of the urban poor, expressed about their condition of poverty, marginality, and subjugation have so far hardly entered the public debate on development and growth, or even more focused discussions of youth, urban development, and marginality (see also Englund 2006). Ethnography is a research method that draws its knowledge from inhabiting discussions and dialogues. As such, it has an important duty to bring reflections, experiences, encounters, and concerns into public debate.

Pervaded by this analytical commitment to witnessing and debating, the book is structured as a journey of how the unfolding of history, the everyday practices of street life, and the life trajectories of my informants intertwined. In each chapter, I discuss the ways the past that my informants recounted to me interacted with the lives they live, and that I myself observed, in the present. The real names of everyone in this ethnography, except known historical figures, have been changed; in some cases, even the pseudonyms have been omitted to protect the identities of my informants.

Chapter 1 investigates the beginnings of my informants' *act of living*. I describe the families of Haile and Ibrahim and their migration from the rural areas into Addis Ababa. I then contextualize Haile's and Ibrahim's experiences of growing up and coming of age in the inner city, Arada, a context shaped by economic stagnation under the pre-1991 socialist regime but then reconfigured by deepening social inequality as economic liberalization began in the 1990s. This chapter follows Haile's and Ibrahim's first entrance into the street economy and examines why *being* and *becoming Arada* were so central in their experiences of marginality. Street life and hustling provided them with a form of economic independence and autonomy. By *being* and *becoming Arada*, they asserted their ability to act on that landscape of social differentiation and exclusion that pervaded their experiences of growing up as poor young men.

Molding *the act of living* on the streets held both a predicament and a promise. It grounded their action into a problematic flirtation with street violence and crime. At the same time, it enabled them to embody models of smartness and toughness on which they based their search for respect, dignity, and recognition. Chapter 2 characterizes action and life as they intertwined with the history and experiences of street life. I trace the history of the street economy and show how street life appealed to generations of young men because it enabled them to assert themselves as a recognizable constituency of urban history. I argue that involvement in street life and crime cannot be understood just as a response to an enduring condition of marginality. People's search for dignity, respect, and recognition on the streets made history and enabled hustlers and thugs to become makers of their own history.

Chapter 3 captures the moments when, between the late 1990s and the mid-2000s, my informants sought to find ways out of street life. The deaths of close friends and the realization that a life of smartness and toughness had taken them nowhere triggered a restless search for a better life. The chapter follows Haile,

Ibrahim, and others among their friends as they engaged with a variety of careers and trajectories. I document how their condition of marginality endured regardless of their efforts and in spite of the moment of promise and change following the opening of the free market in the 1990s. This chapter examines the *act of living* as being caught between the promise of change and the endurance of subjugation. Growth transformed the landscape of Addis Ababa and molded aspirations for a better life in the inner city. However, Haile, Ibrahim, and their peers soon realized that their ability to enjoy change and pursue improvement was contingent on access to useful networks. Lacking this access, their efforts failed. This chapter shows how such a lack of access to relations is itself a relational product, and points out that economic growth has reconfigured, but not challenged, the regime of interconnectedness that enables marginality to persist through change.

Chapter 4 adds another layer to this book's exploration of subjugation and the *act of living*. It shows how my informants' condition of marginality did not result just from the ways patterns of social differentiation constrained their attempts to pursue trajectories of social mobility. I argue that marginality is also a product of the strategies political elites used to ground their power at the bottom of urban society—namely, the ways they carved out the terms and conditions of my informants' membership in wider society, as subjects to be either strategically mobilized or pervasively repressed. The chapter traces how the political history of contemporary Ethiopia played out on the streets, revealing how the concern of the ruling party with mobilizing and developing the street economy deepened forms of political subjugation and reinforced conditions of social exclusion.

Politics and the deepening of patterns of social differentiation have not erased the street economy as a space to live meaningfully through marginality and exclusion. Chapters 5 and 6 focus on the logics and tensions encompassing a "life within limits" (Jackson 2011) experienced when getting by on the streets of inner city Addis Ababa. Chapter 5 shows how people's attempts to navigate their condition of marginality are not lonely endeavors but are carried out by relating to equally and more marginalized individuals. I discuss how hustling is a particular experience of living with others. Success in hustling is contingent on the ability of the hustler to relate to others, and more importantly outsmart them. Hustling, however, is not social Darwinism. While hustling, the protagonists and coprotagonists of this book grounded their *act of living* into a form of situated morality through which they justified their actions, comprehended the predicaments of others as their own, and understood their condition of poverty as something difficult to challenge and question. Getting by on the street transformed hustlers into moral subjects, struggling between the individual demands of making do and the awareness of living a condition of poverty and exclusion that was shared and experienced with others. Chapter 6 shows how this understanding of poverty constitutes the frame of my informants' experiences of enjoyment and satisfaction. Focusing on performances of style and on the consumption of *khat*, a mild narcotic stimulant, I explore how enjoyment revolved around the ability of the hustler to redefine and reimagine what a poor person could do and be while living an existence that is firmly embedded in subjugation and oppression.

My informants continued to nurture and exercise their capacity to live skillfully and smartly through poverty. Yet, as chapter 7 points out, they were far from content to live a "life within limits." Poverty, exclusion, and marginality were seen as difficult to question and challenge but also far from desirable. The chapter discusses my informants' critique of the society they lived in. With these critiques, they made sense of their position in society, as members of the urban poor who were left with nothing. At the same time, they morally disengaged from what they identified as the sources of their condition of marginality and exclusion: the selfishness of city businesspeople, the occult nature of the wealth of the country's rich, and the falseness of the ruling party's politics.

The ruling party's politics and deepening patterns of social differentiation significantly constrained my informants' quests for a better life. Questioning politics and the rich was a way of mitigating the effects of political authoritarianism and social exclusion on their sense of self-worth. Engaging in a "war of words," as James Scott (1985) put it, was not enough. Enduring exclusion and oppression and trying to be something other than their constraints, my informants understood, was a matter of action. In chapter 8, I explore the ways my informants reinstated the possibility of acting and living, and even searching and hoping for a better life through an appreciation of the indeterminacy of life.

I end the book by discussing how examining the tensions of the *act of living* can help us go beyond a temptation to understand agency as made of an act of resistance (de Certeau 1984) or marginality as the outcome of the cunning work of structuring structures and the vicious circle of production and reproduction (Bourdieu 1977). The *act of living* tells how history and becoming unfold as people's attempts to be something other than their constraints coexist with the experiences of being acted upon by marginality, subjugation, and oppression. This is a tension that is never resolved. Accounting for this tension is not only crucial to anthropology and its examination of the desires and actions of the marginalized. It is central for imagining development alternatives. Learning from the tensions and concerns that pervaded my informants' *act of living* and their attempts to achieve a better life, I reflect on the potential options ahead, making the case for an anthropological engagement with a politics of open-endedness.

MIGRANTS, GENTLEMEN, AND THUGS

Relative Achievements

Pure chance dictated that Haile and Ibrahim were born in poor households in inner city Addis Ababa. They were thrown into the world without control of the circumstances of their beginnings (Heidegger [1953] 1996; Jackson 1989, 2005). However, the making of these circumstances was not fortuitous: the randomness of birth assigned them to a place shaped by a history of political subjugation and marginalization. In this chapter I look at the historical foundation of Haile and Ibrahim's beginnings and explore how their condition of marginality and subjugation was a product of a long-term urban history which they sought to navigate as they grew up to become skillful hustlers.

This chapter teases out a central tension in the act of living—namely, the ways people's search to be something other than their constraints is inevitably situated in the contingencies of their presence in the world (Rorty 1989). However, this tension can remain undetected in the study of marginality if life trajectories and actions are narrated exclusively in relation to their outcomes. Adopting this view, Philippe Bourgois (2003) and Paul Willis (1977) examined how the marginalized end up embodying the circumstances of their condition of subjugation as the co-ordinates of their existence and identity, thus contributing to the reproduction of their own condition of oppression. By looking at where Haile and Ibrahim eventually ended up, we might well argue this is the case. Yet we might also miss what it was that Haile and Ibrahim sought to achieve—and, to some extent, did achieve—through their involvement in street life and hustling: economic autonomy, independence, and, as we will see in the rest of this book, a way of experiencing respect, excitement, and enjoyment.

These were undoubtedly relative achievements because, as Bourgois (2003) and Willis (1977) rightly argued, they were embedded in an underlying condition of exclusion. However, these relative achievements were, for Haile and Ibrahim, not just remainders of their constraints but also milestones in their attempts to search for ways of living meaningfully through the endurance of their condition of marginality. In this chapter, and in the book more widely, I seek to document these "relative" achievements to make sense of both the meanings and the outcomes of Haile's and Ibrahim's actions and those of their peers. This tension concerns not only the social analysis of the ethnographer but also the lived experiences of the protagonists of this book as they sought to be something other than their constraints.

This chapter explores this tension by investigating the weight of place and history in the trajectories of Haile and Ibrahim. In particular, I look at how their act of living was molded through their experience of the urban. I define the urban as a repertoire, or rather an "archive" (Barber 1997; Fabian 1978), of performances, expectations, meanings, and identities, the making of which includes, but does not exclusively revolve around, the relations between the city and the rural (cf. Ferguson 1999), and between the local and the global (Weiss 2005, 2009). The urban in Addis Ababa, as in many other African cities, has an internal local history that is "thick" (Geertz 1973) and that we need to explore and understand in its own terms (Pieterse 2010; Mbembe and Nuttall 2004; Simone 2004a; Iliffe 2005). For my interlocutors, in fact, the city, and in particular the inner city, is not just a place among others. Categories, expectations, and identities of urban living constituted their "life space" (Friedman 1994). It shaped the ways they positioned themselves in society and sought to act on the contingencies of their presence in the world.

The protagonists of this book understood their condition of marginality in relation to an expectation of continuous improvement that was embedded in their experience of the city. This was an expectation that was initially grounded in an appreciation of their parents' trajectory of migration—from rural areas to the city—as the achievement of a certain degree of economic improvement, and then in the economic transformations of Addis Ababa during their decades living in the city.

Unfortunately for Haile and Ibrahim, these expectations of continuous improvement went unfulfilled. They soon realized that the city where they were born marginalized them. Their parents' trajectories of improvement were only "relative." It was partly a result of their trajectories of migration and partly an outcome of how the policies implemented in the 1970s to govern the poor delivered a form of secure poverty (Clapham 1988; Di Nunzio 2017). This secure poverty enabled their rural-born parents to get by but did not open opportunities of social mobility to Haile and Ibrahim. In principle, being born in the city, with access to the education from which their parents had been excluded, they were a step ahead of the previous generation. Despite this advantage, they soon found that embarking on a trajectory of improvement that was at least comparable to their parents' was difficult or nearly impossible. Schools were sites for promoting individuals, not for addressing structural problems (Clapham 1988; Mains 2012a; Poluha 2004; Markakis 1974). Moreover, social inequality and patterns of differentiation and social segregation that had persisted throughout the 1970s and 1980s (Diamantini and Patassini 1993; Clapham 1988; see below) deepened after economic liberalization and the opening of the free market in the 1990s (Solomon Mulugeta 2006; Yonas Alem, Köhlin, and Stage 2014), further limiting my interlocutors' prospects of social mobility from below (see chapter 3).

Inner city street life, and hustling in particular, constituted the way Haile and Ibrahim navigated their condition of marginality. While doing so, they achieved a certain degree of autonomy and economic independence through which they sought to balance out the lack of opportunities for attaining either a relative or a more substantial form of social improvement. However, Arada, the inner city area where Haile and Ibrahim were born and grew up, was not only the place *where* the protagonists and coprotagonists of this book happened to experience marginality. Living in Arada shaped *how* they understood their condition of marginality as both relative and relational, and learned to mediate between the meanings and the outcomes of their actions. As I mentioned in the introduction, Arada is not only the name of Addis Ababa's inner city. *Being Arada* conveys notions of smartness and urban sophistication that street hustlers and a great variety of other individuals, including sex workers and middle-class inner city residents, have claimed for themselves since the 1950s.[1] *Arada,* as a notion more than a place, does not consist of a particular inner city "culture" or "subculture" characterized by a certain range of practices, markers of identity, modes of consumption, values and ideologies. Instead, it broadly translates an understanding of the "urban" as a place populated by people from different walks of life and a large variety of discourses, identities, desires, ways of doing and acting. *Arada* gave a name to what Walter Benjamin ([1982] 1999), Georg Simmel ([1908] 1971), and the urbanist Abdoumaliq Simone (2004a, 2004b) captured in their work on cities: the

---

1. As we will see in chapters 2 and 5, *being Arada* is not exclusively a male concept; women, and in particular sex workers, have historically claimed to *be Arada.*

conceptualization of the urban as both a place and a particular kind of experience. *Being Arada* is fundamentally the capacity to both benefit from and navigate the heterogeneity of the urban, either to find ways of getting by or to simply find enjoyment. Haile and Ibrahim, like many others in the inner city, embraced *being Arada* to ground their actions and found meaning in their experience of the city. This intimate relation between meaning, place, and action in their social navigation is not a given, nor is it inevitable. It is a result of the ways a particular understanding of the "urban" became the site for mediating and acting on their condition of marginality and exclusion (Barber 1997; Newell 2012; Cole 2010; Weiss 2009; Gondola 1999). For Haile and Ibrahim, *being Arada* was the outcome of the fact that they recognized their condition of marginality as inhabiting the ordinary spaces of their everyday life in the inner city. *Becoming Arada* was the move that they took to occupy those spaces with their actions, performances, and exploits.

As we will see both in this chapter and in the next, this move itself was not without tensions. Haile and Ibrahim were both proud of and conflicted about *being Arada*, as it bore witness to their capacity to live smartly while exposing their condition of exclusion. At the same time, *becoming Arada* became relevant for Haile's and Ibrahim's life trajectories because it helped them question the particular regime of class, marginality, and interconnectedness that had been imposed on them at birth. By *being* and *becoming Arada* Haile and Ibrahim understood their involvement in street life not just as a relative achievement but as a wider attempt to reshape the ways they related to that landscape of class and social inequality that had contributed to the production of their condition of marginality and exclusion.[2]

The chapter investigates this complex intertwining of place, history, class, identity, and action. I begin with an examination of the social history of Arada. I then situate the positionality of Haile and Ibrahim and their parents in this history and explore the circumstances of the former's entry into street life. I conclude by

---

2. Within Ethiopian studies, accounting for ideas and meanings of *being Arada* and the ways it became central in shaping experiences of marginality and exclusion in the city makes evident that cultural, social, and political dynamics in the capital cannot be fully understood through the exclusive lens of ethnicity and religious difference that has characterized much of the literature on Ethiopia (also on this point see Heinonen 2011; Mains 2012a). Though my informants in Arada came from a variety of backgrounds, both Orthodox Christian and Muslim, and with various ethnic identities, such as Amhara, Gurage, Silte, Tigrayan, Oromo, and Walayta, the very fact of being from Addis Ababa or even Arada constituted the way they defined themselves and made sense of their position in broader Ethiopian society. This is not to underestimate the importance of ethnicity in Ethiopian identities and national and local politics (Dereje Feyissa 2006; James et al. 2002; Vaughan 2006; Watson 2002). I suggest, however, that the categories people use to describe, make sense of, and experience social marginality in the city reveal other political and social dynamics that characterize urban contexts in Ethiopia and that an overemphasis on ethnicity might conceal.

discussing how Haile and Ibrahim embraced *Arada* as the existential, social, and spatial coordinates of their act of living.

Arada

Arada is the old city center, and, for a long time, what happened here roughly corresponded to what happened in Addis Ababa. The imaginary boundaries of Arada have long been shifting, but in the current administrative structure, it is one of the ten subcities of the capital. In 2007 it was home to 212,009 people, or 7.78 percent of the population of Addis Ababa (Population Census Commission 2008). When I started fieldwork in late 2009, Arada was characterized by a highly varied mixture of economic activities. Cafés, restaurants, hotels, and shops selling expensive clothes were concentrated on the main roads. The side roads were lined with what remained of the old houses of merchants and the Ethiopian aristocracy, small shops, *khat* vendors and chewing houses (*khat bet*), video parlors, and cheap restaurants. Spreading out from the side roads, a wide extension of tin-roofed houses accommodated most of the area's population.

When viewed from these tin-roofed houses, Arada is undoubtedly a poor area. Housing and water and sanitation facilities are of poor quality. Pictures of the area and accompanying data on living conditions have featured frequently in government, NGOs (nongovernmental organizations) and UN-Habitat reports decrying the high proportion of slum areas in the Ethiopian capital and around the country—in 2005 some 81.8 percent of the Ethiopian population was believed to be living in slums (UN-Habitat 2008a, 106). Such images and data support powerful crisis narratives, as in Mike Davis's (2006) description of landscapes of urban destitution and radical poverty in *Planet of Slums*. A more careful look at Arada, however, along with similar areas across the continent, reminds us that urban poverty is not interpretable and understandable only through narratives of crisis. A variety of arrangements and historical trajectories shape life in, and the geography of, poor settlements in African cities (Simone 2004a; Myers 2011).

In this section, I discuss Arada by examining three intertwining trajectories of urban change. The first was not directly experienced by Haile and Ibrahim, but it significantly shaped the Arada they grew up in and concerns the interaction between the heterogeneous social geography of the old city center and deepening forms of social differentiation, especially between the 1940s and the 1970s. The second revolves around how the emergence of a suburban attitude in Ethiopian elites in the 1960s and the worsening of housing conditions since the mid-1970s transformed Arada from the city center to the inner city of the Ethiopian capital.

The third is the sharpening of social difference after the introduction of the free market in the early 1990s.

Agglomeration and Differentiation

Historically, one of the key features of the landscape of Arada was the proximity of the houses of the Ethiopian aristocracy to poorer homes. This was because in the early history of Addis Ababa, the residences of the Ethiopian aristocracy, and even the royal palace, were surrounded by settlements where their retinue and followers lived. This arrangement was embedded in a social geography of interdependence linking masters to clients and vice versa. Aristocratic households and the royal palace were independent economic units that included workshops, farms, and factories, the activities of which tended to meet the demands of the master, his family, and numerous followers.

The political centralization of the state, initiated by Menelik and radically pursued by Emperor Haile Selassie after the end of the Italian occupation in 1941, resulted in a gradual disengagement of the elites from their retinues. Haile Selassie worked to accumulate power by targeting and reducing the power base of the old aristocracy. He attempted to create a "new nobility" out of the old aristocracy: one that was freed from regional interests, whose political behavior aligned with the royal will (Levine 1965, 183–184), and whose legitimacy was based on the political and administrative positions held in the bureaucratic structure of the state (Markakis 1974; Donham 1986). The increasing centrality of the state as the terrain of political interaction between the emperor, who granted positions based on loyalty, and the elites corresponded with a transformation of the dynamics of patron-client relations. As the new urban-based elite came to ground their resources in their engagement with the state bureaucracy, they shifted away from their duties to support peasants in the countryside (Levine 1965). Patron-client relationships in the city also weakened. Older people in my field site remembered when rich Ethiopian families still organized banquets and invited their poor neighbors during religious festivals, but this was far from offering a reliable source of support for the poor. Many came to understand that they had to look elsewhere in order to get by.

The declining importance of patron-client relations triggered a range of social transformations, such as the expansion of the wage economy and, simply, the fact that those who lived around the houses of the aristocracy were no longer dependents but workers, or even tenants, on the properties of the aristocracy. Even early in the history of the city, a decrease in the support of the elite for followers and clients manifested in the growth of the market in Arada from the end of the nineteenth century, when the city was established, and the 1930s, before the Italian occupation. The increasing volume of transactions, the diversification of the goods sold in the market, and the growth of the community of foreign merchants based in the city, including Greeks, Armenians, Italians, and Indians, was mainly due to two factors. First, the palace and aristocratic households increasingly relied on the market for their supplies instead of the work of their dependents. Second, those who had previously been supported by the aristocracy now turned to the market as sellers or buyers, and sometimes both, for their survival (Daniel Tesfaye 1991). As Chapple (1987) suggests, the people who relied on the market for their food supply were "modern type wage workers"—salaried government employees, merchants, craftsmen, and foreigners who were not directly dependent on the palace or on aristocratic families.

This deep transformation in the relations between the aristocracy and their followers was far from smooth. The decreased importance of patron-client relationships and the increasing relevance of the market economy molded a changing understanding of social difference. The presence of rich foreigners and the enrichment of the Ethiopian elite showed that wealth was available, but the strategies these privileged groups used to distinguish themselves from the rest of society made clear that this wealth was not for all (Garretson 2000). Once in Addis Ababa, the preexisting practices of ostentation and mannerism that the nobility cultivated in rural areas as a "distinction" from the peasantry acquired new meanings (Levine 1965). The new urban-based nobility developed a set of symbols and social paradigms that stressed consumption, the performance of a Western lifestyle, and engagement in commercial enterprises as the main means of the production of wealth. During these transformations, the central neighborhood of Arada was the site of a complex interaction between patterns of "differentiation" and "agglomeration" (Horvath 1970), a long-standing nodal point around which new arrivals in the city clustered. Rich people continued to live side by side with poor people, but the persistence of this spatial proximity did little to change the endurance, or hardening, of political and social hierarchies in the city.

Meanwhile, the bureaucratization of the state also resulted in the emergence of a new political and social constituency of the city and Ethiopian society writ large. The making of this bureaucratic state opened up opportunities for social mobility through which an increasing number of newcomers could achieve status through education and employment. As Donald Levine (1965) and John Markakis (1974) described, an Ethiopian middle class emerged, with its own system of values and social paradigms based on meritocracy and self-achievement, as opposed to the hereditary prestige of the old aristocracy.

The newcomers' quest for grounds for cultural and political legitimization and the concern of Haile Selassie to continue to be seen as the center of Ethiopian politics and society corresponded to a period of increasingly institutionalized culture production—a golden age of Ethiopian urban society. This period saw the establishment of schools and, later, Haile Selassie I University (now Addis Ababa University). Theaters and music bands were established with the support of the police, the Imperial Bodyguard, or the Municipality (Falceto 2001; Simeneh Betroyannes 2008). The emperor granted scholarships to talented young people abroad, and he attended performances and the openings of art exhibitions. A generation of intellectuals who were sent abroad in the late 1940s returned to Ethiopia in the first half of the 1950s, and included a small group of writers, playwrights, actors, and artists who were directly or indirectly linked to the emperor or at least to his paradigm of modernization (Shiferaw Bekele 2006).

The quest of this new middle class for new grounds of cultural legitimation occurred within the ongoing tension between agglomeration and differentiation. It exacerbated the landscape of social difference in Arada and, notably, in those emerging public spaces where people went to enjoy, experience, and imagine a modern and urban "lifestyle." Throughout the 1940s and 1960s, during Haile Selassie's politics of centralization of the state, cafés, drinking houses, cinemas, bars, and restaurants[3] came to constitute an autonomous public arena where meanings and performances of urban sophistication took shape, ideas and the notion of *being Arada* gained momentum to describe this experience of urban living.

However, as clubs, bars, and restaurants continued to increase in number and social inequality deepened, leisure in Addis Ababa, and in particular in Arada, just as in many other African cities at that time (cf. Iliffe 2005; Suriano 2009; Martin 1995; Akyeampong and Ambler 2002; Gondola 1999), became not only a platform for elaborating ideas of urban sophistication but also the site of performances of social distinction and differentiation. The clubs in Arada, for instance, were not affordable for all. Dereje Tekle, a local historian, long-term resident of Arada, and acute observer of Addis Ababa's local history, made me aware of these internal cleavages: "A girl in *Dejacchu Bet* [the name of a drinking house in Arada] cost 1 or 2 birr, in Taytu [a hotel patronized by intellectuals, artists and government officials] she cost 20 birr, the salary of a soldier at that time." Girma aka Girma *Dinare* [ten cents], a singer and a performer during the socialist regime, was a poor young man in the 1960s and remembered those days in this way: "People were just spending money on food, house, clothes and enjoyment, nothing else. If you could have money, nice clothes, you would be a *geta* [lord]

---

3. Enjoyment and urban lifestyles in Arada have a long history, going back to the very beginning of Addis Ababa's history, in the 1890s and early 1900s, when the neighborhood was the city's market-place (Pankhurst 1961). As the market attracted people coming from rural areas to buy and sell various products, small restaurants and hostels emerged, offering places to rest, and drinking houses multiplied (Garretson 2000). Though the market was forcibly moved to Merkato in the western part of the city during the Italian occupation in the mid-1930s, the number of drinking places in Arada continued to grow.

and get *kibur* [respect]." Getachew Debalke, also a singer in the 1960s, agreed with Girma's description of life in Arada: "If you did not have any money and you could only pay for a soft drink, people would look upon you as a poor man. Then, you would fight to show who you were; women liked this." I naively asked him, *Are the Arada poor then?* "What do you mean?" he replied. "Rich are rich and poor are poor. What the poor should do is try to be like the rich!" In the words of Getachew and Girma, rich and poor juggled with class differentiation through the performance of style, fashion, and conviviality. However, alongside this juggling act, existing distinctions remained undeniable frames of the social interactions that shaped this segmented conviviality.

Differentiation, Scarcity, and Segregation

Social inequality persisted throughout the 1960s and 1970s (Levine 1965; Markakis 1974) while Arada witnessed a shift in its place from Addis Ababa's center to its poor inner city (Bahru Zewde 2005). This was a process of urban change triggered by the intertwining of two very different ways of dealing with social difference: the emergence of spatial segregation with the appearance of a suburban attitude in urban Ethiopian elites by the 1960s, and the ways the question of housing the poor was tackled after the establishment of the socialist regime in the mid-1970s.

These two trajectories of urban change stemmed from the social and political transformations of the 1960s and 1970s and the increasing emphasis on elite discourses on urban sophistication. As the urban "middle class" expanded, both state and society came to be loaded with expectations the economy could not fulfill. Both Levine, in 1965, and Markakis, in 1974, pointed out the emergence of the contradiction that the former labeled the "Ethiopian Dilemma": a growing tension between calls for modernization advanced by the middle class and the centralization of power in the hands of Haile Selassie. As the anthropologist Donald Donham (1986) said, the process of centralization was "of a very particular type, and the whole administrative system operated only as long as a strong man occupied the center. In the absence of a rationalized, impersonal bureaucracy, the working of government depended on paternal guidance from the emperor at the top" (33). As Levine (1965) and Markakis (1974) emphasized, the modality of recruiting this new urban "middle class" and their future involvement in running the state was the central critical question of Haile Selassie's process of modernization and centralization. As such, the recruitment of newcomers was not primarily motivated by the encouragement of social mobility but by the establishment of new forms of control over society.

However, contrary to the expectations catalyzed by the emperor's declared commitment to modernization, the capacity of the system to accommodate the aspirations of newcomers remained limited. Members of the Ethiopian aristocracy remained holders of most of the highest positions in the state. Moreover, by the 1970s, the decline in resources and in the positions available for an increasing number of newcomers with secondary school and university degrees showed that the political aims of the Emperor to control the structure of the state and the expectations of the new educated generation that they would join the middle class were no longer compatible. This new generation, Markakis pointed out, "matured in a milieu that . . . [was] no longer mesmerized by the aura of the benevolent Emperor" (1974, 187). The education they received and their perceived or actual inability to achieve their expectations made this generation more critical of the regime than ever before. Foreshadowing events to come, Markakis wrote at the time: "While it does not now constitute a major political force in the political system of Ethiopia, the educated class is laying the foundation for such a role by gradually taking over control of the apparatus of the state, including its defence and enforcement branches" (191).

Amid the postcolonial struggles of the 1960s and 1970s and the student movements in Europe and the United States, this new generation of students and intellectuals employed the discourse of Marxism-Leninism to express their frustration and call for a radical transformation of Ethiopian society (Messay Kebede 2008; Bahru Zewde 2010). Marxism provided a collective narrative through which students could relate their sense of marginalization to a broader quest for social justice encompassing other segments of society. The Leninist idea of a "revolutionary vanguard" suggested how this intellectual elite could lead a process of political transformation and claim an elite status that Haile Selassie's regime could no longer grant them.

However, the student movement was not able to define and initiate an organized political structure to deliver revolutionary change. In January 1974, a minor rebellion over food and drinking water in a small garrison in southern Ethiopia triggered a snowballing of events that led to the deposition of Haile Selassie and transformed Ethiopia into a socialist country led by a military junta—the Derg (Donham 1999). The army was initially perceived as different from other state institutions, which were widely considered corrupt, encouraging some students to see it as the engine of a genuine socialist revolution. Soon, however, the students realized that the military was not so willing to hand over power to the civilian left. Meanwhile, for their part, the leaders of the Derg became increasingly suspicious of students and revolutionary intellectuals. Ideological differences and the attempts by each faction to claim leadership of the political process created the conditions for what followed. Fractures within student groups and a power struggle within the Derg itself resulted in one of the most dramatic and violent periods in Ethiopian history, the Red Terror. Many young people and students, as well as cadres of the regime, were killed in widespread everyday violence. Although the Red Terror ended in 1978, the wound it left in Ethiopian society remains raw (Tronvoll, Schaefer, and Girmachew Alemu Aneme 2009).

Transformations in the urban space reflected the social tensions framing and characterizing the "Ethiopian dilemma" in the 1960s and 1970s. Already in the 1960s, as the city continued to expand, the city center, as the place where new architectural construction represented the making of urban space, shifted away from Arada (Bahru Zewde 2005). More significantly, the upper strata of the Ethiopian elites began to move to the suburbs; in the 1960s and early 1970s new settlements emerged on the southern and western edges of the city as elites distanced themselves from the mixed and socially heterogeneous fabric of the old city center (Bahru Zewde 2005; Himmelreich 2010). As a result, social differentiation coincided with an incipient form of spatial segregation. Exclusive clubs and bars opened in newly developed areas and became the favored destinations of the upper crust (Simeneh Betroyannes 2008), leaving the clubs and drinking houses of Arada to university students, middle- and low-level government officials, sex workers, and poor young men.

When the regime changed and the Derg took over, its political elite did not return to the inner city. In the mid-1970s, the socialist regime brought about a significant transformation in the inner city with the nationalization of land and housing. Former owners of land and homes were allowed to keep the place where they lived, but any additional houses were confiscated and managed by newly established urban dwellers' associations, the *kebelle*. As the state gained ownership of a large number of housing facilities and plots of land, house rents fell, enabling a significant part of the poor population of the capital to find a stable home.

However, nationalization only partially solved the problem of housing the poor. Indeed, in the long run it only worsened housing facilities in old neighborhoods like Arada since maintenance and repair of existing structures was not a political priority and was consequently underfunded (Lefort 1983). Deteriorating housing conditions, dwindling availability, and, more generally, the lack of investment in construction did not stop the flow of people from the countryside to Addis Ababa (Assefa Damte 1983). Despite widespread economic scarcity, the city continued to grow (Assefa Damte 1983; Diamantini and Patassini 1993; Clapham 1988), reaching nearly 1.5 million inhabitants in the mid-1980s (UN-Habitat 2008b).

Segregation and Exclusion

By and large, the economy of the city after the 1974 revolution witnessed a contraction in production and the increasing significance of the state bureaucracy and state enterprises as the main employers and economic actors (Krishnan, Tesfaye Gebre Selassie, and Dercon 1998). However, low-level private business—predominantly drinking houses, small restaurants, retail shops, and petty trades—continued to exist and provided livelihoods for a significant part of the urban population (Diamantini and Patassini 1993). In the final years of the socialist Derg regime, an incipient opening of the economy began as the military junta attempted to build new alliances after the collapse of the Soviet Union and East Germany, which had supported Ethiopia since the 1974 revolution. However, it was only the fall of the regime in 1991 that triggered transformations that, in time, radically reshuffled urban economies.

The opening of the free market led to an unprecedented inflow of media and goods. The volume of private investment gradually grew, and the private sector expanded. Construction activities also resumed, initially concentrated in the southeastern part of the city, particularly Bole, which had already seen some development in the last years of the socialist regime. This expansion of the urban economy, however, did not entail equal access to the benefits of economic growth. By the end of the 1990s, social inequality had skyrocketed. Real incomes in urban areas had increased, but while the wealthiest households saw significant increases in their income, poorer households saw a decline (Bigsten and Negatu Makonnen 1999). As a result, while poor households experienced increased availability of goods and services, their ability to actually access them decreased.

Concurrently, the liberalization of the economy resulted in the revival of Arada during the 1990s. The night curfew, imposed to enforce order during the socialist regime, was abolished. Once again, fashion, style, and nightlife fascinated a generation of young people who had grown up amid cultural sobriety. Cafés, bars, and clubs reopened on the main roads, shaping ideas of leisure and enjoyment. On the side roads, alongside the existing drinking houses, video parlors and *khat bet* blossomed. Nevertheless, despite these transformations, the Ethiopian urban elites continued to stay away from the inner city, mainly residing in the expanding southeastern district, Bole, or in newly built suburban areas such as Ayat and CMC (Himmelreich 2010).

Although forms of spatial and social segregation hardened, the inner city was not left just to the poor. A section of the educated middle class had stayed on in Arada after the 1974 revolution and included not only low- and middle-level government officials but also artists and intellectuals. After the opening of the free market, the old city center witnessed the growth of a local business community running small shops and businesses. The resulting heterogeneity produced an intricate social geography. As we will see, the sharpening of social inequality within the

FIG. 1.1   A partial view of Arada © Marco Di Nunzio

inner city constituted the first site of my informants' experiences of social exclusion (see next section and chapter 3), while the social and spatial distance between the inner city and Addis Ababa's business elites triggered a deep sense of incommensurability and inexplicability, nurturing my informants' suspicions about the morality of the city's growth and wealth (see chapter 7).

Migrants' Sons

Haile and Ibrahim experienced this changing history of space, social difference, and class from a particular positioning: as descendants of the large number of people who moved from their home regions across the country to Addis Ababa between the 1960s and the 1980s; as poor residents of the inner city who had learned to understand their condition of marginality as an experience of secure poverty in a landscape of social difference, segregation, and inequality; and as targets of policies that aimed to govern rather than empower the urban poor. These three sets of relations constituted the *regime of interconnectedness* that defined the terms of Haile's and Ibrahim's integration into Ethiopia's society at birth. The following chapters examine how this regime of interconnectedness was reconfigured under the impact of the liberalization of the economy and economic growth. In the rest of this chapter, I explore how such a positioning in the city's landscape of social difference shaped Haile's and Ibrahim's experiences of marginality while constituting the circumstances that made street life and *becoming Arada* the terrains of their search for being something other than their constraints.

The wave of migration that brought Ibrahim's parents (Muna and Ahmed) and Haile's mother (Wubit) to Addis Ababa was unprecedented in urban Ethiopia. In the 1960s and throughout the socialist regime in the 1970s and 1980s, these new arrivals came to constitute the bulk of the city's population (Diamantini and Patassini 1993; Getahun Benti 2007). This migration was important not just because of the number of people involved[4] but because of their social characteristics and motivations. The largest group (36 percent) of in-migrants in the late 1960s, as Getahun Benti (2007) pointed out, was composed of people aged fifteen to twenty-four. They were mostly those who had left school, both graduates and dropouts, as well as young men and women attracted by the concentration of activities and economic opportunities in the city. As Getahun Benti argued, "Contrary to the conventional theory that people migrate to towns from areas where social services are poor, inadequate or even non-existent" (2007, 106), the new arrivals often came from areas and provinces where urbanization had already begun and where, for instance, educational facilities and health services were expanding. They came to the city with expectations and ideas about the opportunities available.

Muna, Ibrahim's mother, was born in a village in the Gurage region, nearly three hundred kilometers southwest of Addis Ababa. She had arrived in Addis Ababa in 1973 with her husband, Ahmed, who was born in the same village but had grown up in Addis Ababa. Ahmed had left the village to look for a job when he was just a kid. As a young Muslim from the Gurage region, Ibrahim's father followed a historical route of migration that, since the early history of Addis Ababa, has taken Gurage men to the Ethiopian capital to work as seasonal workers or as merchants, making them one of the main ethnic groups in the city (Garretson 2000; Getahun Benti 2007). Ahmed started as a shoeshine boy and then found a job as a waiter in the pastry shop where he has worked ever since. When he got the job in the pastry shop, he went back to his village and married Muna. They were both very young, she remembered. When she arrived in the city, Muna began selling milk on the street and gradually moved into a more profitable business: buying kitchenware and plastic containers in Merkato, the main market in Addis Ababa, and reselling them to her neighbors. After they arrived in Addis Ababa, they moved home many times, until Ahmed, when Ibrahim was just seven months

---

4. In his study of migration and the history of Addis Ababa, Getahun Benti (2007) reported that in 1967 the population of Addis Ababa reached 637,831, of which 54 percent was migrants. More significantly, one-fourth of the population in 1967 consisted of migrants who had arrived in the city only after 1961 (42).

old, obtained the house where they have lived for the past thirty-eight years through the local government office (the *kebelle*).

Wubit, Haile's mother, came to Addis Ababa from the Amhara region, in the north of the country, when she was very young. Once in the Ethiopian capital, she became involved in commercial sex work to support herself and, later, her sons. Her social trajectory was similar to those of the many other young women who moved to the city. For many young Amhara women in the 1960s and 1970s, migrating to the city was an established and viable option for avoiding early marriage or for looking for means of survival after a divorce (Getahun Benti 2007). Many of these women from the countryside as well as those born in the city turned to sex work because it paid more than other opportunities available to them, such as working in a factory or in a private household, and because it was a route to still-better incomes for those determined and lucky enough to become a "madam" who owned her own bar and counted the rich and the notable among her customers (Laketch Dirasse 1991).

Ahmed, Muna, and Wubit arrived in Addis Ababa during the increasing social inequality of the 1960s and 1970s, which I have described as a combination of patterns of differentiation and segregation. They took their place at the bottom of urban society in a context where their condition of social subordination was no longer defined by their dependence on specific patrons but through their insertion into the wider, looser, and diversified sets of interactions that composed the city's economy and labor market. Notably, it was that expanding economy of leisure and enjoyment that provided them with ways of getting by. Ahmed found a job as a waiter in a pastry shop that is now among the oldest in the city. Wubit engaged with the sex economy, which at the time was at least sixty years old, and closely linked to the blossoming of drinking houses in the very early history of Arada (Pankhurst 1968, 1974, 1985; see chapter 5).

The experiences of Haile's mother and Ibrahim's parents provide a glimpse into how a significant part of this generation of migrants seeking work in the city came to permanently occupy the lower or lower-middle sections of urban society. Unlike those who, for instance, had significantly benefited from the bureaucratization of the Ethiopian state and the modernization of society, such as university graduates who could earn a starting salary of 500 birr[5] a month in 1970 regardless of specialization (Markakis 1974, 183), Ahmed and Wubit earned salaries that remained low. In 1970, the majority of people employed in the formal labor market, including Ahmed, earned between 50 and 150 birr a month (Laketch Dirasse 1991, 98). In 1974, a woman like Wubit, working in a small drinking house, earned

---

5. In 1970, one Ethiopian birr (also called Ethiopian dollar) was equivalent to US$0.40 (Markakis 1974, 119).

no more than 44 birr a month. Wubit could have risen in the trade, first as a young woman in a bar working for a madam and earning 65 birr monthly, to become a madam running her own small place and earning 100 birr a month, and, finally, to a freelance prostitute at 130 birr a month (Laketch Dirasse 1991, 44–47). Even at its height, however, her income would remain low.

However, Wubit never became a madam and eventually quit sex work when she became very ill. She turned to selling bread and vegetables outside her house to support herself and her sons. Meanwhile, after many years of working as a waiter, Ahmed opened a small retail shop. He worked there for a while, hoping for a better income, but the business did not prosper. Ahmed rented the shop out while continuing to work as a waiter. This lasted until the mid-1990s when the newly established EPRDF government granted ownership of retail shops to those who worked in them. Ahmed lost the shop and relied on his work as a waiter and Muna's small business to support his five children: four sons (including Ibrahim) and one daughter.

Despite their condition of subjugation, Ibrahim's and Haile's parents felt that they had achieved a small but valued social improvement relative to the radical scarcity of the rural areas they came from. For Ibrahim and Haile themselves, the positions that Ahmed, Muna, and Wubit had achieved in urban society were proof of their parents' cleverness. Although Haile's relationship with his mother was never easy, he never questioned the fact that his mother had been very smart in navigating the challenges of her life. Likewise, Ibrahim told me, "My father has been very clever. He opened his own shop when he was young and he managed to get our house from the *kebelle*. [At that time] you did not get it if you were not paying someone."

Ibrahim had tremendous respect for his father's success. But he was aware that he and his father had very different understandings of the society they lived in. While both Ibrahim and his father significantly engaged with urban life, his father conceptualized and experienced the city in comparison with rural areas, reckoning that going to the city had provided him with valuable opportunities to raise a family. Although his job at the pastry shop had not made him rich, Ahmed valued his investment in the city as signaling a degree of relative success away from the rural areas. Ibrahim recalled how his father brought this history up in conversation with his son: "My father asked me why I was wasting my time. [He said] 'When I was your age, I had rented a house, a wife and a work and I came from the rural area. What about you? And you even have grown up in Addis Ababa.'"

However, he had mixed feelings about his father's economic stability. Talking about his father's job at the pastry shop, for instance, he exclaimed, "He killed his age working there," as if to say that by working as a waiter for more than forty years his father had missed out on the opportunities available to improve his life and his family's lives. Moreover, while Ibrahim was proud of his Gurage and Muslim background, he did not speak his father's language and had seldom visited his father's hometown. He saw himself as a "plastic Muslim" who knew much more about Orthodox Christianity than about Islam.

Having been born in Addis Ababa without particular connections to his father's hometown, Ibrahim made sense of his position in broader society exclusively by relating to the social reality of growing up in a poor neighborhood in the capital. For Ibrahim, the city, and particularly the neighborhood where he grew up, was not a place for hardworking men and women such as his parents, but for gangsters and crime. The inner city, he argued, "is the place where you learn to become a gangster." "There are prostitutes, drinking places, *khat bet* and a lot of gangsters, just gangsters!" He made a similar point on another occasion, talking about a guy in his neighborhood who had studied at a good school but ended up a thug (*duriye*): "When you don't have money and you have grown up in [Arada], it is impossible to become something else!"

Ibrahim's understanding of the inner city as a place of gangsters and prostitutes was not only the result of the fact that Ibrahim—born and bred in Addis Ababa—had a different range of expectations from those of his rural-born parents. The difference between his parents' and his own experiences of the urban milieu reflects the broader historical transformations that have shaped Ethiopian urban society over the last thirty years—a period of great change during which Arada, the old city center, became Addis Ababa's inner city and interventions to govern urban poverty shaped opportunities available to Ibrahim, Haile, and their contemporaries.

The government measures that fostered their parents' improvement were ineffective in opening up social mobility for the city-born poor of Ibrahim and Haile's generation. This is not because the policies were badly designed or poorly implemented, but because they were not concerned with enabling mobility out of poverty. To echo Simmel ([1908] 1971), government interventions were primarily concerned with managing deficiency (the "too little") while containing excess (the "too much"). The Ethiopian state could not afford to have large numbers in radical poverty in the capital, but left it up to the urban poor to find additional resources to achieve something better.

After Emperor Haile Selassie was deposed in 1974, the Derg established a greater policy focus on the livelihoods of the urban poor. However, the urban poor entered state political projects not as a political constituency but as imagined beneficiaries of policies implemented from above and on their behalf. As a result, while the poor remained poor, the socialist state expanded its apparatus of social control by making people dependent on its system of distribution (Clapham 1988). City property was nationalized, providing stable homes at low rents, and, over the years, a socialist distribution system gave people access to rationed food-stuffs at controlled prices (Clapham 1988). These initiatives provided people like my interlocutors' parents with a measure of economic security. Secure poverty did not, however, mean greater opportunities. Government measures left people in an enduring condition of poverty.

Growing up in secure poverty did not enable Haile and Ibrahim to pursue trajectories of social improvement. As members of the generation that came of age during the socialist regime, they were meant to be beneficiaries of an expanding education system. But the visions of progress and social mobility that had long characterized discourses on education were hardly reflected in their experiences (Mains 2012a).

As Haile put it, school was "fake": it was a place to avoid rather than one where a vision of a better future could be cultivated. Ibrahim remembered studying in overcrowded classes led by underpaid and undermotivated teachers. Ibrahim's neighbor Yibeltal, a minibus driver, echoed many disenchanted and resentful recollections of school days: "Teachers were *cold*." In these circumstances, Haile and Ibrahim soon left school. Haile did not remember himself as a great achiever and dropped out in eighth grade. Ibrahim dropped out before the twelfth grade exam, which could have given him a chance to go to the university.

Looking at my interlocutors' trajectories at school, we could easily blame them for their poor performance and lack of commitment. They were, in fact, already busy "working" and getting by on the streets. In his teens, during the early 1980s, Haile sold chewing gum and potatoes on the street. A neighbor helped him procure his wares in exchange for a cut. About ten years later, when Ibrahim was in his teens, his father sent him to work with a mechanic after school, providing Ibrahim with what his father thought was valuable work experience.

Child labor in Ethiopia and elsewhere has often been blamed for students' poor performance and high dropout rates (Yisak Tafere and Camfield 2009). In Addis Ababa's inner city, however, working after school was not uncommon even among those who did well in school. Some university graduates and would-be professionals with whom I sometimes spent my time off mentioned that during their childhood they had occasionally earned money by selling chewing gum and tissues on the street—without their parents' knowledge, they emphasized—as proof of their dedication to work and to family responsibilities. Childhood, for both my key informants and these university graduates, was a time where they were active social and economic actors, contributing to the income and activities of their households.[6] In this context, engaging in work while in school was a fundamental

---

6. The image of childhood as a playful and care-receiving period, free of work and responsibility, is often placed in potential opposition to adulthood, when a person assumes responsibilities and

aspect of their past lives as children in the way it enabled them to assert their position in the family and, potentially, find the means for a certain degree of economic autonomy (cf. Tatek Abebe 2008; Heinonen 2011).

Yet there was a fundamental difference between these university graduates and people like Haile and Ibrahim. This difference did not lie in whether they had worked after school but in whether they had access to the resources and networks that would have supported and encouraged them to pursue their education even when they were not performing well. My research assistant, a university graduate in anthropology who grew up in the same neighborhood, had once been a street vendor and hustler. Passing the tenth grade national exam, he told me, was what steered his life toward the university and away from the streets. He admitted, however, that he passed the exam not only because of his own willpower but also because his brother hired him a tutor. Haile and Ibrahim did not have access to such resources, and when a student does not perform well, continuing school is burdensome and holds little promise for future betterment.

The school system that Haile and Ibrahim attended was inspired by a principle of individual achievement. It could not give, or, rather, was not concerned with giving, the support they needed to do better in school. Established under Haile Selassie, it was designed to mold a bureaucratic elite (Markakis 1974). Its expansion under socialist and, notably, postsocialist Ethiopia was informed by a similar concern: filling the ranks of the state's expanding bureaucratic machinery (Clapham 1988; Mains 2012a). As the school was a channel for recruitment, low academic performance was rarely tackled in the classroom (Poluha 2004). The school system was mainly concerned with fostering those among the urban poor who were hardworking and determined enough to rise above the circumstances of their birth.

Change had come and reshaped the experiences of my interlocutors and their parents. Living in the city, my interlocutors' parents were better off than their rural kin, and Haile and Ibrahim were more educated than their parents. Cheap housing, cheap goods, and free education shaped the terms of their integration into wider society, but they also configured marginality as a secure form of poverty, one with limited opportunities for social mobility. Haile and Ibrahim were thus caught in a predicament. They were "securely" included in society, but in a way that significantly constrained their chances to get somewhere better.

---

achieves maturity and economic independence. As studies on children and life courses in both urban and rural Ethiopia have already shown, this opposition is fundamentally misleading and clouds our ability to understand how people define and experience their life trajectories (Nieuwenhuys 2001; Poluha 2004; Tatek Abebe 2008; Heinonen 2011). Indeed, many communities in highland Ethiopia, for instance, do not arrange the life of an individual through this well-defined linear and gradual succession of steps. The process of growing up has long been perceived as a continuum of responsibilities and social experiences (Levine 1965; Molvaer 1995).

Entering Street Life

The centrality of street life in Ibrahim's and Haile's lives cannot be fully appreciated merely as a necessary consequence of the fact that other opportunities were not available to them. Their long engagement in the street economy makes sense if we consider that it was the most viable trajectory offered to them since they were very young. Such a relation between viability and the persistence of marginality constituted the central node of the tension between outcomes and meanings that this chapter seeks to tease out.

Entering street life offered Haile and Ibrahim a means of getting by. This relative autonomy and economic independence was the very first achievement that they experienced as teenagers in the face of their condition of marginality and exclusion. While they valued this achievement, they also had mixed feelings. As Haile and Ibrahim looked back on their experiences and compared them with the outcomes of their life trajectories, they saw their quest for independence and autonomy through engagement in street life not only as bearing witness to their smartness and ability to rely on themselves but also as embedded in the tensions that encompassed their existence. After all, similar to Ahmed's, Muna's, and Wubit's experiences of rural-urban migration, the promise of independence and autonomy that street life held for Haile and Ibrahim was relative and inevitably embedded in the condition of exclusion and subjugation they were born into.

As school dropouts, Haile and Ibrahim could hardly expect to gain employment in the state administration, as generations of motivated, hardworking but still numerically limited "newcomers" had done since the early 1960s. In addition, coming from families who could not support them, Haile and Ibrahim could not "wait" in unemployment for something better to come along, as more privileged young people would do in Addis Ababa and other towns in the country (cf. Mains 2012a). They had to "move around" (*inqisiqase*), taking what was available, because, as Ibrahim put it: "When you are young, your family pay for your food and for your clothes. But once you turn twenty, what do you do if you don't have a job? Are you going to ask your family for money for your clothes?" Many among my informants had a similar view. Fasil, a street tourist guide, told me: "Young people in Addis Ababa are lazy, they bother their families for everything. They ask for money even for *khat* and beers. I don't like this. You have to be independent and rely on yourself."

Their engagement with street life tapped into these notions and expectations of independence and autonomy and, notably, was perceived to be in continuity with their earlier engagements with part-time work. In this regard, leaving school constituted a key conjuncture in my interlocutors' lives. Leaving school put them in an entirely new routine: Haile and Ibrahim no longer had obligations to the school and its timings and had to begin "moving around" to get by. Such moments of "transition" have often been interpreted as those instances when the social agents' actions wittingly or unwittingly contribute to the reproduction of wider social structures. For Pierre Bourdieu (1977), this is a *conjuncture*—that is, the moment when wider social structures are enacted and reiterated through action. Seen from this perspective, when Haile and Ibrahim left school and moved to find ways to get by, they were adapting their practices to the social structures that generated their practices. But my interlocutors' trajectories and the wider patterns that their experiences reflect suggest a different reading of the dynamics at play.

Leaving school and finding themselves out there, looking for ways to get by, was a conjuncture of potential change. This was a *vital conjuncture*, a moment not when wider structures are enacted but when social agents try to mediate between "structured expectations" and "uncertain futures" (Johnson-Hanks 2006, 24). After leaving school, Haile and Ibrahim were left to themselves to fashion the ways they would navigate a condition of marginality they could hardly challenge. With their practice, they were not enacting wider and underlying social structures; they were simply trying to act on the relationships of force acting upon them (Jackson 2005).

Viability, however, does not mean success. For my interlocutors and their peers, viability had more to do with what they could realistically hope for in a landscape of power relations that they could not navigate effectively. For Haile, for instance, the comparison with better-off children was the reason he stole at a young age: "When you are poor, you see other kids who come from better families who have things you don't have. You want them, but you cannot get them, then you steal them." Comparison with others, by itself, cannot explain the whole range of reasons why the street economy became a viable option for achieving autonomy and independence. However, the comparison with better-off children was relevant because it voiced Haile's deeper sense of frustration with the circumstances of his existence and his own quest for autonomy and independence: the very fact of being born poor and in a family that could not care for him.

Haile described his history and engagements with street life as being directly linked to his, as he put it, "family case." His mother was a sex worker, and, for this reason, Haile told me, he had to spend time away from his house because his mother received her clients there. Already when he was eleven, Haile was often on his own, learning how to look after himself. Haile felt very bitter about this. When I asked him to tell me more about what his family thought about his engagement with street life, he skated over this part of his story, saying: "Families don't understand anything."

As Heinonen (2011) suggests in her book on street children in Addis Ababa, conflicts could sometimes emerge in a family when children and young people achieved relative forms of independence and autonomy. Heinonen argues that children and young people may come to claim and perform roles that directly question and erode the authority of their parents, potentially leading to conflict as the latter try to enforce their role while the former attempt to maintain their positions of independence and autonomy. With his bitterness while talking about his childhood, Haile reenacted for me the conflicts that had pervaded the circumstances of his involvement in street life.

Haile's resentment toward his family was shared by his peers. For Ibrahim, for instance, persistent conflict and confrontations with his father were an important part of existence. On the one hand, his father's actions were often motivated by a concern that his son was gaining his independence and autonomy by becoming a thug and an offender. From Ibrahim's own account, Ahmed was, in his way, a caring father. Ibrahim remembered one incident fondly, when Ahmed took him to the zoo and then to the university compound nearby. He wanted to show him where he could go if he kept focusing on school. "This is when he told me what money is for," Ibrahim remembered.

On the other hand, Ibrahim interpreted and sometimes encouraged the conflict with his father by resenting the fact that he found himself looking for autonomy and independence in the first place because of his family's inability to provide him with the means for social improvement. For instance, when I asked him why many young people I interviewed were reluctant to talk about their families, he replied: "They don't because families don't give them what they want or because they are poor." A few days later, when I asked him to explain what he meant, he told me about a recent quarrel: "I was very angry with my father. . . . I told him that he did not teach me anything and he did not show me anything. How could you make five children without thinking about the future? He replied to me that he made me strong, healthy and even told me to go to school. . . . I told him 'fuck you.' . . . He did not like it."

Being Arada

By engaging with street life, Haile and Ibrahim embraced the conflicts encompassing their experiences of marginality and exclusion to find a ground for action and achieve a relative form of economic independence and autonomy. By *being* and *becoming Arada*, Haile and Ibrahim went a step further. They placed their frustrations pervading their involvement in street life at the very center of the public arena of city and inner city life. As I argued in the introduction to this chapter, the nexus among experiences of marginality, place, and meaning is not a given. In principle, Haile and Ibrahim could have become hustlers investing only instrumentally with what happened in the inner city. Instead, Arada—as both a place and a category of urban living—became central in the ways they described themselves, made sense of their condition of marginality, and gave meaning to their practice and action. In the words of the anthropologist Henrik Vigh (2006), the urban was the terrain of their experience of *being* and *becoming*. Such a process of *being* and *becoming Arada* inhabited the domain of the ordinary as a move that Haile, Ibrahim, and many others among their friends and peers took to occupy or even disrupt the everyday spaces of their existence (de Certeau 1984). In this regard, by claiming to *be Arada*, hustlers and thugs were not just putting forward a claim of territoriality or belonging. They sought to ground their attempts to live meaningfully through their condition of marginality into a place and a set of notions that had been central in the definition and experience of the urban in Addis Ababa.

Earlier in this chapter I discussed how, already by the 1960s, *being Arada* denoted the sociality that pervaded Addis Ababa's cafés, bars, and restaurants. In the words of Ato (Mr.) Mekonnen, a man in his sixties and a long-term resident of the inner city, the *Arada* were those who patronized these places. They could dance and drink, and were smart in their understanding of what was happening around them. Hence, in this wider definition, an *Arada* is a person of fashion, leisure, and style. Sharing, joking, generosity, and conviviality are also commonly believed to be features of an *Arada*. An *Arada* is also a social hero who fights back in a bar brawl, often to take the side of those who cannot defend themselves; he is a trickster, a street-smart person who knows how to make things happen and, sometimes, not happen. As Ato Brahanu, a man in his sixties when I met him in 2010, and an alumnus of the General Wingate School (a boarding school for the best students of the country who received scholarships from Emperor Haile Selassie himself), put it: "I remember the *Arada*, they were clever as well, good at fighting. They always ate together and they never ran away from sharing and loving each other. It was about pure friendship! *Arada* is not about a place. It is a soul, a spirit [*manfas*]."

At the same time, however, as inner city residents argued, not all *Arada* were the same and not all *Aradas* could equally claim to be "true" *Arada*. There were "gentlemen *Aradas*" (*denbegna Arada*) and "thug *Aradas*" (*duriye Arada*). *Denbegna*, in Amharic, means "customer," "buyer," or even "patron" (Leslau 2005), and *denbegna Arada* conveyed the sense of properness, manners, gallantry, and style that made a person a proper *Arada*. Being a proper *Arada* and being in Arada embodied ideas of sophistication that an emerging urban middle class, made up of students, intellectuals, artists, singers, members of the aristocracy, government officials, and army officials, claimed as symbols of its distinctiveness between the 1940s and the mid-1970s. Tesfaye Gessessie, a playwright in the 1960s, explained that the *Aradas* were the vanguards of urban society, those who were ahead of everybody else, those who had a talent and used it to produce something.

Duriye, meanwhile, is the Amharic word for "thug." *Duriye Arada* reflected that street life and the street economy existed alongside the society of gentlemen and their ideas of sophistication and properness. For my informants among hustlers and thugs, a pickpocket, a con artist, and a robber are *Arada* because they master street smartness and street knowledge. Andare, a street tourist guide, told me: "*Arada* are the ones who understand other people. Pickpocket is a smart way of *being Arada*. First you have to understand the brain of the person and also his stature, then you will choose your target." Similarly, Ibrahim often reminded me: "A smart person could also be a criminal, but you already know this."

Middle-class ideas of urban sophistication and thugs' street smartness represented two ways of conceptualizing *being Arada* and *being in Arada*. And that a clear distinction was made between gentlemen and thugs reveals that there was not just a divergence of views between the two. Between "gentlemen" and "thugs" there was a long history of differentiation and exclusion, a history that made *being* and *becoming Arada* so central for both gentlemen's strategies of distinction and the ways inner city marginalized men (thugs) sought to navigate their condition of exclusion.

The value of this history becomes evident when we consider that "gentlemen" celebrated and praised the *Arada* of the past, in particular those frequenting the bars, cafés, and theaters of the 1960s, as the ultimate embodiment of bravery, smartness, and urban sophistication, while questioning whether "thugs" could ever rightfully claim to *be Arada*. As Ato Teferi (a friend of Ato Mekonnen and Ato Brahanu's), an educated middle-class gentleman in his sixties and a long-term resident of the inner city, told me: "Nobody would call a *duriye* an *Arada*." Exploring the reasons why a "gentleman" questioned the *Arada* credentials of thugs would require an entire book exploring the fortunes of a segment of Ethiopia's urban middle classes that Haile Selassie's regime nurtured and that both his and subsequent regimes failed to accommodate. Suffice to say that for Ato Teferi, Ato Mekonnen, and Ato Brahanu, talking about *Arada* and, in particular, the "*Arada* of the past" (*yeduro Arada*) did not involve just praising the ideals of education, chivalry, and cultural sophistication on which these gentlemen had grounded their sense of distinctiveness. By questioning the thugs' *Arada* credentials they guarded their own sense of distinctiveness from the poorer segments of the inner city in the face of the fact that they, as inner city gentlemen, had themselves experienced relative forms of marginalization and exclusion.

As discussed earlier, already by the 1960s the elites had begun to leave Arada. The section of the middle class that continued to live in the inner city subsequently experienced a process of political and cultural marginalization that fueled nostalgic celebrations of the 1960s as a period when they could claim to be among the cultural elites of the city. The Red Terror, with the deaths of many intellectuals and the impoverishment of urban society that followed, further frustrated the urban middle classes' sense of distinction. When the Red Terror ended, the Derg sought to co-opt the urban middle classes through university education, scholarships to study in other socialist countries, and employment in the expanding bureaucracy (Clapham 1988). Yet the performances of style and urban sophistication that had characterized ideas of *Arada* in the 1960s were publicly banned as symbols of the culture of the bourgeoisie that the regime wanted to fight, a policy that stripped the middle class of the status of "cultural vanguards" (Simeneh Betroyannes 2008). Even the end of the socialist regime did not result in a rehabilitation of the inner city middle classes. Instead, the shrinking of the public sector under the impact of neoliberal policies and the suspicion that the governing EPRDF felt toward the intellectual middle class reduced the resources and opportunities for gentlemen to rethink their political and economic role. Today, the ideas of distinctiveness that the gentlemen cultivated have been replaced by other paradigms through which members of the urban upper-middle class seek to find their role in Ethiopian society, including affiliation with the ruling party, employment in international NGOs, and economic engagement in trade and business ventures (see chapter 7).

In these circumstances, inner city gentlemen used *being* and *becoming Arada* to cultivate a sense of distinction in relation to both those who excluded them in the city (the new urban economic elites) and those who occupied the spaces that gentlemen felt were theirs (inner city thugs). Still, for these thugs and hustlers, as with *les bluffeurs* in Abidjan (Newell 2012) and *les sapeurs* in Kinshasa (Gondola 1999) or marginalized inner city young men in New York (Bourgois 2003), *being* and *becoming Arada* was less about achieving a sense of distinction and more about asserting their presence in the urban space. Ultimately, this was why gentlemen were so concerned with questioning thugs' claims of *being Arada*. In fact, as we will see in more detail in chapter 2, the thugs had effectively and successfully occupied the spaces of the inner city. This occupation, however, was not so much about competing with the inner city gentlemen, as the latter ones saw it. By claiming to *be Arada*, a generation of inner city young men, including Haile and Ibrahim, sought to navigate their condition of subjugation by fashioning their presence in a city that marginalized them, as descendants of poor rural-born migrants, as inner city residents, and as only marginal beneficiaries of the state policies on development and education.

FIG. 1.2   A bar in Arada © Adelaide Di Nunzio

Becoming a *Duriye Arada*

The occupation of Arada, both as place and as an "archive" of meanings and identities of urban living, was partly a joyful enjoyment of the sociality and the practices of leisure that inhabited the places of the inner city—from bars and restaurants to the informal video houses and *khat bet*. But it also constituted a presence in the inner city that asserted itself through the illicit and, to some extent, the criminal (see chapter 2). Haile's and Ibrahim's presence on the streets of Arada combined this joyful experience of the urban with a forceful occupation of the urban space.

Ibrahim often told me about the sense of wonder and fascination that caught him when he first encountered street life in Arada, and over the years I could tell that this remained an important dimension of his commitment to *being Arada*. One of his earliest memories is from the mid-1980s, when he was just seven. On Sundays, he would spend his time guiding an old blind man he knew from his neighborhood and who made his living begging. "He gave me 1 birr a day. Fuck! 1 birr a day for me at that time was a lot of money!" At the end of the day, the man sometimes took Ibrahim to the *taj bet*, a honeywine drinking house. The man ordered some food for Ibrahim and drank *taj*. "That was an amazing place. People fighting, people drinking and shouting. I really liked it. From then, I hated begging, I always wanted to go to the *taj bet*. My father had taken me to restaurants, but they were Muslim restaurants, nothing like that happens there."

"Once then," Ibrahim recounted,

> the power went off at my house. It was night and dark, I rushed to my father's wallet and I took some money. I thought it was 1 birr, but, instead, I got 100 birr. Fuck! This was the first time that I saw 100 birr. How could I spend it? I asked myself. Then, I went to the blind man. We were begging. I told him "*abbat, abbat* [father, father], I found 100 birr." The old man threw his stick: "Son, where is it? Where is it? Take it!" Then, he told me "Son, today we don't beg, we go to the *taj bet*." I was so happy. He ordered me food and he drank. He drank so much that he said "Son, I am so sick, take me home, son." He was so drunk. I took him home and he gave me 10 birr. Fuck, again. What should I do with this? I asked myself. I bought some biscuits, a lot of biscuits and I went home. My mother and my father were furious with me, they understood I had taken the money. They searched me and they found some birr. They shouted at me and pulled my ears, then when I saw my father taking the *dula* [stick], I told them everything. "I gave the money to the blind man!" We went together to his house, we found him lying on the floor. He was still drunk. He told my mother and my father that he had spent all the money. My father was so mad. He put me in the house for six weeks. I could not go out, I could not play with my brothers. Sometimes my father was taking us to the cinema. When they went there, I stayed home.

Nearly seven or eight years later, Ibrahim's fascination with life in Arada transformed into a long-term engagement with street life. At that time, he was still in school, and Addis Ababa had just seen the fall of the socialist regime and the initial effects of the liberalization of the economy. In inner city Addis Ababa, one of these effects was the blossoming of video houses (*video bet*), especially in the 1990s (Emrakeb Assefa 2005).[7] This is where Ibrahim first met Haile, who, between 1992 and 1998, worked as a manager of video houses in the inner city. "He was one of the coolest guys in the *sefer* [neighborhood]," Ibrahim recalled, remembering Haile standing by his *video bet* wearing his Michael Jackson–style jacket and trousers.

---

7. Video houses were opened in the back of houses or replaced former businesses. Owners and managers of video houses were often different people. The owner usually rented the space from the *kebelle* and received a fixed amount or a percentage of profits from the manager who ran the video house and screened the movies.

In the memories of Haile and Ibrahim, video houses were not exclusively places where people went to watch movies and participate in the flow of images and the imaginations from Hollywood movies, which were increasingly available after the liberalization of the economy (Emrakeb Assefa 2005). Like drinking houses in the early history of Addis Ababa, video houses were a public arena in which a generation born in the decades immediately before and after the downfall of the socialist regime performed, embodied, and practiced ideas of street smartness and toughness. In fact, in the reckonings of Haile, Ibrahim, and Gizachew, a manager of video houses in his late thirties whose story I will tell later, running a video parlor in the early 1990s was a business for thugs (*duriye*). Knowing about movies was undoubtedly important—Haile and Gizachew became managers of video houses because they had spent time watching movies. Yet, being smart and tough was also necessary if managers wanted to keep their business going and ensure their customers behaved. Whereas the copyright for non-Ethiopian movies is still highly unregulated and pirated copies of freshly released blockbuster movies are openly sold from street stalls, at the very beginning of the business of video houses managers needed to rely on their knowledge of the informal economy to find movies to show and, in some cases, to run side businesses for extra profit. Notably, Getachew Bongar, a gangster (*hardegna*, literally "hard man") and, as we will see in the next chapter, a quasi-mythical figure in the 1970s and 1980s, owned a small video house during the last years of his life, which he used as a base for fencing stolen goods and selling marijuana.

Ibrahim also became closely involved in the business of video houses. In the beginning, when he was around fifteen, he would play hooky and go watch movies. By the time he was nineteen, at the end of the 1990s, he had met Haile and already had significant experience in managing video houses. The number of video parlors in the inner city had rocketed, and getting customers depended on the ability of the manager to find the latest movies. Ibrahim, Haile, and a few other managers of video houses sniffed out a new and promising, but illegal, business: showing pornographic movies. This paid off for a while, until they all got caught. The video houses they managed were shut down, and Ibrahim and Haile spent some time in prison.

When they were released some months later, Ibrahim and Haile needed to find ways of getting by. For a while, they helped Noah, a man who had just returned from Saudi Arabia, run a *video bet* that he had opened at the back of his parents' place, where he showed movies in the morning and sold *ganja* in the evening. After discovering the illegal trade, Noah's parents closed the video house. But by that time Ibrahim's and Haile's networks on the street had expanded, and the two started aggregating in a bigger group that included Mikias, a contemporary of Haile's whose biography I will tell over the course of the book. Over the years, they became part of a stable group of friends who became known as the *yemot midib*, the group of "those who are destined to die." The emergence of this group opened a new phase, especially in Ibrahim's life, that revolved around fighting and stealing.

Haile's early encounters with the street economy differed from Ibrahim's. While Ibrahim became closely involved in the criminal economy of the street in his early twenties, Haile, who was ten years older, entered the street economy directly through hustling and stealing. Ibrahim's first steps in street life demonstrate a fascination with the opportunities for enjoyment it provided, intertwined with ways of getting by (see chapter 6). Haile's experiences remind us that the street economy was not just a place for leisure but was deeply embedded in crime and forms of street violence (see chapter 2). In the mid-1980s, when he was fifteen, Haile was already "doing business" on the street. He started with two friends, one who ended up immigrating to Saudi Arabia and one who died when he was just twenty. They started by stealing watches, explained Haile: "The best ones were the Seiko 5. We could get 100 birr for one of it, and 70–100 birr in the Derg time was like 1,000 birr now!" Then, they moved on to robbing people on their way home at night by committing *čebu*, a technique of stealing in which a robber makes a victim lose consciousness by hitting the person's neck. This was a very dangerous and risky technique, as it could end with the death of the victim. On top of this, the police soon started taking notice of them. Haile and his friends decided to move to a safer occupation—pickpocketing. Haile reckoned that being caught pickpocketing would lead to a less severe sentence than if he were caught doing *čebu*. Eventually they grew overconfident and went from pickpocketing to burglary. They were caught, and Haile spent his first long spell in prison. Wubit, Haile's mom, was shocked, he remembered. She did not realize that her son had turned into a professional thief.

Navigating History and Marginality

Engagement with street life constituted a particular way of navigating history and marginality. It consisted of an attempt not to challenge exclusion and oppression but to live meaningfully through a condition of marginality that they understood they could not challenge. By engaging with street life, Haile and Ibrahim were not simply coping with failure or the impossibility of achieving the relative improvement their parents had experienced. Instead, they sought to refashion the terms of their presence in the urban space by establishing a valued form of economic independence and asserting themselves as part of a visible constituency within the fabric of the city.

However, this is only a partial portrayal of Haile's and Ibrahim's engagement with history and how contingency pervaded their experience of the act of living. In these pages, I have shown how they and their peers acted primarily within their circumstances. I have also described street life and the street economy as a sort of aggregate of individuals' quests for autonomy, recognition, and enjoyment. In the next chapter, I examine how street life constituted a collective reality and how engagement in the street economy was not only the experience of being acted upon by history. It was also an attempt to shape history through the search for being something other than one's constraints.

A THUG'S LIFE

The Productivity of Street Life

Being and *becoming Arada* offered Haile, Ibrahim, and generations of inner city young men ways of asserting their presence in the urban space and encouraging action amid exclusion. At the same time, they faced a predicament: they grounded their actions in flirtations with street violence and engagement with illicit activities and, sometimes, criminal offenses. This predicament, Philippe Bourgois (2003) argued in his ethnography of Puerto Rican drug dealers in Harlem, New York, shows how the search for ways of navigating oppression and subjugation comes to reinforce the same condition of marginality. In this book I seek to propose a slightly different interpretation of this predicament. Rather than a vicious circle, I see the relation between action and marginality as a tension. People's attempts to navigate their condition of marginality are a fertile terrain for the elaboration of modes of being and acting, which are grounded in a condition of exclusion but, crucially, are not reducible to it (Berlant 2011; Butler 1997). As I showed in chapter 1, Haile and Ibrahim did not create their condition of subjugation. Instead, they were simply trying to act on a condition that had been imposed on them (Jackson 2005). What eventually reinforced their condition of marginality was not their actions but how their actions and the terrains of their practice were governed (see chapters 3 and 4).

This chapter seeks to characterize action in the midst of marginality and exclusion. As Philippe Bourgois (2003) aptly pointed out, street life appeals to generations of young men, including in inner city Addis Ababa, because it holds a promise: it enables them to elaborate meaningful ways of living through marginality, obtain a sense of respect and dignity, and shape what happens in the everyday spaces of their existence (Jensen 2008; L. Ralph 2014; A. Goffman 2014; Venkatesh 2006; Gondola 1999; Newell 2012; Friedman 1994; Steinberg 2004). This production of meaning and achievement of respect, I agree with Bourgois, does not put the marginalized in a better place. However, this search for meaning and respect is not what contributes to the persistence of marginality. While marginality persists as a result of the ways the actions and the lives of the marginalized are governed, the search for meaning and respect produces a certain kind of change. It makes thugs agents of the history of their city and their community.

To appreciate this relation between action, marginality, and history, I contend that involvement in street life and, specifically, in the street economy of hustling and thieving should not be exclusively conceptualized as a consequence of unemployment (Cruise O'Brien 1996; Glaser 2000; Newell 2012; Mains 2012a) or as a descent into subcultures of deviancy (cf. Akyeampong and Ambler 2002; Decoudras and Lenoble-Bart 1996; Heap 1997; Glaser 2000; Vigil 2003) triggered by necessity in the face of hardship and poverty. To be sure, engagement with crime is often situated in experiences of social exclusion. However, by assuming that involvement in street life is exclusively driven by privation and deprivation, we risk missing the "productive" dimension of street life as a site of action and social practice.

By acknowledging the productivity of street life, I am not trying to romanticize the street economy as a site of social justice. Flirtations with performances of male bravery and physical toughness made street life a gendered place as well as a violent one (Iliffe 2005; A. Goffman 2014; Bourgois 2003; Jensen 2008; Pype 2007). As we will see in this chapter, however, thugs might be tough but not necessarily rough, nor were they invariably rogues. Being recognized as a smart thug *Arada*—and not just a violent thug—meant embodying a certain balance that, though problematic, regulated and mediated performances of toughness and street violence. Through this mediated and regulated street violence, street life appealed to young men like Haile and Ibrahim not because it gave them an opportunity to be violent or masculine. Street life gave marginalized young men a way of asserting their presence in the city while obtaining a certain degree of respect, recognition, and fame on the streets and in the community.

Again, pointing out how involvement in street life could deliver respect does not mean endorsing toughness and street violence as legitimate grounds and paradigms for action. Conversely, it means recognizing the existential quest and struggle behind it. With Frantz Fanon ([1952] 2008), I read the appeal of crime, hustling, and street violence for Haile, Ibrahim, and many others in the inner city as embedded in the search "for somewhere else and for something else" (170) that this book tries to tease out. As Fanon acknowledges, this is no joke. It can be a "savage struggle" in which one must be "willing to accept the convulsions of death, invincible dissolution, but also the possibility of the impossible" (170). I argue that this temptation to play with the possibility of the impossible appealed to Haile, Ibrahim, and generations of marginalized young men before them. Involvement in street life gave them an opportunity to experiment with what poor persons could be and do (possibility) in the face of a condition of marginality they could hardly challenge (impossibility).

This attempt to claim possibility out of impossibility did not put thugs in a better place, but it made them agents of their own history and the history of their community. Thugs shaped history, but not as "breakers" or "vandals"—those agents of rupture, disruption, and crisis that have populated scholarly discussions on the agency of young people and marginality in Africa (Honwana and de Boeck 2005; Abbink and van Kessel 2005) and beyond (Maira and Soep 2005; Nilan and Feixa 2006). Instead, similarly to what Jennifer Cole (2010) argued in her study of history, generations, and life trajectories of sex workers and religious converts in Madagascar, street thugs made history by imposing a continuity. Generations of inner city young men made history by creating a recognizable and enduring constituency in the urban space: a community for elaborating, learning, and embodying ways of living through marginality and exclusion. This community had its own history and an appeal grounded in the continuity of that history.

This chapter examines how this continuity was achieved on the streets of Addis Ababa and how it shaped experiences of marginality. I begin by discussing the history of the street economy and show that loose networks of criminal activities and street actors had long characterized the underworld in the inner city, while the emergence of organized "groups" was a relatively recent phenomenon in Arada. This long history suggests that to study the street economy and the history of the street, as Fourchard (2005) wrote in reference to crime, we should examine them as cumulative phenomena. I argue that this cumulative production of the history of the street economy is what made street life appealing to generations of young men. The street economy is a viable and productive terrain of social practice because, over time, an increasing number of people have produced and expanded the repertoire of ways of being on the street. By joining the street, young men were not there to invent new ways of getting by, but could rely on a wider range of techniques and modes of action through which to find means of making do and imagining trajectories toward respect and recognition.

Remembering the history of street life enabled my interlocutors to take advantage of this cumulative history. By recalling and recounting the deeds of generations of street thugs, they learned street smarts. By marking a historical continuity between the thugs of the present and the thugs of the past, inner city young men embodied valued models of toughness and smartness, defined themselves as worthy of respect, and sought to navigate their condition of marginality. This twofold practice of remembering and reenacting the deeds of the thugs of the past made thugs of the present actors in history. As Geoffrey White (2000) might put it, thugs remembered history as made through individual actions and biographies and, at the same time, claimed to shape history through their own individual actions and biographies.

A Cumulative History of the Street Economy

A comprehensive history of crime and the street economy in Addis Ababa is yet to be written. Through the few historical sources available, such as the now-defunct police magazine *Policena Irmejaw* (Police and Enforcement), studies on crime in urban Ethiopia, and oral histories, however, we can analyze the fundamental features of the history of the street economy.

Thieving and Hustling

Thieving and "hustling," as some of my informants called it, are the bread and butter of the street economy in inner city Addis Ababa. Hustling is slippery and elusive, not only for those who deal with it in their everyday lives but also for the scholar, the historian, and those more generally interested in keeping records of what happens on the street. As Wacquant (1998) pointed out in his work on the black American ghetto, hustling refers to an incredible variety of activities "from the relatively innocuous and inoffensive . . . —to the felonious" (4). Similarly, the Amharic term *mella* (literally, a "means," "formula," or "system") is used to describe a wide range of activities on the street. A *mella* is a trick, or, more simply, a way of getting by. Ibrahim told me he was doing a *mella* when he helped one of his friends sell a mobile phone. A "hustler" is doing a *mella* when he is trying to persuade someone, even a friend, to treat him to a meal, a full plate of *injera* (Ethiopian pancake), a couple of beers, or a bag of *khat*. A *mella* also refers to specific street businesses, such as stealing, fencing stolen goods, touting minibuses, and showing tourists around. An analysis of any of these activities can easily be overwhelmed by the intricacies of their histories and of the arrangements they entail; I discuss more of these details in chapter 5.

Thieving is also a complex "business." The term for "stealing" (in Addis Ababa's street slang, *laboro*, from the Italian *lavoro*, literally, "work") was used as a generic category including a wide repertoire of techniques that each had their own name and specificity. *Čebu*, as I have already mentioned, is a form of assault, literally hitting the victim's neck. *Belbela* is a house burglary conducted by breaking in and out from the roof. *Ankte* is a house robbery conducted by breaking in through the door. *Setete* is a daylight house robbery, sometimes carried out by showing up at the house of the victim pretending to be looking for someone. *Quč'laquč'* means pickpocketing on minibuses, but is termed *šwawešwawe* if the driver helps the thief steal by jolting the passengers with a rough driving style. Pickpocketing on the street is *qaste*, and *git't* is a way of pickpocketing by tripping up the victim. *Mančku* is bag snatching, and *nabu* is car theft.

It is difficult to know when precisely a particular stealing technique appeared on the streets of the inner city. A few are mentioned in newspapers, but we may imagine that a particular technique of stealing already existed before it was actually mentioned. *Setete*, for instance, was the nickname of a certain Kefyalew, after his favorite business. He was caught by the police in 1964 (1957 in the Ethiopian calendar) after he tried to break into the house of an American working for the Peace Corps in Addis Ababa.[1] Meanwhile, *Addis Reporter*, a monthly English-language magazine published during the end of the 1960s and the beginning of the 1970s, reported in January 1969 that a group of "neck hitters" (*čebu*) were caught by the police while "robbing a gentleman of his watch."[2]

Whereas we cannot say anything certain about the history of stealing techniques, we can confidently argue that the rich terminology associated with it is the product of a long, cumulative history of thieving and stealing. In the early history of Addis Ababa, Zewdu Temtime (1995) reports that theft was very common in the market in Arada. Traders from the countryside were usually the easiest targets. The presence of shops, the houses of rich Ethiopians and foreigners, drinking houses, and, later, clubs provided thieves, pickpockets, and robbers with potentially rich pickings. At night, burglars robbed rich houses and foreigners' shops while on the street, robbers attacked drunks going home from the drinking houses. Banditry also existed: in the areas where the woods were thick, bandits, sometimes servants from the palace (Berhanu Lameso 1983), ambushed convoys of rich people going toward the king's palace.

By the time the first issues of *Policena Irmejaw* appeared in the early 1960s, thieving and burglary were not the only activities taking place on the city's streets. An incoherent army of hustlers, cheaters, and forgers, together with pickpockets, robbers, and snatchers, populated the "criminal underworld" in

---

1. "Meqetat yalebachew berikash yemigezugn nachew," *Policena Irmejaw*, Tekemt 15, 1957 Ethiopian Calendar (hereafter EC) (October 24, 1964), pp. 1, 3, 9.
2. "Addis Muggers," *Addis Reporter*, January 10, 1969, p. 22.

Addis Ababa. Already by the late 1960s and 1970s, thieving—in particular, robbery, but also the management of a wide range of illicit activities, including fencing stolen goods and protection rackets—had become the domain of organized groups. These groups, however, tended to be short-lived since their activities often easily attracted police attention—a history I return to below.

Less organized and professionalized forms of thieving and hustling persisted longer, even through moments of intense political conflict (cf. Andargatchew Tesfaye 1988), during which security forces paid particular attention to what happened on the streets (see chapter 4). Petty theft and hustling endured through these difficult circumstances because they were low-key, situational, and not professionalized. Hence, it is not pure coincidence that petty theft and assault, especially at night, are historically the most common offenses in urban Ethiopia (Brown 1971, 1973; Daniel Wondimu 2004). Those engaging in petty thievery turned to it occasionally and opportunistically and combined it with equally opportunistic and situational involvement in other activities, such as hustling or cheating, and licit activities in the informal and formal economies, such as wage labor and self-employment (Daniel Wondimu 2004; see chapters 3 and 4). The variety of stealing techniques, I argue, was both the result of and the reason for the endurance of petty theft on the streets of Addis Ababa. It enabled thieves to move from one technique to another, as, for instance, Haile and his associates did when they were looking for better businesses or trying to avoid police investigation and imprisonment. As we saw in chapter 1, Haile and his companions shifted from "hitting the neck" to pickpocketing when they realized the police had taken notice of their activities.

Tough Men and the Economies of Respect

Although petty theft and hustling were low-key, situational, and not particularly professionalized, thieves and hustlers did not act in a vacuum. The street economy has historically been encompassed by a complex sociality where "respect" (*kibur*), or being respected and recognized as a smart hustler, a skillful thief, and a brave street fighter, constituted the symbolic capital that hustlers could mobilize in transactions and exchanges in the immediate, and also, my informants believed, rely on to establish a more durable and stable position on the street (see also chapter 5). Within this landscape of regulated transactions and interactions, the deeds and the activities of "tough men" (*hardegna*) have long been important features of the street economy.

In the memories of my informants, the names Getachew Bongar, Mesfin Redi, and Mamush Kuchere resonated as being among the most important and well-known tough men in Arada's history. There is little documentary information about these three individuals, and many of the stories about them are shrouded in legend. Nevertheless, as depicted in the memories of my informants and many others in Arada, the behavior of these tough men constituted a particular modality of street practice, closely linked to the street economies of hustling and thieving.

The lives of Getachew, Mesfin, and Mamush overlapped but marked different periods in the history of the street. Getachew was active in the period after the Red Terror and throughout the socialist regime. He was born in the neighboring area of Arat Kilo but grew up in Arada. Ato Tesfay, a resident of Arada and an old friend of Getachew's, remembered that before the socialist revolution Getachew worked as a shoeshine boy. Twenty years later, Getachew was a tough man. Still later, he sold drugs and ran a video house in Arada until he died in the early 2000s. Mesfin, meanwhile, was positioned in the transition between the Derg and the TPLF. He grew up as a street child and then became a dangerous thief and snatcher. Haile told me that Mesfin heartily disliked Tigrayans and Eritreans when they came into Addis Ababa with the TPLF. He began targeting them and their properties, especially the Tigrayan-owned jewelers' shops in Arada. For this reason, many people in my field site believed, a TPLF official shot and killed him in the early 1990s. Finally, Mamush was a tough man and street fighter in Arada. He died of tuberculosis (or, as some think, of HIV/AIDS) in the mid-2000s.

Getachew, Mesfin, and Mamush shared many similarities but manifested significantly different ways of being tough men. Mesfin was a thief, often described as a Robin Hood–like figure. He targeted the rich and shared the booty with his friends. Getachew and Mamush, on the other hand, despite walking the streets of Arada at different times, were believed by many of my informants to be *joffe*, professional hustlers or even "racketeers."

Ibrahim helped me understand the concept of *joffe*. Coming from Naples, where the Camorra is more than a criminal phenomenon, I told Ibrahim: "Where I come from, the street has a rule: the economy of the street is organized, and if you do something wrong, you could even get shot!" Ibrahim replied, "Marco, we do not have such a thing, here. The only thing that exists around here is *joffe*. In Naples you call it gangster, here we call it *joffe*." He continued, "When you see someone doing a business, you would ask him to give you a part, this is a *joffe*." The *joffe*, however, is not necessarily a practice of largesse or mere generosity. Just as friends might share with or even "steal" from each other (see chapter 5), the *joffe* inhabits the micropolitics of the street. First, a *joffe* is able to profit because of the illegal dimension of the street economy and because complicity is sometimes necessary. A thief can be persuaded to share because the person demanding a share could be a potential witness to the illegal act the thief has just committed. Second, *joffe* sometimes corresponded to the role particular individuals played in the street economy. The *joffe* were those who could bank on their reputations as brave street fighters to claim a cut of other people's transactions and exchanges.

To be on the safe side and avoid a beating, thieves preemptively gave a cut of their booty to Getachew, Mamush, and another young man whom I will call Ash and who was an active *joffe* during my fieldwork. Ibrahim explained this to me about Ash: "He is a fucking dangerous snatcher [*manču*]. He could steal a lot of mobile phones. There are some other guys who usually hang out with him, they are also snatchers. When they get something, they would give a part to him or they would involve [Ash] in the business by selling the mobile they stole through him; this is *joffe*." Snatchers preemptively gave money to Ash thanks to the street credit he enjoyed as a dangerous young man. As Bourdieu would say, the position of Ash as *joffe*, similarly to the positions of Getachew and Mamush, rested on the particular symbolic capital that he had acquired on the street, capital that was grounded in respect and the mastery of street violence. This not only granted the successful *joffe* room for maneuvering on the street but also provided a way of steadily controlling the money and resources circulating in the street networks of which he was a part (cf. Newell 2012, 118).

With their activities, "tough men" occupied a middle ground between low-key hustling and organized groups. Tough men were active agents in the production of a certain internal hierarchy within the economies of hustling and petty thieving. Yet their positions as tough men and *joffe* were far from institutionalized. Tough men succeeded each other, but not as heads of a criminal syndicate with particular functions of leadership and administration. Skillful hustlers became tough men because of the strength of their personality and their ability to command respect and recognition. Their careers as tough men were expressions of the endurance of the economies of respect on the streets, not an institutionalization of the world of hustling. When Getachew, Mesfin, and Mamush died, they left no clear institutional and organizational legacies, only the memories of their brave deeds and gestures, as discussed in the last section of this chapter.

The History of Street Groups

A higher level of professionalization and organization than that embodied by individual tough men existed on the streets of Addis Ababa, though it was achieved on shaky grounds. Already by the late 1960s and early 1970s, the activities of organized groups and street fights between different groups made it into the pages of *Policena Irmejaw* and *Addis Reporter*. One of these groups was the China Group, which, Yeraswork Admassie, a sociologist at Addis Ababa University, described to me as a "mafia in the making" that extorted protection money from merchants in Merkato, the city marketplace. The history of these groups and the confrontations between them is significantly different from that of petty theft and hustling because while hustling and petty theft persisted and many could claim to be tough men throughout their lives, groups did not last for long. They blossomed in the late 1960s, disappeared in the mid-1970s, reappeared in the mid-1980s, only to disappear again a few years later to reemerge during the 1990s and again in the early 2000s. As I discuss further in chapter 4, these moments of contraction and expansion were primarily due to the ways state politics penetrated street life at particular moments of Ethiopian urban history. The China Group, for instance, came to an end during the Red Terror in the late 1970s as it became engaged in the violent struggle between the squads of the EPRP (Ethiopian People Revolutionary Party), which opposed the military regime, and the Meison (All Ethiopian Socialist Movement), which initially supported the military regime. The conflict led to the deaths of many members of the China Group and similar gangs (see chapter 4).

Organized groups reemerged and resumed their group fights a few years after the Red Terror. In the mid-1980s, *Policena Irmejaw* (then called *Abiotawi Police*) reported that a new generation of robber groups had appeared, this time using machine guns and cars to commit their crimes.[3] Simultaneously, the city witnessed the reemergence of street fights between different groups. These events were not reported in the police magazine, but memories of the fights remained vivid for my informants as well as ordinary residents of the inner city. Haile, for instance, began stealing watches with his two friends in the early 1980s. However, he rarely participated in these fights. He was among the many hustlers and thieves who preferred to keep low and find ways of getting by on the street—a tactic that helped him avoid prison only to a limited extent, but meant that when he did get caught, his sentences were brief. Yet Haile had clear memories of what happened during those years of intense street violence, and he described to me a violent fight between the thugs of Arada and those of Kera, the neighborhood where the city meat market was situated. "Five buses full of people came to Piassa [Arada] to challenge the *Arada*," Haile remembered. Kera was the theater of even more violent fights between its group, the *bombard* (those who fight with stones), and the *filatew kuratew* (those who do things sharply) from Kirkos, the second most important market area in southern Addis Ababa.

The early 1990s witnessed another reemergence of street economy. The downfall of the military junta and the limited experience of the new regime in dealing with street life increased the room that hustlers and organized groups had to maneuver and set their *mella*. Street crime, organized groups, and group fights blos-

---

3. "BaAddis Ababa yezerafiwoch budin tegalete," *Abyotawi Police*, Hamle 15, 1977 EC (July 22, 1985), pp. 1, 5, 7.

somed during this time, including in Arada. An article in *Policena Irmejaw* published in 1995 (1987 in the Ethiopian Calendar) drew a comparison between group street fights in the late 1960s and what the city's streets had begun to witness in the early 1990s: a series of street fights between competing groups of young men from different neighborhoods.[4] These continued until the late 1990s and, as we will see in chapter 4 in more detail, emerged again in the early 2000s.

Groups of Arada

Unfortunately, no scholars have yet recounted and examined the history of street life in Kirkos, Kera, and Merkato. The stories of these groups remain only in the memories of the residents living in those neighborhoods. Although the streets of Arada had not seen the existence of powerful organized groups such as the China Group, they were characterized by loose networks of illicit activities and small-scale "organized groups."

Ibrahim described group life to me, recounting a vignette that he located in an undefined historical moment before the early 2000s. "All the *yeArada lijocc* [literally, "the guys of Arada"] used to go to Giorghis Hotel. It fucking looked like a party house." Each group had its own table. The guys from different neighborhoods, from Arada, Arat Kilo, and yeAmerica Gibbi (literally, "the American compound") next to Merkato, used to hang out there. At Giorghis Hotel, "the groups were fighting to get the most wonderful women, usually bar ladies," Ibrahim recounted. The *yemot midib*, Ibrahim's group, did not have their own table. "We used to take things from the table of those who were not from Piassa [Arada]. If something happened, the people from Piassa would have never allowed people from other areas to beat us up."

This image of groups from different areas sitting at their own tables, sipping drinks, and keeping an eye on each other vividly evokes the dynamics between them. I have thus far used the term "group," which Ibrahim and others among my informants used, because the category of "gang" often evokes an idea of a formalized, stable, hierarchical, and well-defined street unit that does not often reflect the social reality of the street economy in Addis Ababa, let alone Arada. The term "group" refers to two kinds of street units: on the one hand, situational entities that aggregated when there was something or someone to fight for or against, and on the other hand, more stable and organized groups that emerged around specific street businesses.

---

4. "Besefer simet yetenesasu goremisoch bechube tewegagu," *Policena Irmejaw*, Terri 15, 1987 EC (January 23, 1995), pp. 1, 5, 6, 7.

Let us start with the situational groups. There was a commonly held belief among my informants that if a neighbor was fighting someone from another area, it was likely that his neighbors would take his side. This did not mean that neighbors did not fight each other. Paraphrasing Evans-Pritchard's (1940) examination of the Nuer political system, on the streets of Arada each network of friends and neighbors was itself segmented and prone to conflict, violence, and brawls. These same networks might unite for conflicts with adjacent groups of the same order, and unite with these adjacent groups against larger sections (142).

Social obligations of reciprocity encompassed these situational alliances between neighbors. Ibrahim, for instance, once told me that he would not be happy to have the "young snatchers" fight alongside him in a street fight because, in the future, he would be expected to reciprocate by fighting with and for them. Unlike the Nuer, however, these social obligations of reciprocity were not expressed through kinship or specific idioms of belonging, such as ethnicity. It was the street itself that, as Bayat (1997) argued in his examination of street politics in Iran, "possesses this intrinsic feature, making it possible for people to mobilize without having an active network." "Such mobilization," Bayat contended, "is carried out through passive networks—the instantaneous communication among atomized individuals, which is established by the tacit recognition of their common identity and is mediated through space" (19). Passive networks, Bayat stated, constitute the range of informal contacts, interactions, and communications that incoherently and situationally link people on the street. What mediates between passive networks and common action is often what is perceived to be a common threat, causing networks of people who share only a geographical location in their everyday life to engage in unplanned and instantaneous cooperation.

Considering situational groups as "passive networks" in action is key to understanding why a large number of people joined violent street fights in the past. Haile and Ibrahim recalled that in the early 1990s many people in Arada joined a raid on yeAmerika Gibbi in Merkato, in the western part of the city. The fight was because the people of yeAmerika Gibbi were trying to take over the business of the minibus touts run in Arada by Saladin, a man from the inner city, and his group. Saladin organized the raid on yeAmerika Gibbi to fight back. Because the number of people in the group was not enough, Saladin turned to his neighbors and friends. People joined the fight for different reasons, Ibrahim and Haile remembered. To encourage his friends and neighbors to help him, Saladin treated them to a meal. However, a plate of *injera* was far from the only reason people participated in the raid. Some fighters wanted to join Saladin and did so after the raid. Others continued with their dealings. "At that time we were not interested in getting involved in the *tara* [minibus touts], we had our own *mella* [street business]," Ibrahim told me. The reason why people like Ibrahim joined was simple.

Having street businesses controlled by people from other areas was considered a threat because an increasing number of thieves and hustlers would flow into Arada from all over the city, stepping into existing street businesses run by locals. Thus a situational group "formed" to fight yeAmerika Gibbi.

These occasional fights between situational groups, however, constituted only one aspect of group life on the streets of Arada. Organized and more stable groups, like Saladin's group of minibus touts, are an important part of the history of the street economy in Arada. Among these a distinction may be made between two kinds of groups. One kind emerged around specific tough men and had already existed by the 1970s. These were usually composed of groups of friends who fought with and for the tough men, or of the circle of thieves from whom the tough man took his cut. Getachew Bongar, Mesfin Redi, and Mamush Kuchere had their own groups who fought with them and, throughout the early 1970s, *Policena Irmejaw* reported on robber groups that were organized in a similar way.

This kind of group had a long history, despite periodic disappearances. For instance, in the late 1990s and again in the early 2000s, in a neighborhood adjacent to the one where Ibrahim and Haile lived and Getachew, Mesfin, and Mamush had their base, the Ashanti group had its base. It included Gizachew, Kassaye, and Wondimu, men in their thirties whom I came to know well during my fieldwork. Ashanti was a pseudonym that the leader of this group had taken from a violent and wicked character in an Indian movie. His elder sister lived in India and this, perhaps, suggested the Bollywood connection. Ashanti was a tough man similar to Mamush and Getachew. As Kassaye, Gizachew, and Wondimu remembered, the group counted over forty members at its peak with Ashanti as *joffe*. This group, however, was not an organized gang. It members did not, in fact, always *work* together but sometimes expressed themselves as a group through collective action. Wondimu, for instance, remembered that a raid on a shop would follow if the shopkeeper had not given something for free or paid a couple of birr to a member of the group when asked.

The *tara askabari* (literally, "queue keepers"), or minibus touts, were a second kind of group. They appeared in the mid-1980s when minibuses began to circulate in Addis Ababa. From the very beginning, the business of touting minibuses was characterized by two main features, which soon made it significantly different from other street groups. The first feature was that the activities of the *tara askabari* were centered and structured around the control of a specific and well-defined business, while other groups mainly navigated the situational character of the inner city street economy. The second was the existence of a clear and recognizable leadership within each group. Haile and Ibrahim told me how the control of the minibus touts in Arada went back and forth between individuals who belonged to the same networks of friends, neighbors, and even relatives, out of whom, eventually, Saladin, the man who led the fight against the yeAmerika Gibbi, emerged as the strongest leader.

The *Yemot Midib*

Ibrahim and Haile had their own personal experience of being part of a group. They had just been released from prison at the end of the 1990s, having served a sentence for illegally showing porno movies. At first, Haile and Ibrahim went back to their old business, running Noah's *video bet*. There, they met Mikias, still a good friend, as well as Kebedde, Samson, Stefanos, Wube, and Taddesse. They were all regular customers of Noah's video house, where they came to smoke *ganja* and watch movies. When the video house shut down, they found themselves hanging out together on the street. This is when Ibrahim, Haile, and their new friends grouped together to look for "business," and the history of the *yemot midib*, the group of "those who are destined to die," began. The *yemot midib* was a clique of eight friends having fun together on the streets of Arada and often helping each other with stealing, cheating, dealing drugs, and so on. The group gained certain fame on the streets: indeed, its name was not self-assumed. People in the neighborhood called them this because of their defiant style, smoking *ganja* and heavy drinking, as well as their ability to navigate Arada's street economy.

The *yemot midib* was of a different type from those of the situational and organized groups in Arada. It was not organized around a tough man or a particular street business. This was a group mainly because its members spent time together. It was a network of friends woven around the different opportunities of the street economy. They alternatively, and sometimes individually and independently, engaged in stealing, cheating, fencing stolen goods, and selling *ganja*. Haile and Kebedde, for instance, picked the pockets of minibus riders. Ibrahim and Haile occasionally robbed people on the street. These were not organized activities; Ibrahim, Haile, and their friends just took "businesses" as they came. This may be the reason for the paradoxical fact that, when money was tight, guys in the *yemot midib* often robbed each other. "If you were sleeping, it could happen that someone else would take your shoes and would sell it to have something for a drink or a meal," Ibrahim remembered. Yet, the fact of being a group had a particular relevance in the lives of Ibrahim and Haile and in their positions in the street economy. Getachew Bongar and Mesfin Redi liked them. "They thought we were funny," Ibrahim remembered. Being part of a group of young men who were "destined to die," both dangerous and entertaining, provided them with a collective symbolic capital that was qualitatively similar to the one of the *joffes*. The tough men of the area, Ibrahim remembered, rarely claimed a cut in the booty of the *yemot midib*. This happened only if the group stepped into someone else's business—namely, a more powerful street actor who dealt with bigger and more profitable businesses.

Generations of Heroes

In his seminal work on honor, Frank Henderson Stewart (1994) argued that we can make a distinction between an inner honor and an outer honor, or in simpler terms, between "dignity" and "respect" (Johnson-Hanks 2006). Respect consists of a public practice concerning the fact of being greeted and honored (Iliffe 2005). Dignity is an internal feeling through which individuals feel and stay true to themselves (Bourgois 2003; Jensen 2008). As Jennifer Johnson-Hanks contended, there is "much analytic purchase" in analyzing respect and dignity separately (2006, 60). Individuals might find their way toward dignity, without achieving respect and recognition from others. In inner city Addis Ababa, this was often the case. While gentlemen disrespected the thugs, the thugs claimed for themselves a sense of respect and smartness. Likewise, even where economies of the streets are dominated by logics of respect, the fact that individuals might become targets of hustlers, thieves, and *joffes* does not mean they lack a sense of dignity and self-worth.

At the same time, however, searches for respect and dignity coexist, as the quest for self-worth and recognition is often grounded in understandings, notions, and meanings that individuals share with the wider society or with others populating the domains of life they feel (willingly or unwillingly) attached to (Johnson-Hanks 2006). It is not pure coincidence that in the words of my informants, the Amharic term for respect, *kibur*, referred to both their sense of inner honor and the recognition they pursued on the streets. Their quest for both respect and dignity was embedded in a specific repertoire of practices and meanings: the fact of *being* and *becoming Arada*.

Notably, as I learned by spending time with Haile and Ibrahim, to be an *Arada*, it was not enough to be able to navigate economies of respect by being a skillful hustler or a brave street fighter. It was the deeper capacity to embody valued models of smartness and toughness that led to a hustler and a fighter being recognized as an *Arada*. These ideas of smartness and toughness did not come from nowhere: just as thieving, for instance, had a cumulative history, so did smartness and toughness. Generations of inner city young people had attached themselves to this cumulative history when they entered the street economy; through this history they sought to navigate economies of respect and pursued their search for self-worth, all the while in a context where poverty and social stigma challenged the grounds on which they could claim both respect and dignity. Making sense of the intertwined quest for respect and dignity can help us understand why street life was so attractive to Ibrahim, Haile, and many others in the inner city.

Haile was sitting at the back of the room when I first went to hang out with the parking guys at the house of another parking guy, Najeeb. Ibrahim and Haile were the oldest in the cooperative of parking guys, and witnesses of a "history" that most of their colleagues, who were mainly in their early twenties, had not experienced. In early February 2010, when Haile began to talk to me about the history of the groups and tough men, the topic of my research was still not clear. I knew it would be about the attempts of the ruling party to control the street in the aftermath of the 2005 riots. When I met people for the first time, I introduced myself as a researcher who was interested in what had happened in 2005. I did this when I first talked to Haile. Haile mainly saw me as a student interested in "history" (*tariq*). Thus, it was history, and more importantly, the history to which he thought he belonged that he recounted to me. This was a history populated by tough guys, fights, and street businesses.

When Haile recounted the history of the tough guys, he, like many others, made a clear distinction in terms of "generations." He rarely used the Amharic term *twilid*, usually preferring the English term. In Haile's narration, generations were a chronological distinction between three cohorts of tough guys and *Arada* from the 1960s to the early 2000s. The succession of cohorts corresponded to the period when a particular tough guy dominated the streets of Arada. Getachew Bongar was the "hero" of the first generation. The passage from the first to the second generation took place when Getachew Bongar went to jail and Mesfin Redi took over. The story of this generational transition is interesting. Getachew Bongar was put in prison, Haile reckoned, because he was dealing in mercury. The trade of mercury is something of an urban myth in Addis Ababa, and it is difficult to know whether it actually existed. It is a common belief that the mercury was smuggled out during the first years of the EPRDF from the Derg's disbanded weapons factory and that the business was a dangerous one. Getachew was caught because the traders in the yeAmerica Gibbi in Merkato tricked him and snitched on him to the police.

Mesfin Redi then took over, but for just a few years. Mesfin had already proved himself to be a brave Arada, and not just a skillful thief, when he fought the people from yeAmerica Gibbi who had initially been controlling the business of the minibus *Arada*. Listening to this story I realized that the confrontation between Arada and the yeAmerika Gibbi that I described earlier, with the case of Saladin in the early 1990s, had historical roots. On a day Haile placed somewhere in the mid-1980s, Mesfin went to yeAmerika Gibbi and stabbed Yared, the then leader of the minibus touts. A fight followed, and people from Arada took over the minibus business. However, Mesfin preferred to continue his activities as a "dangerous thief" in the area and gave control of the business to the people of Arada: "'Arada work now!' Mesfin said," Haile remembered. I asked why Mesfin did this. The gesture, Haile argued, was simply the most visible example of Mesfin's generosity toward other *Arada*.

The killing of Mesfin, allegedly by a TPLF official in the early 1990s, marked the passage from the second to the third generation. This, as Haile recounted, roughly concurred with the end of the socialist regime, drawing a correlation between a change in the political scenario and a transformation in street life. After Mesfin's death, a third generation, "our generation," as Haile called it, followed. This was the time in the early 1990s when not only a famous (*tawaki*) thug such as Mamush Kuchere dominated the streets of the inner city, as Getachew and Mesfin did in earlier years, but also a period when, Haile reckoned, a significant and unprecedented number of young men turned to the streets and became *duriye* (thug) *Arada*.

While Haile was narrating the stories of three generations, the broader "history" of the country ran along, almost in the background, with successions of cohorts of tough guys, heroes, and thugs in Arada. That Haile narrated Arada's history by focusing on the cohorts of tough guys does not mean that he was unaware of broader Ethiopian history. On many occasions, he mentioned the Red Terror and discussed the 2005 riots and postelection violence. His focus on the tough guys and the heroes was a claim for making the stories about Getachew and other thugs part of the country's history with a capital *H*. Haile's history was not independent and disconnected from broad historical events. For him, the stories of tough guys and thugs were an important and crucial part of the making of history.

Others among my informants also expressed this claim on history. Wondimu was a contemporary of Haile's and a thug in the Arada neighborhood opposite where Haile and Ibrahim were born and grew up. Like Haile, he was one of the many gatekeepers of memories of Arada. He used the term "generation" to describe not just the succession of tough guys but also what he felt were the historical and cultural transformations that Arada had gone through and that somehow reflected the periodic appearance and disappearance of groups and street fights. For Wondimu, the first generation consisted of the tough guys during Haile Selassie's reign, before even Getachew Bongar, when tough guys, football players, and boxers populated the fighting scene in Arada. In Wondimu's words, this was fighting for "respect": bar brawls to claim the title of best fighter. For him, the second generation was that of Getachew Bongar, which survived the Red Terror and fought and made business during the socialist regime. The third generation, "our generation," was the one that emerged after the TPLF took over. "This was not the time of the gangsters, the *gangster* mood was over," Wondimu said. "This was the time of the brain game, of the business of using the brain rather than the fists. This was the time of the business."

Haile's and Wondimu's chronologies on Arada differed. And, notably, they were not the only versions of the history of Arada that did so. Spending time on the streets of the inner city listening to people remembering the past, I heard different and often discrepant versions of the stories of Getachew Bongar, Mesfin Redi, and Mamush Kuchere. This heterogeneity and inaccuracy, historians have argued, is a characteristic of oral histories as a narration of the past but also of the wider production of historical memory (Passerini 1987; Portelli 1991; Kennedy 1995; Perks and Thomson 1998). Debating and comparing different versions of the same story is not just an activity of the historian or the scholar. Haile, Wondimu, Ibrahim, and many others in the inner city debated and compared versions of history as well, when they told me a story or when they heard a version of a story that differed from theirs. Spending hours and hours debating and comparing stories and memories of Getachew and other tough men of the past was the process through which the collective memory on street life was made.

Identifying cohorts, narrating historical events such as the transition from one regime to another, making sense of the transformation in the ways people stayed on the street—the fights for respect, the fights for survival, and, lately, the brain game and business—all intertwined in defining the generations of Arada. Cleavages marked the different "stages" of history, but, just as in Haile's narration, the succession of generations also emphasized its continuity. The claim for history and continuity in these narrations had to do with the way my informants conveyed, thought about, and made sense of their "position" in society. As I mentioned in chapter 1, members of the urban intellectual middle class celebrated the chivalry of the gentlemen *Arada* as a way to distinguish themselves from the political events of the socialist regime and from the current transformation of Addis Ababa's history. Meanwhile, poor people who were engaged in the street economy of Addis Ababa's inner city—those whom government organizations, NGOs, and members of the new and old middle classes described as thieves, thugs, and destitute youth—narrated how at least since the 1960s generations of *Arada* had succeeded in grounding their sense of smartness and bravery in the continuity of their history and within a legacy that intertwines with the broader history of Addis Ababa.

For this reason, my informants spent hours and hours, often unprompted, talking about Getachew and other tough men of the past. Listening and becoming knowledgeable about the history of the street were an important part of how the protagonists of this book learned how to be smart and how to act as a "proper thug." Haile, as he remembered, became an *Arada* by learning from what people told him in the drinking houses. This value of learning smartness through remembering the past was still crucial when I carried out my fieldwork. "We learnt a lot today," a young man who worked at a printing company told me after Haile and Ibrahim had spent hours recounting the history of the tough guys.

History populated the streets, shaping both everyday discourses and practices. It was a form of street knowledge that was built cumulatively in a similar way to the slang of the *Arada*, *yeArada kwankwa*. For instance, while policemen described the *yeArada kwankwa* to me as a code language used by thieves to deceive targets and call the attention of other "street actors" when policemen were around, in reality it was not secret. It was a linguistic corpus of terms and categories that people became socialized in as they engaged in economies of the street. In a similar way, smartness and toughness have been molded through an archive of narratives, discourses, and paradigms that people became aware of by remembering and learning about the history of the street. By mastering the knowledge of the past, my informants claimed to *be Arada*. By remembering generations of gangsters, my informants claimed to be part of that history they deeply valued. By acting out lessons from these stories of famous men, they learned how to deal with poverty and exclusion.

Getachew Bongar was not only a "gangster of the past" (*yeduro Arada*) but also a model of toughness. Melaku aka Melaku *Čista* (literally "broke"), a singer and performer during the Derg, remembered him as a "true *Arada*." People at Sefru's knew him as a *denbegna Arada*—a proper *Arada*—or as *Gashe* Yirga, a comedian of the old days, said, "half *denbegna* and half *duriye*," that is, half gentleman and half thug. Getachew was believed to be able to eat a whole sheep. He was a good street fighter. Policemen respected him and usually backed off when he was around. Many people in my field site remembered that he once knocked down six policemen who wanted to capture him. Getachew was also a man of the community. Mothers would ask him to scold their sons if they were becoming "thugs" and were "naughty"—Ibrahim's own mother did this to discourage her son from becoming a *duriye*. Families turned to him to get back what had been stolen from them by thieves.

As the story of Getachew shows, *becoming* and *being a thug Arada* did not mean being out of control, a maverick. Rather, it consisted of being able to embody the models of toughness and smartness that Getachew himself personified. Getachew was respected, remembered, and celebrated because he was able to use his reputation as a fighter to engage in different street businesses and have influence in different domains of the life of the community. Many among my informants looked at heroes such as Getachew as a source of inspiration. Ibrahim, for instance, saw himself as a *duriye* and an *Arada*. As he told me, he *became Arada* because he grew up in Arada, learning from what other people were doing. For him, *being an Arada*, a thug (*duriye*), and even a strong man (*hardegna*) were not just ways of behaving; they were the cultural scripts that intertwined with the way he thought about and acted on his social reality. Smartness, thug-ness, and tough-ness were thus "thick," recognizable, and remembered models of social practice.

If we zoom out from the social reality of the street and situate the actions of the thug *Arada* within broader society, we realize that thugness and smartness are social practices of a particular kind. People like Getachew Bongar, who both engaged in illegal activities and enjoyed respect and social recognition, exist not only in Arada but also in other areas of the African continent and beyond. The "bandit" in the rural areas and the *picaro*, or rather, the confidence man, in the cities, Ralph Austen (1986) pointed out, achieved fame and respect or were even considered heroes for their deeds. The legitimacy of their heroism, Austen ar-gued, rested in the fact that the poor resented the rich and that, importantly, the acts and the lifestyles of the bandit and the *picaro* challenged the hegemony of the existing political system over both rich and poor (89).

Getachew Bongar shared the heroism of the *picaro* and, like the *picaro*, lived by his wits. Getachew was a fighter, a hustler, a *joffe*, and a community man but also a grotesque character who, people believed, could eat an entire sheep by him-self. Yet, Getachew's heroism—and the enacted heroism that the stories about him inspired in my informants' everyday lives—did not speak to power, voicing the opposition of the poor to the rich, or more generally, inspiring defiance against class hegemonies. When people remembered Getachew, they did not picture him fighting the Ethiopian elites. They described him stealing, making a deal, and fighting on the street. In this regard, Mesfin Redi, perhaps, was a unique case in the history of Arada: his Robin Hood deeds, robbing Tigrayans and the Eritreans in the early 1990s, were interpreted as emerging from his deep dislike of the new elites. Yet Mesfin was inimitable and his heroism was not replicated in the streets of Arada. When Haile, Ibrahim, and Wondimu recounted the history of the street, they did not mention any new "versions" of Mesfin, while Getachew had his "ideal successors" in Mamush and the young Ash. Their heroism was embedded in the everyday life of the inner city and expressed in their smart deals, their mastery of street knowledge and street violence, and their capacity to get by and "shine" as famous and respected people. This is what made the heroism that Getachew em-bodied appealing and replicable. Getachew was a "hero," and those who followed could then also claim to be so, not because he questioned his own condition of poverty but because he bravely lived through it every day. Such was the promise that living smartly and toughly held for Ibrahim, Haile, Wondimu, and many others in inner city Addis Ababa.

Street Life and Marginality

This chapter has argued that street life, crime, and hustling should not be understood as the inevitable consequences of poverty—or as the moment when the marginalized reproduce their condition of marginality. Adopting an ethnographic and historical approach to street life helps us appreciate how people's attempts to act on the circumstances of their lives might lead to a flirtation with street violence and crime. Street life became the site of my interlocutors' search for a meaningful way of living a condition of marginality because it gave them the opportunities to play with the possibility of the impossible and pursue already tested and celebrated paths to respect and recognition. In the next two chapters, I explore the making of my interlocutors' condition of marginality as a product of the ways patterns of differentiation, increasing inequality, and the ruling party's politics of mobilization, repression, and control codified the terms of poor people's membership into Ethiopian society and their participation in economic growth and development.

DONKEYS WITH ASHES

Gains and Benefits

Being a member of the *yemot midib* brought Ibrahim respect and recognition. He remembered how the defiant style of the group made him and his friends a model of toughness and smartness in the inner city: "We had a place in front of a school where we used to hide. There we were chewing [*khat*] and smoking marijuana. Sometimes we were standing in front of the school. Many of the boys who went to that school were fascinated by us, and some of them wanted to be like us. I don't know why, perhaps they saw that kind of life from the movies but I can tell you that thirty people dropped out of school because of us."

The *yemot midib*, like many other street groups in the history of Addis Ababa, did not last long. Just a couple of years after Haile, Ibrahim, Mikias, Kebedde, Samson, Stefanos, Wube, and Taddesse met at Noah's *video bet*, some of them met the destiny spelled in the name of their group: "those who are destined to die." Wube was among the youngest in the group. He was just nineteen when he was found hanged from the ceiling of his house. Samson and Stefanos soon followed when the spread of HIV/AIDS hit Arada.

Members of the *yemot midib* were not the only ones to die during those years. Important pieces of the history of the streets of Arada were vanishing. Already in the early 1990s, the gangster Mesfin Redi had been shot to death, allegedly by a security official (see chapter 2). Others followed as the new EPRDF government tried to establish its rule on the streets of Addis Ababa (see chapter 4). Some thugs succumbed to serious illnesses, including Getachew Bongar, Mamush Kuchere, and Noah, Ibrahim and Haile's close friend and the manager of the video house where the *yemot midib* met for the first time. The causes of their deaths were debated, with some of my informants blaming tuberculosis and others pointing to HIV/AIDS or arguing it was a combination of the two. What their memories agreed on was that these three men had become weak, confused, and lost. During the last years of his life, Getachew Bongar spent most of his time hiding in his video house. Mamush Kuchere drank too much. Noah slept on the streets.

Looking back to the days of the *yemot midib*, Ibrahim and Haile remembered that the deaths of their close friends and heroes seemed like both a warning about the risks inherent in living a tough life and a push to find a way out of street life. At such moments the attainment of respect and recognition in the streets was felt less as an achievement and more as a reminder of the predicament of living in a condition of enduring marginality and exclusion. The death of close friends, however, was just one of many "vital conjunctures" (Johnson-Hanks 2002, 2006) they discussed when they found themselves questioning the direction their lives were taking. Like when they got out of prison, determined to look for a change, or when their respective partners gave birth, they found themselves wondering about alternative life trajectories. These critical moments prompted Haile and Ibrahim to seek other possible lives, by going back to school, leaving the country, embarking on a career in business, or climbing the ranks of the construction sector.

This chapter adds another layer to the book's understanding of the *act of living* as a tension between people's attempts to go beyond the contingency of their circumstances and the persistence of marginality. I follow Haile and Ibrahim on their quest for social improvement as they attempt to overcome their constraints and go beyond living meaningfully within a condition of marginality. I document why, despite their restless search for a better life, their condition of marginality endured.

For Haile and Ibrahim, their search for alternative possible lives was weighed down by a range of constraints. Migration is a risky venture. The types of wage labor available to the poor may simply lock them into poverty. Education for the urban poor can be useless without access to valuable connections that provide job opportunities that meet academic credentials (Mains 2012a). And success in business is contingent on relations more than dispositions.

In this chapter I examine these constraints on Haile's and Ibrahim's ability to achieve social improvement. In particular, by seeing the role that relations play in effecting economic success or failure in the inner city, I provide a more nuanced appreciation of the relation between historicity, marginality, and action we have explored so far. Chapters 1 and 2 examined Haile and Ibrahim as they effectively acted within historical circumstances of their own making, shaping the terms of their presence in the urban space. Here I follow them as they fell short of acting in tune with the changing historical circumstances of their country.

Haile and Ibrahim's search for a better life did not occur in a historical vacuum but at a moment of radical historical transformation. The socialist regime that had delivered stable but enduring poverty collapsed in the early 1990s with the military victories of the TPLF and the withdrawal of Soviet support (J. Young 1997; Donham 1999; James et al. 2002). The victory of the EPRDF, a coalition of regional parties led by the Tigray People's Liberation Front (TPLF), was followed by the liberalization of the economy, opening a conjuncture of economic growth that, over the course of a decade, would transform Ethiopia into the paradigmatic Africa success story.

By emphasizing the potential disjuncture between this moment of historical transformation and the outcomes of my interlocutors' quests for change, I show that while the *act of living* is historically situated, experiences of becoming remain contingent on the ways relations and relationships of force—what I describe in the introduction as "regimes of interconnectedness"—define people's positioning even during moments of change. Chapter 1 examined how Haile's and Ibrahim's place in urban society was produced by the ways the policies of the Derg and the patterns of social differentiation in the city molded their condition of marginality as an experience of secure but enduring poverty. This chapter explores how in a moment of economic growth and promise their condition of marginality was reconfigured as an experience of exclusion, deprivation, and abjection.

Already by the early 2000s, just a few years after the end of the *yemot midib*, Ibrahim and Haile were witness to the first moments of Addis Ababa's remarkable and unprecedented urban expansion. Capitalizing on the increasing ability of Ethiopian elites and returnees from the diaspora to afford life in a city with world-class amenities, real estate developers and local construction companies began to make exorbitant profits (Himmelreich 2010). Expensive housing facilities and gated communities were built in the expanding suburbs toward the eastern and southern parts of the city (Yeraswork Admassie 2008) while high-rise office buildings and shopping malls continued to multiply, dominating the central business districts (Stroll 2010).

This moment of economic and political change informed Haile's and Ibrahim's quests for change. Haile attempted to take advantage of the country's political instability on the eve of the Derg's collapse to make his way to Kenya. Subsequently, as Ethiopia's economic boom took off, both men tried to find ways to seize a share of the expanding market economy. Ibrahim tried to start a business and sought better educational credentials. Aware of the large investments transforming

Addis's built environment, they saw a career in the construction sector as a potential avenue for change. These quests for a better life were embedded in the historicity of a moment of change. By seeing the possibility of individual change in Ethiopia's economic awakening, Haile and Ibrahim sought to transform their experience of living in a historical "open moment" (Lund 1998) into a "vital conjuncture" (Johnson-Hanks 2002, 2006).

Unfortunately for Ibrahim and Haile, economic growth soon became the historical background of their existence, without foregrounding opportunities for change. In the words of urbanist Susan Fainstein (2010, 38–39), growth offered the urban poor "diffused benefits" but not "material gains." Growth delivered benefits in terms of living in a better-serviced city and access to a diversified market, including the availability of cheap clothing and mobile phones. However, within a landscape of accrued social inequality (Solomon Mulugeta 2006; Bigsten and Negatu Makonnen 1999; UN-Habitat 2010), the achievement of material gains, in terms of economic opportunities for social mobility and improvement, was profoundly unequal (see chapter 1), deepening people's sense of abjection and deprivation (Yonas Alem, Köhlin, and Stage 2012). While sections of Addis Ababa society have grown richer, opportunities for enjoying the fruits of economic growth and achieving social improvement have remained unequally distributed. Opportunities existed, but not for my informants to seize. For them, the African success story was seen from afar: a spectacular landscape enticing and exciting to gaze upon, but fundamentally out of reach.

But if abundance was available, why could Haile and Ibrahim not access it? Structuralist and liberal understandings of marginality and exclusion come to a similar conclusion: poverty and marginality persist because poor people lack capacities to imagine and pursue trajectories that would enable them to achieve social improvement and economic empowerment (Sen 1999; Appadurai 2013; Bourdieu 1977). This chapter shows that people in inner city Addis Ababa had a sophisticated understanding of the terrains they sought to navigate. What they lacked, however, was access to the range of relations that could have enabled them to succeed. This lack of access to relations, I argue, is itself a *relational* product. As James Ferguson famously wrote, disconnection, abjection, and abandonment imply "a relation and not the absence of relation" (1999, 238). This is the case because, as Caroline Bledsoe (2002) pointed out, existence is the experience of being related to and dependent on the effects of the actions of both known and unknown individuals. As such, marginality is not just the result of the relationships in which the marginalized are involved via face-to-face relations. Marginality is enforced through the imposition of forms of relatedness and interconnectedness that exclude, disconnect, and expel (Agamben 1998; Sassen 2014; Butler and Athanasiou 2013).

This chapter explores how relations can be agents of exclusion by focusing on the microsocial environment in which my informants lived: a social space where exclusion and marginality were experienced and reiterated through a landscape of relations and interactions. This microsocial environment—as we will see as we follow Haile to Kenya, and other young people from inner city Addis Ababa to Dubai—was not localized in a specific place but existed as a "cloud" of interconnections that followed (or, rather, haunted) my informants as they tried to pursue trajectories of social improvement.

I begin by giving theoretical and ethnographic strength to a relational understanding of marginality vis-à-vis the weary convergence between structuralist and liberal readings of the reasons of its persistence. I then follow Haile and Ibrahim as they turned to education, migration, and the inner city's business communities to pursue their quests for a better life. I document why these potential alternative lives failed to deliver the improvement that Haile and Ibrahim so desired, and show how success, even in favorable economic times, is not a matter of dispositions or capabilities but of relations.

"Relatives with Relatives, Donkeys with Ashes"

Social theorists like Bourdieu have taught us that "practices and representations are 'objectively' adapted to their outcomes without presupposing a conscious aiming at ends" (1977, 53). In other words, the position that people occupy in wider society inevitably affects what they imagine, what they consciously or unconsciously leave out from the horizons of the conceivable, and what they think is possible (or impossible) for them to achieve.

Embracing liberal ideas on poverty and exclusion, the anthropologist Arjun Appadurai (2004, 2013) has given us a slightly different formulation of Bourdieu's theorization on the apparent coincidence between "practices" and "outcomes." Appadurai goes so far as to argue that poor people are poor because they have a limited "capacity to aspire." This is the capacity to map, plan, and then enact ways to achieve a desired social goal (Appadurai 2004, 2013). The more privileged, he argues, have access to a wider range of networks, resources, and opportunities that enable them to explore and experiment and gain a sense of the pathways that might effectively enable them to realize their aspirations. "Where these pathways do exist for the poor, they are likely to be more rigid, less supple, and less strategically valuable, not because of any cognitive deficit on the part of the poor, but because the capacity to aspire, like any complex cultural capacity, thrives and survives on practice, reputation, exploration, conjecture, and refutation" (Appadurai 2013, 189).

I agree with Appadurai that people develop a sense of the pathways and trajectories to avoid as they encounter opportunities to experiment with possible and potential lives. However, unlike both Appadurai and Bourdieu, I argue that my informants' inability to pursue alternative lives is neither the result of a lack in capabilities (also Sen 1999) nor an apparent coincidence between their sense of the possible and their position in broader society. Conversely, their attempts at achieving a better life bear witness to the effort they made to imagine and "aspire to" a better life, well beyond their condition of social exclusion. As we will see in this chapter, the protagonists of the book have a well-developed sense of the pathways and steps to take, and the trajectories to avoid. This sense was developed through an appreciation of the trajectories of those who had succeeded or failed and, more importantly, in experimenting for themselves with possible and potential lives.

The reason why my informants were unable to pursue (rather than imagine) possible and alternative lives needs to be found elsewhere. A different route to understanding why my informants' lives could not have been otherwise is provided by a proverb, commonly used by people in the inner city to describe their society: *zemed ka zemedu, aya ka amdu*. The phrase literally means "a relative with a relative, a donkey with ashes," but it might be more appropriately translated as the English proverb "birds of a feather flock together," with an undertone of "blood is thicker than water." In short, people of the same sort will be found together, and more importantly, people who are connected are likely to help each other, leaving those outside their networks with nothing but "ashes."

As this proverb suggests, relationships matter, because they determine who gets what, how he or she gets it, and through whom. As people distribute access to resources and opportunities through their personal networks, they wittingly or unwittingly exclude those outside these networks. Likewise, those who are able to pursue imagined trajectories of social improvement by taking advantage of their networks wittingly or unwittingly contribute to excluding or at least limiting the trajectories of others who do not belong to those networks.

Possible Lives

Haile often wondered what his life could have been had he taken other paths—would he have become rich had he pursued his career as a football player? His team was not of the level of Kidus Giorghis (Saint-George) or Ethiopian Bunna

(Ethiopian Coffee), the top teams in the Ethiopian Premier League, but he and his teammates often played some good matches. Haile had always been very good at football, he reckoned. However, he did not turn pro. While he was playing, he continued doing business on the streets. And *suse*, literally "addiction," drinking, smoking, and chewing *khat* limited his ability to play. After four years as an amateur, in his mid-twenties he quit the sport.

My informants' perception of alternative career paths did not exclusively depend on exceptional trajectories like becoming a sports star. They also engaged with more conventional life paths such as going back to school or trying to get out of the country. For instance, after leaving school at age sixteen, Ibrahim resumed his studies in his mid-twenties, attending evening classes with the hope of making his way out of street life and going to the university. Haile had done the same earlier, when he was in his early twenties during the last years of the socialist regime. Then later, in the early 1990s, he left Ethiopia and spent nine months as a refugee in Kenya.

What triggered the decision of engaging with these alternative lives was often a series of events that had made each of them question their current trajectories. Ibrahim decided to resume school after spending his first long sentence in prison. Being locked up was a revelatory moment for him: he realized that he could not take any more of the life he had lived until then. By resuming school, he was trying to go back to the moment in his life that, he felt, marked his first engagement with street life: when he first began playing hooky to spend time in Arada's video houses. Haile's search for an alternative had similar motivations, but wider political circumstances gave him the impetus to take a much bigger leap. Haile left prison when the days of the socialist regime were nearly over. As the TPLF approached, many young people decided to take advantage of the political instability and relatively unguarded borders to leave the city and then the country to claim asylum in Kenya, hoping to be relocated somewhere else. Haile took the chance. He crossed the Ethiopian-Kenyan border through Moyale, continued to Isiolo, and then down to Thika, close to Nairobi, where he spent nine months in a refugee camp together with many Ethiopians who had fled the civil war as well as Ethiopian Jews—Falashas—who hoped to be sent to Israel. Haile himself tried to navigate this historical conjuncture by trying to pass himself off as a Falasha: "There were 900 Falashas in the camp. Some were Falashas, others were fake Falashas."

These moments of imagined change soon closed down, however. Ibrahim found that doing well in school was extremely difficult, especially after nearly ten years away from the classroom. Moreover, he could no longer rely on his parents' financial help since they were focusing on his younger siblings. He thus needed to fend for himself financially, which further limited the time he could spend studying. Haile left Kenya when he realized he was not going to be relocated to the United States, Europe, or Israel any time soon. As he remembered, the then president of Kenya, Daniel Arap Moi, said that Ethiopia was at peace and Ethiopians did not have any particular reason to stay in Kenya as refugees. Haile agreed to return to Ethiopia, with the promise of a small cash payment and a free lift home.

Looking back on these experiences of potential change, Ibrahim and Haile were left wondering whether they would have actually improved their lives had they persisted with these alternative trajectories. Haile was sure he would have. Ten years after his return, the friend with whom he had gone to Kenya and had decided to stay was relocated to Canada. In his friend Haile saw not only a trajectory of progress and change but also what he could have achieved. Ibrahim was more skeptical about the potentialities of their experiments with alternative trajectories. Not only did he doubt that gaining a degree would have enabled him to get a better life; he also refused to follow many others from the inner city (including his sister) who had gone to work in Dubai, Qatar, and other countries in the Gulf. His mother had found a contact to get him a work visa, but he continued to refuse: "I am not going to be a slave in Arab countries!!"

The different views these men held depended on their personal experiences, but also on the fact that education and migration are symbolically charged social horizons. For more than a century, education has been branded as a pillar of contemporary society and the solution to poverty. In Ethiopia, education has historically embodied ideas of modernity, sophistication, and self-achievement; and during the reign of Haile Selassie and the socialist regime, holding a university degree was a near guarantee for employment in the public sector (Markakis 1974; Clapham 1988). However, the opening of the free market and the downsizing of the government bureaucracy in the early 1990s resulted in limited public employment opportunities for the increasing number of university graduates (Mains 2012a). Nevertheless, as the economy has come to expand and diversify, education and a degree are still considered to be a means to navigate the labor market and pursue better-paying and higher-quality jobs. In particular, a university degree is necessary to apply for office jobs in international development organizations, NGOs, or international private companies.

Migration also has a long history in urban Ethiopia. Haile and Ibrahim were sons of the generation of rural migrants who came to Addis Ababa in the 1960s and 1970s looking for a better life (see chapter 1). International migration has a shorter but increasingly relevant history, as the vision of the Ethiopian diaspora returning from the United States and Europe to invest and live in Addis Ababa's wealthy suburbs continues to trigger imaginations of progress and success for many people in the city. The experiences of young people from poor families making their way to Europe, the United States, and the Gulf countries have triggered a wider understanding of the possibilities of migrating and the kinds of routes and arrangements involved.

One prominent option, winning the Diversity Visa Lottery for the United States, for instance, was considered too unreliable a way for imagining trajectories of social improvement. Yet, many of my neighbors in the inner city continued to apply and reapply to the Visa Lottery to keep the option open.[1] Illegal migration to Europe was believed to be extremely difficult and potentially expensive, and stories of young people drowning in the Mediterranean were always received with deep distress. Yet, there were many people who were still willing to embark on this trajectory, and there were a significant number of brokers and fixers to whom they could turn for assistance. Other options also existed. One was to try to find a foreigner to marry. As we will see in chapter 5, in the inner city this was the niche of a few female "players." Another option chosen by many was to migrate to the Gulf countries. As the number of people who traveled to the Gulf to work as guards, waiters, babysitters, and maids increased, people in my field site could rely on the advice of friends, relatives, and neighbors to find reliable brokers for work visas. More importantly, knowing that they would find fellow Addis Ababans at their destination gave people hope that they would have emotional support as well as access to information to help find better jobs once in the Gulf.

As these visions of progress spread, the idea that social improvement could be achieved was validated by the trajectories of those who had made it. Hence, it is easy to understand why Haile, for instance, looked at his experience of migration with regret, and why many people in the inner city continued to place their bets on going abroad. Likewise, the number of people engaging in education and, especially, entering the university was ever expanding. Despite the uncertainty of graduates' ability to get lucrative employment, nobody would voluntarily opt out of the opportunities that education could offer.

Yet we still need to understand why Ibrahim and, like him, many others in the inner city looked at education and migration with skepticism. One explanation may be that skepticism was a way of dealing with memories of failure and despair. Another is that what Ibrahim and others in the inner city observed from other people's life trajectories often reinforced doubts about education and migration.

---

1. According to the U.S. Department of State website, in 2010 a total of 745,372 people from Ethiopia applied for the 2012 Diversity Visa Lottery (http://travel.state.gov/content/dam/visas/Diversity -Visa/DVStatistics/DVApplicantEntrantsbyCountry%202010-2012.pdf). Of these, 4,902 were selected for further processing (https://travel.state.gov/content/travel/en/us-visas/immigrate/diversity-visa -program-entry/dv-2012-selected-entrants.html), and only 1,419 were granted visas to the United States (http://travel.state.gov/content/dam/visas/Diversity-Visa/DV-Instructions-Translations/DV-2014 -Instructions-Translations/FY12AnnualReport-TableVII.pdf). (Websites visited July 19, 2018.)

While a degree was a necessary requirement to apply for well-paid jobs, it did not mean that graduates had easy access to those jobs. In the inner city, many believed that a *wafra zemed*, "a fat relative," or at least an insider, was needed to get any job, but particularly those that were the most valuable and appreciated. Students could jump to the top of the list if they had a foreign university degree, but this was very difficult to achieve, as scholarships were not easily available and application procedures were hard to navigate without informed advice. Some college and university graduates "waited" in unemployment to see what jobs were available (cf. Mains 2012a). But "waiting" was an option only for those who could afford it; family resources, especially if limited, quickly dried out. Some joined the EPRDF in the hope of getting a job within one of its branches or in government offices. Others turned to low-paid work as teachers in private schools. Some managed to get an office job without enrolling in the party or having an inside contact, but they were considered a sort of invisible minority.

Besides, not all those with university degrees found jobs that met their educational credentials. One of these was Abiy. A good friend of Ibrahim and Haile's, Abiy was in his mid-twenties during my fieldwork, and a graduate of Addis Ababa University. He did not choose his degree: it was assigned to him by a centralized system. Abiy was unlucky and ended up in the Applied Physics Department— what he said students at Addis Ababa University called the *yemot department*, the "department of death," because its graduates never found jobs. In addition, he came from a poor family in the inner city, so he could not afford to "wait" for a job matching his credentials. Hence, together with Ibrahim and others he had known while hanging on the street opposite his house, he enrolled in government entrepreneurship programs for unemployed youth. In 2009, he became a member of a cooperative of "parking guys," or car attendants. After a year, Abiy found an opportunity to work for a rich neighbor, a member of the inner city business community, whose family owned a gas station in the city center. When I returned to Addis Ababa in 2013, he was working twenty-four-hour shifts as an attendant at the gas station.

Abiy's social trajectory is revealing. It shows not only that the networks that people have access to are relevant in gaining employment, but also that education has little benefit if individuals cannot rely on useful information and contacts to help them capitalize on their credentials. Abiy was smart enough to graduate with a degree in applied physics from one of the best universities in the country. Yet, he came from a poor family. His friends were equally poor and, more than that, less educated than him. His only useful contacts could not help him gain a position that matched his academic knowledge. Even when his rich neighbor approached him, he was not offered an office job, only low-paid and low-quality employment.

In these circumstances, when even university graduates struggled to find jobs, migration was eventually considered to be the only good opportunity to improve one's life. This was not because university graduates, for instance, would find suitable employment opportunities for their academic credentials once abroad. It was because a low-paid job in Dubai pays much more than the exact same job in Addis Ababa. This difference gives Ethiopian migrant workers room for sending remittances home and for saving money to pursue a trajectory of social improvement upon their return home. This sense of planning and progress was an incentive for both those who felt destined to work low-paying jobs in Addis Ababa and educated youth who were unwilling to take these kinds of jobs at home (cf. Mains 2012a).

Back in the inner city, aspiring migrants like Zennebesh, a young woman in her early twenties who worked as an accountant earning 600 birr a month (US$44.66), thought this ideal plan could work: "Look in two years here, I could get 15,000 birr [US$1,116]. There, for instance in Dubai, I could get 40,000 birr [US$2,977]." She gave the example of a friend of hers who had worked in Dubai for a while and then upon returning to Addis Ababa opened her own beauty salon. At the same time, however, Zennebesh had a sense that success was highly contingent on working hard and saving in Dubai. There were many others who, once they were back home, soon spent the little money they had saved, enjoying themselves with relatives, friends, and neighbors—as if to recover from the years of restrictions, limited means, and homesickness. "Why did those guys go outside to work if after they behave at the same way as before they left?" Zennebesh asked me and herself.

For people like Ibrahim, their skepticism did not revolve around whether this ideal plan of working hard and saving could work. True, working as a guard in Dubai paid more than being a parking guy in inner city Addis Ababa. However, the Dubai guard lived in a far more unequal society than the one the parking guy inhabited, with far less respect. When Ibrahim said, repeating it like a mantra, "I am not going to be a slave in Arab countries!!" he was not necessarily disengaging from the possibilities of doing hard work. He was refusing to sign up for further marginalization and stigmatization. His concerns, as I understood only later in my fieldwork, were grounded in a perception held by an increasing number of people in the inner city that places like Dubai were not easy for migrant workers.

When I was in Addis Ababa in 2014, Ibrahim and his neighbors were mourning the tragic death of a young woman who had been trying to make her way in Dubai. She had worked there for four years, starting as a maid, then finding ways of getting by as best she could when faced with unemployment. Something had not worked. A few days after her family stopped hearing from her, she was found hanged from the ceiling of her home in Dubai. As stories like this traveled back from the city that had inspired Addis Ababa's architectural visions of development, families were beginning to wonder. How could they send their kids to work and die there?

Why Do Hustlers Not Become Businesspeople?

The liberalization of the economy in the 1990s resulted in the revival of Arada and its economy, providing a boost to its business community. Commercial activity blossomed, and long lines of shops in the inner city came to offer a view of what the free market had availed to Addis Ababa's residents. Twenty years later, as the economy continued to grow, many among my informants believed that running a shop or a business was the key to success and wealth. Whereas migration and education had failed them, business, they thought, could give them a chance. "Once you open a shop, you are a rich man!" Wondimu, a parking guy and a former member of the Ashanti group (see chapter 2), told me, standing in a square lined with busy shops.

Ibrahim had the opportunity to become a businessman in his mid-twenties when, in 2003, the Addis Ababa city government launched a campaign to boost income-generating activities for the poor by establishing "container shops" all around the city. At this time, Muna, Ibrahim's mother, was a long-standing member of the Women's Associations linked to the ruling party. Her contacts at the *kebelle* helped her get a container shop. She thought she would give an opportunity to her troubled firstborn son, who had begun to prove he was willing to change his life. These were the years that immediately followed the efforts of Ibrahim and some of his closer friends in the *yemot midib* to resume schooling and enter the construction sector (see also chapter 4). At the time, Ibrahim was in a long-term relationship with a woman who a few years later would give birth to their son, Yassin. In this conjuncture of Ibrahim's life, change seemed to be in reach.

Ibrahim thus took his shop business seriously. He quit chewing *khat* and stayed focused. He sold women's shoes, and many remembered him as a skillful and relatively successful shoe seller. As he recounted, he got hold of fashion magazines that people brought from abroad or sold on the streets. From these, he developed a sense of the shoes women wanted and gave suggestions to his suppliers on the styles they should import from China. But Ibrahim's success did not last. As soon as his business started going well, he resumed chewing *khat* and smoking *ganja* after work, and with his old friends on the street he squandered the money he

FIG. 3.1 A line of container shops © Marco Di Nunzio

had earned: "Everything changed when I started smoking that shit," Ibrahim told me. "I was not interested in anything. I was chewing and smoking. I did not pay attention to money." The business slowly went downhill, and by the mid-2000s he had lost his shop and his relationship with his partner soon broke down.

Why did street actors like Ibrahim hardly ever become successful business-people? We could argue Ibrahim had a limited capacity to aspire. His behavior seems to prove the point of Arjun Appadurai and, broadly, liberal views on poverty and poverty reduction: Ibrahim failed because he lacked skills and capabilities. However, if we see how businesspeople succeed in Addis Ababa, it becomes clear that Ibrahim's failure does not fall entirely on his shoulders. In fact, differently from what entrepreneurship evangelists argue, being and becoming a businessman, just as *being* and *becoming Arada*, is not an individual endeavor. It is a social trajectory that is experienced while relating to others. And, as business-people in the inner city often told me, spending time with other businesspeople, as well as sharing skills and knowledge, is crucial when starting and carrying out new businesses and trades. Then why did Ibrahim not hang out with other busi-nesspeople? Because, as the proverb I mentioned earlier about "relatives and rela-tives, donkeys and ashes" suggests, social networks, especially those that grant access to resources, are not always inclusive. Ibrahim did not manage to become a "relative"—he was left with the "ashes."

However, exclusive networks in business are not just a matter of catchy prov-erbs. They are built in practice, enforcing and reproducing social hierarchies encompassing the economies of inner city Addis Ababa. Wondimu, a parking guy and a former member of the Ashanti group, gave me a sense of these social hierarchies. After telling me that once you open a shop you can consider yourself a rich man, he outlined for me a rough sociology of the inner city. Poor people, he argued, are parking guys like him and Ibrahim, those who work for owners of shops, or waiters, managers of small retail shops (*suq*), or managers of video houses. The ones in the middle are those who own those small shops. He did not mention those who are at the top, implying that elite businesses did not populate the inner city streets. As we will see, Wondimu was wrong about this. But, let us first use his rough categorization as a tool to navigate the inner city's economies and sociology.

Parking guys, Wondimu argued, were at the bottom. They were organized as cooperatives established throughout the capital since the late 2000s by the local government offices to provide jobs to unemployed youth. As we will see in the next chapter, this initiative was part of a wider government campaign on micro-finance and small-scale entrepreneurship. These cooperatives were situated by Wondimu at the bottom of his sociological map for a very simple reason: park-ing guys do not earn much. As a parking guy, Wondimu earned no more than

FIG. 3.2 A *suq* (retail shop) © Marco Di Nunzio

250 birr (US$15) a month in 2010. Ibrahim was working for a cooperative that was assigned to busier streets and could rely on 400–800 birr (US$24–$48) a month in 2010 and 1,000–1,500 birr (US$50–$75) a month in 2014. This, as we will see in the next chapter, exceeded the income of other types of enterprises that the local government office had established in the inner city. However, Ibrahim's salary was still comparable to the monthly wage of those at the bottom of Addis Ababa's labor market, such as daily laborers in the city's construction site, rather than the earnings of other "businesspeople" in the inner city.

Along with the parking guys, Wondimu contended, there was also a wider and more diverse number of people whose earnings were not much higher than those of Ibrahim's cooperative, but who were part of the inner city business community, albeit its lower rungs. Gizachew and his partner Fatima were two of these neighborhood businessmen, as we might call them. Gizachew was in his thirties and, like Wondimu, had been part of the Ashanti group between the late 1990s and early 2000s. He was a *duriye* (thug), as he remembered, until he got his job as a manager of the video house where he had been working for more than a decade.

As we learned in chapter 1, running a video parlor in the early 1990s was considered to be a business for thugs. In the aftermath of the 2005 riots, video houses, like *khat* chewing houses, had become targets of police repression because they were believed to be places where thieves hid and political opposition recruited supporters (see chapter 6). As the ruling party neutralized political opposition (see the introduction and chapter 4), however, video parlors gradually became part of the inner city economy. But those who managed these places still needed to watch out, making sure that customers did not smoke *ganja* or chew *khat* while watching movies. *Ganja* is illegal; selling *khat* is permitted, but managing a public space where people chew *khat* is illegal.

Gizachew was able to do his job as manager of a video house because he knew about movies. He had watched them since he was very young and claimed to have a collection of nearly six hundred movies in his house. He had watched them all, he boasted. When he found a new movie, he told me, he would watch it to determine whether it fit his customers. Luckily for Gizachew, competition for finding new movies was no longer as fierce as it had been in the past when Ibrahim and Haile decided to illegally show porno movies to attract more customers (see chapter 1). The repressive police campaigns targeting video houses had effectively limited the number of Gizachew's potential competitors.

Running a video house, Gizachew told me, has a standard formula: "You rent a place with two rooms for 1,000 birr a month. You buy a stereo with good sound boxes. You take someone working for you. At the beginning, you would call your friends and, after a while, you will have your customers. You could end up getting 100 birr a day, that is 3,000 birr a month. 1,000 birr for the rent, some money

FIG. 3.3   "Gizachew" © Marco Di Nunzio

for the workers and the rest is yours." I followed Gizachew for nearly four years. In 2014, his business was making more than 100 birr a day. The entrance fee to his video house went from 1.50 birr in 2010 to 3.00 birr in 2014, and none of the screenings, from early in the morning to 10 p.m., went without a customer. Yet Gizachew and Fatima enjoyed only limited benefits from this increased income as the cost of living also increased significantly. They felt they needed to rely on "side businesses" to support themselves and their young daughter. Fatima sold *khat* at the front of the video house, making sure that none of her customers chewed it during Gizachew's screenings. She did not sell large amounts like *khat* retailers in the inner city, but she could get 40 birr profit out of one kilo of *khat*. The other side business was Gizachew's public toilet, a hole in the wall not far from the video house where young men stopped to pee. "It was very smelly. Now I clean it every day and I take 0.25 cents for each person who goes to pee there. . . . This is creating your business . . . day by day."

As with running a video house, a "shop" is a formula—or in Arada slang, a *mella* (system)—for making money (see chapter 2). Walking through the inner city, following the lines of shops running along the streets, makes this clear: long lines of shops sell exactly the same thing, competing for the same customers. This is not a peculiarity of inner city Addis Ababa; we might find similar patterns in many commercial districts around the world. In Arada, as in other places, this is because, despite the glorification of the market economy as a site of innovation, many businesspeople rely on standardized formulas to pursue economic success: accumulating money in one trade, then moving to another that is believed to be more profitable. Sitting on a bench near the corner where Wondimu told me about rich people, shops, and social hierarchies, Kadir, a businessman in his thirties, could recount the history of the business activities in the neighborhood just by recalling the trades each businessman had gone through. Turning from side to side as he described the history of one shop after another, he said: "Look at that. It used to be a barbershop. Now it is an *arakie bet* [a drinking house]. They are making a lot of money." "Look at that restaurant over there. Before it was a small *shay bet* [tea room]. He made a lot of money and he opened a restaurant." Kadir worked in his "family shop," as he called it; it had a similar history under his father's ownership. "At the very beginning, it was a barbershop. Then we changed into a *khat bet*, and five months ago, we started this *juice bet* [juice parlor]."

That shop owners rely on formulas to conduct their business does not mean that Gizachew, for instance, could easily move from managing a video house to running a profitable business. Gizachew's business enabled him to get by, but he was far from being able to accumulate enough capital to move up to a more profitable business. Moreover, Gizachew could not consider himself a "shop owner." As manager of the video house, he was running a business chosen by the person who owned the shop. He could hope to become the owner of his business and the shop he worked at. But to do this, he would have to navigate a thick landscape of arrangements and connections.

"Owning" or simply "running" a shop remains a complex matter. Many of the "shop owners" (*bale suq*) are in reality "shop holders" renting from either the government or private investors. Since the nationalization of property in the mid-1970s, the Ethiopian government has owned the land and many of the buildings built at least up to the demise of the socialist regime in 1991. Owners were allowed to keep ownership of the house where they lived, and small-scale commercial activities were allowed to continue. When the economy was liberalized in the early 1990s, the demand for business activities rose. Construction activities in the inner city remained limited, however, and the availability of space for commercial use did not increase accordingly, affecting the outlook of the inner city business community. Some current shop holders were thus long-term traders who had rented their shop from the government for more than a decade. Others rented from those who kept the ownership of a house after the nationalization of the mid-1970s. Meanwhile, new shop holders emerged in two main ways. Those lucky enough to live in a house facing the street could start a business by carving a small shop out of the front wall of the house they rented from the government. Those who were less lucky but resourceful could open a business by renting or taking over from shop holders who had previously rented from the government and then privately rented out or sold the "key" of their shop to others.

This complex landscape of arrangements, and the cost of buying or renting from former shop holders, could be enough to discourage newcomers. Aware of this, in the early 2000s the city government launched its "container shops" campaign as a springboard for new commercial activities and poverty reduction. Those involved in the program paid a small annual rent to the government. Yet, the number of people who could actually join the program was de facto limited by the belief that having contacts with the local government office was required. Despite the odds, and drawing on the financial and political help of his mother, Muna, Ibrahim was among those who joined the program. More than ten years later, some container shop holders still endured, serving customers seeking cheaper prices than the shops. Others, like Ibrahim, failed, revealing other variables at play besides ownership issues and people's capacity to gather start-up capital.

What really mattered, many businesspeople I interviewed agreed, was having been "exposed" to business as a way of learning how to run a specific trade and deal with the competition. Ibrahim had, putatively, been exposed to business. His father, Ahmed, had run a small retail shop. Muna also had a business, buying and selling kitchenware to the neighbors. Yet, when he opened his shoe shop, Ibrahim was not building on his parents' enterprises and connections. Muna's business did not make her part of the inner city business community, and Ahmed had lost his shop in the mid-1990s, nearly ten years before the container shops. Ibrahim was basically starting from scratch.

Interviewing businesspeople who were contemporaries of Ibrahim's and running profitable commercial activities, I realized that they did not start from scratch, even though some liked to describe themselves as embodying the myth of the self-made man who had gone from shining shoes to owning a profitable business—a myth that many in the inner city believed, Ibrahim included (see chapter 7). Dawit was a man in his late thirties who loved to see himself as a self-made man. He first worked as a "shoeshine boy," then he moved up to selling to restaurants mutton that he slaughtered himself. As he accumulated money and customers, he bought the key to a butcher's shop in the inner city. With the profits from this shop, he opened a second shop in another neighborhood. Dawit's trajectory is remarkable. Yet, what he pushed into the background when he recounted his business trajectory to me was that, while he was working hard to find his way up, his father owned a butcher's shop in the inner city, leaving me wondering about the extent to which his father's resources, or at least his father's connections, helped Dawit thrive.

Some businesspeople had no problem admitting that they had inherited their business from their parents. Kadir, the man who summarized decades of business history in just a couple of sentences, was working in his "family shop." Ermias, a man in his thirties, ran a retail shop (*suq*) he had taken over from his father, who had worked there since the mid-1970s. Comparing his own and his contemporaries' trajectories with what his father had managed to achieve, Ermias believed that moving from rags to riches was not as simple as many believed: "It is not like before that you could go up by starting with selling chewing gum. Now, if you do not belong to a family who has its business, it is difficult to start a new one from nothing. These guys selling chewing gums on the street will hardly manage to open a shop like my father did. Things are different now."

Talking about the past is often a way of making sense of differences that are particularly visible in the present. Yet, keeping in mind that Kadir's, Ermias's, and Dawit's fathers were all long-term businesspeople, we should ask ourselves to what extent this older generation of businesspeople built their careers from scratch, or perhaps more accurately, pursued their careers depending entirely on self-determination. The dynamics of the inner city business community between the 1960s and the early 1990s is outside the scope of this book, but we may still approach an answer by making sense of the fact that the connections and relationships that enabled Dawit, Ermias, and Kadir to "start" their businesses were also key in keeping their businesses going.

In accordance with his image of a self-made man, Dawit believed that outsiders who did not grow up in a business family could easily become part of his clique and hang out with other businesspeople for advice and for opportunities to grow: "People have to work and if you have the right attitude, you could do things. . . . You could share your ideas and make money. . . . You should hang out with businesspeople so you can learn how to make business. You have to speak frankly and clear, and you could learn things from them." Rukia, a woman in her mid-thirties who ran a family "boutique" selling clothes on one of the main roads in Arada, held a similar belief. Yet, she emphasized, "you have got to have money if you want to hang out with businesspeople." This, she explained to me, is not a matter of luxury and conspicuous consumption. Doing business and keeping commercial activities running entail a certain element of cooperation, as fellow businesspeople might join efforts to support each other and imagine future business ventures. Rukia and ten of her friends, for instance, had grouped together to save money every month. This was different from the *equb*, the saving associations many among my neighbors relied on to buy a television, a fridge, and the like. The fee in Rukia's group was significantly higher than that of my neighbors: 500

birr (US$30) a month for Rukia's group against the 100 birr (US$6) a month that my neighbors paid into their saving association. Unlike the members of the *equb*, one of whom would receive a fixed amount of money each month, the members of Rukia's group could access money from the common pot only in case of troubles or if they wanted to start a new business.

Access to capital, networks, and business knowledge is necessary to succeed and, arguably, has long affected success and failure in business in the inner city. Unequal access to those skills and resources was inherent in the ways business was conducted, but also directly encouraged by businesspeople as they pursued their own trajectories of economic success. The case of Ibrahim is a clear example of this, but this unequal access to capital, networks, and business knowledge also affected inner city businesspeople like Dawit, Ermias, and Rukia when they sought to move up or to engage in more profitable ventures in the inner city, let alone in the city or the country at large. Looking at the inner city, for instance, Dawit, Ermias, and Rukia could not easily gain access to the business networks of the jewelry shops in Arada, which sold items costing thousands of birr and were among the few in the inner city that accepted credit cards.

Guish, on the other hand, was in his early thirties and worked in his father's jewelry shops. His family was originally from Tigray, in northern Ethiopia. Like many other Tigrayans, his father and extended family owned jewelry shops in Arada. This was a business many believed to be firmly grounded in the dominant role that Tigrayans have played in Ethiopian politics. It is hard to say whether this perception is right or wrong, but what remains is that the proverb "relatives and relatives, donkeys and ashes" had a particular resonance in the sector.

However, for Guish, just as for Dawit, doing business in still-higher spheres with access to the city and country's elite was not easy. Dawit was already thinking big, looking to scale up, and capitalizing on the profits from his two butcher shops, but did not know how to go about it. When I interviewed him, Dawit asked if I had any advice. "You are a researcher and you could come up with some ideas," he encouraged me. After I told him somewhat helplessly that having spent most of my life in school I was the least qualified person to give him that advice, he told me what his own thoughts were. "Construction," he said, "is not free [available for entry]." "The government is into this." He said: "The best business now is in agriculture. Flowers and coffee, if you export [them], you make good money." Guish, on the other hand, did not even know where to start. Everything, he said, depended on the kind of opportunities he would be able to get through the people he knew: "I would do something different, if someone comes to me and tells me something about another field that is good and with which I could make more money."

The Limits of Smartness

Those "someones" who could bring Guish business were not just fellow business-people. They also included brokers and fixers who, when they work at higher levels, mediate the acquisition of shares and companies. Mubarik was a professional broker in his mid-forties who helped me understand how the market worked. He brokered the sale and rent of property, one of many other potential businesses in the inner city, like selling cars. The big money, he said, was in the deals that brokers made in Bole, a rich neighborhood in the southern part of the city. His income in the inner city, however, was far from low; he earned between 5,000 and 6,000 birr (US$308–$370) a month, nearly five times what Ibrahim made. "I was a taxi driver, but you don't get much by doing that," he said. To start working as a broker, Mubarik argued, is easy. You walk around and help people find things. Over time, you learn more about the business and you gain trust. Word of mouth, Mubarik continued, is central.

In this regard, Mubarik's job was not that different from what hustlers did when they looked for their *mella*. Yet the arrangements that Mubarik relied on to make money reveal how different hustling and professional brokering actually are, bringing into question analyses of informal economies of brokering and fixing as platforms for poor people's empowerment. In fact, Mubarik, like other brokers I interviewed, was not a free-floating agent, earning a living in the interstitial spaces of society and the market while producing new connections and creating new platforms for future collaborations and ventures, as, for instance, Abdoum-aliq Simone (2004a) envisioned. He did float around, sifting the inner city for business opportunities. But a significant amount of his income as a broker de-pended on the special relationships he had developed with a few businesspeople. These were not just relationships between established business partners. Rather, these patron-client relationships enabled Mubarik to get by and his "patrons" to make some extra money. Whenever Mubarik came across a good business op-portunity, he turned to his patrons. "They would buy everything I tell them to buy. They will buy it and sell it through me." In exchange, Mubarik could turn to them if business and money were lacking.

Why could thugs and hustlers not enter businesspeople's networks and act like brokers? After all, with their deals, hustlers inhabit similar economies of broker-ing and fixing, running errands, and mediating petty transactions for a fee (see chapter 5). One reason for the divide was that many businesspeople avoided thugs, even though they recognized their presence in the inner city with "respect," as the owner of a retail shop in the inner city told me: "I know the thugs [*duriyocc*], but I never do business with them. . . . I don't want trouble. But, of course, I respect them and they respect me. If there is no respect, things do not work here." Respect, as we learned in chapter 2, constituted the symbolic capital that thugs mobilized to make money on the street. This symbolic capital had little currency outside the street economy, however. That businesspeople respected the thugs did not necessarily bridge the gap between the two: respect in this case was a practice of social distancing.

Indeed, even when businesspeople did "business" with thugs, mainly fencing stolen goods, this distance continued to be cultivated. Fencing in the inner city involved wide networks of sellers and buyers that included thieves and occasional customers as well as shop and business owners seeking quick profits. Within these networks, often inhabited by occasional players, one group of fences in the inner city was considered the biggest, with buyers and sellers with enough money to deal with "hot stuff" such as cameras and laptops and, more importantly, jewelry and gold.

Although this group of fences drew on a long history of fencing and stealing in the inner city, they were perceived to be such a novelty that Ibrahim liked to describe them as the "new mafia." The organizational structure of this group of fences was different from that of the groups that had historically populated the streets of Arada: it was a tight-knit organization with a clear division of labor aimed at running the trade while shielding itself from the police. While "lookouts" were "checking" the areas, the "brokers" and "dealers" of the groups bought and sold the goods that thieves brought to them. Becoming part of this group of fences was difficult unless you knew a fence or had grown up in their neighborhood. This did not just bear witness to existing hierarchies within the street economy (see chapter 2); it enabled the group of fences to keep competitors away and build relationships of trust with both thieves and buyers. As these fences were known and established, businessmen in the inner city "knew" who the "legit" fences were and avoided dealing with others. This de facto neutralized the work of undercover policemen (*civil*) who pretended to be fences to catch fences and their accomplices in the business community. Despite these arrangements, however, fences still often faced imprisonment. In these circumstances, the relationship of trust that fences had built with businesspeople turned out to be crucial. In practice, if a fence is caught, he will not reveal the shop owner with whom he is doing business. In exchange, the shop owner will bail out the fence. As a result, the business of fencing continues, as does its capacity to respond to the offer of stolen goods.

This cooperation reveals that the world of business and the world of hustling were much more intertwined than the failure of Ibrahim's business trajectory might suggest. However, that fences and shop owners cooperated did not mean that the boundaries between the street economy and inner city business were redrawn. The logic of the relatives with relatives and the donkey with ashes still applied. "Thugs remained thugs" (*duriye duriye naw*) and fences remained fences. First, as Legesse, a member of this group of fences, revealed to me, the cooperation between his group and the shop owners ultimately benefited the latter more than the former. For instance, Legesse reckoned a fence got around 40–50 birr profit per piece of stolen jewelry, while the jeweler would potentially make a profit of 400 birr by melting and reselling just a gram of gold. Taken on a broader level, despite being a member of one of the most entrepreneurial niches of the inner city street economy, Legesse found becoming a full-time broker like Mubarik, dealing in cars and houses, fundamentally difficult. Even though he dealt with and knew businesspeople, he lacked the access to pursue such a career: "I don't know about the businesses, the information just does not come to me."

Relationality and Marginality

By examining the tension between Haile and Ibrahim's search for a better life and the persistence of their condition of marginality, I have given a reading of the *act of living* that is opposite yet complementary to the one I offered in the previous chapters. In chapters 1 and 2, I followed Haile and Ibrahim as they sought to live meaningfully *within* oppression and subjugation. Here, I examined how marginality endures in spite of people's attempts to challenge that condition with their actions, desires, and motivations, and notwithstanding the promise of economic growth.

This persistence of marginality, I argued, cannot be explained by seeing the limits of poor people's actions and capabilities—as both structuralist and liberal understandings of marginality suggest. What made Haile's and Ibrahim's condition of marginality persist was not their allegedly limited sense of the pathways available but how the forms of relatedness and interconnectedness that molded their place in the city ultimately affected how far they could go with their search for a better life.

The next chapter continues to explore the groundings of my interlocutors' condition of marginality. I focus on how the strategies that the ruling party used to ground its power and boost economic growth have deepened existing patterns of marginality through the imposition of pervasive forms of political subjugation and control. I complement this chapter's analysis of marginality as a condition of exclusion, abjection, and disconnection with an appreciation of how marginality is also a "positive" product: the result of the ways policies, interventions, and other acts of government can make oppression and subjugation the terms of poor people's inclusion into wider society.

DO NOT CROSS THE RED LINE

The Politics of Marginality

As alternative life trajectories failed to materialize, street life continued to characterize and define the lives of the protagonists of this book. By persisting in their engagement with street life, they relied on the productivity of the street economy to get by and find ways of navigating social exclusion. Yet the streets were far from being disconnected political and social terrains where poor people took refuge from the patterns of social differentiation that limited their ability to embark on trajectories of social mobility and improvement. Marginality, subjugation, and oppression also marked the streets as products of a long history of political authoritarianism that has shaped the lives of thugs and hustlers, including Haile and Ibrahim.

This chapter narrates this history of political authoritarianism on the streets of Addis Ababa. Chapter 2 discussed how generations of inner city young men had grounded their search for respect and dignity in a flirtation with street violence, illicit activities, and, sometimes, criminal offenses. Surprisingly, this centrality of crime in street life and the range of the state's responses to involvements with illegal activities per se were not the critical nodes in the making of the history of political authoritarianism in urban Ethiopia. Differently from what ethnographies of street life and the politics of mass incarceration in neoliberal North America, Europe, and South Africa have suggested, crime in Arada did not emerge as the master narrative through which the state articulated its punitive and repressive approaches to the poor (cf. Wacquant 2009; Fassin 2013; Comaroff and Comaroff 2006; Jensen 2008; Garland 2001). Rather, the ways thugs and hustlers were portrayed to be forming an identifiable constituency of the *politically* dangerous made the streets a central terrain in the history of authoritarianism in urban Ethiopia (Toggia 2008; Awol Allo 2017). Punishment in Addis Ababa's inner city has been more about politics and political control and less about the moral panic around poverty, crime, and the criminal.

Because of their involvement in crime and illicit activities, Ibrahim, Haile, and many others in their circle had experienced "prison life," as they called it, either from a couple of weeks or months in a common cell at a police station to longer sentences at the city prison, Kaliti, in the southern suburbs of Addis Ababa. Being locked up, Ibrahim told me, is the worst thing that could ever happen to a human being: "Prison is terrible! You eat one *injera* a day . . . , always the same people, you share the bed with a lot of people, you cannot go anywhere . . . sometimes your family does not respect you . . . it is fucking bad." Still, he and many others continued to walk that fine line between engaging in street life and risking jail. The reason was simple. Being caught was not always a direct consequence of illegal activities: going to prison was an event that might occur, but also might not. That margin of probability made engaging with crime a "job," as street hustlers in the inner city told me, paraphrasing a possibly apocryphal aphorism attributed to the late Meles Zenawi, the longtime prime minister of Ethiopia and secretary of the EPRDF: "Stealing is a job, but if you are caught, it is an offence."

However, there were certain moments when being sent to prison seemed more likely. These occurred at historical conjunctures when the streets became terrains of political conflict and the politics of the Ethiopian state became more visible than ever. At such times, those involved in the street economy became potential targets of the state's attention, not because of specific crimes but because they were considered members of a large political constituency that the government believed it had to either strategically mobilize or pervasively repress. Unlike crime, however, politics did not allow my informants margins of probability. Politics was rather the experience of a limit or, as one of my informants described it, again paraphrasing a pronouncement by the late Meles Zenawi, a "red line that once you cross you are caught."[1]

This chapter examines how state repression and control molded my informants' experiences of politics and how politics and, in particular, the strategies political elites used to ground their power in moments of unrest and conflict have had a long-lasting effect on shaping marginality on the streets of Addis Ababa. By exploring how the relations between the street and the Ethiopian state

---

1. During the 2005 riots and demonstrations, Meles Zenawi warned the youth with terms such as *bichamebrat* ("yellow light," meaning "you are in the danger zone") and *keymebrat* ("red light," meaning "you will be taken out"). Kjetil Tronvoll, personal communication with the author, 2009.

configured my interlocutors' experiences of oppression and subjugation, I show how marginality is not just a result of patterns of social differentiation (see chapter 3). Marginality, I argue, is a political product (Das 2007; Gupta 2012).

While this chapter includes an analysis of the relations between the state and street life since the 1970s, it focuses on the conjuncture of change and promise following the liberalization of Ethiopia's economy in the 1990s. As we saw in chapter 3, the unequal distribution of the benefits of economic growth revealed how the making of Ethiopia's success story was a vision of abundance and wealth that remained out of reach for many. However, the marginalized did not just accept exclusion and abjection as given. The persistent lack of opportunities for social mobility resulted in wide discontent, triggering a wave of protests in Addis Ababa and in the country's major towns since the early 2000s. In April 2001, protests occurred first on Addis Ababa's university campus and then in the city streets (Balsivik 2007, 143–56). In the months following the national elections in May 2005, young people took to the streets in support of the opposition and protested an election that many believed the ruling party had rigged (Abbink 2006).

These riots and demonstrations set the pace of the relations between the state and the street. The government first responded to unrest and dissent with a punitive approach. It labeled protesters as "gangsters" and "lumpen youth" in 2001, and "dangerous vagrants" and "unemployed youth" in 2005, and exercised heavy-handed repression on the streets on both occasions. In 2001, 30 people were killed, and in 2005, two hundred people died in the clashes. Yet police repression and criminalization were not the EPRDF's only responses to political dissent. Especially after 2005, the ruling party effectively expanded its structures of political surveillance, involving the creation of a network of informers based on their affiliation to the EPRDF and through which the ruling party collected information about the activities of individuals or groups on the streets and in communities (Di Nunzio 2014b). At the same time, development programs, in particular the implementation of small-scale entrepreneurship schemes, targeted what the government believed to be the main reason for political and social unrest among young people: the lack of employment. With these programs, the ruling party sought not only to tackle the predicaments of Addis Ababa's marginalized but also to mobilize them. Small-scale entrepreneurship schemes worked as springboards for the ruling party's attempts to increase the number of people who were directly or indirectly dependent on the state for their survival (Di Nunzio 2014a, 2015a).

These interventions were a political success: in 2008, 2010 and again 2015 the ruling party achieved overwhelming electoral victories in Addis Ababa and in the country at large (Di Nunzio 2014; Tronvoll 2011). Small-scale entrepreneurship schemes and the expansion of the EPRDF's apparatus of political surveillance enabled the ruling party to expand its reach at the bottom of urban society and secure the political stability that national politicians and international observers described as the foundation of Ethiopia's economic growth and development (Kelsall 2013; Devereux and Whyte 2010; Nino-Zarazua et al. 2011; Jones, Soares de Oliveira, and Verhoeven 2013; Booth and Golooba-Mutebi 2012).

However, political stability did not necessarily benefit those who were involved in government programs, including Haile, Ibrahim, and many others in their circle. The greater ability of the ruling party to mobilize, control, and surveil resulted in a wider sense of vulnerability on the streets. For many, punishment had become more likely than ever. In these circumstances, many former hustlers and thugs, as well as ordinary marginalized men and women, joined government programs, either from opportunism or with the hope of shielding themselves from the enhanced machinery of state repression. In doing so, they witnessed a process of greater integration and inclusion that reconfigured their relations with the Ethiopian state. However, this was a process of inclusion that deepened rather than challenged marginality on the streets of Addis Ababa. As I argued in the introduction, inclusion can marginalize. In fact, the opportunities that these programs offered continued to fail to provide ways of achieving social mobility or even relative improvement. Moreover, participants in these government programs were expected to show allegiance to the ruling party and refrain from siding with the opposition if they wished to keep their jobs. As a result, marginality persisted, not so much as a condition of abjection and exclusion but as the experience of being integrated and connected, yet with a limited ability to negotiate and challenge the terms of one's inclusion.

With this focus on the relationship between street life, marginality, and the politics of the Ethiopian state, this chapter seeks to characterize the *act of living* politically. The tension between trying to be something other than their constraints and living an existence that was firmly embedded in experiences of oppression and exclusion is not just a generic feature of the lives of the marginalized. Similarly, impositions and constraints on people's abilities to challenge their condition of marginality, both collectively and individually, are not just the outcome of invisible hands operating through invisible structures. Limits, constraints, and tensions are reinforced through actions, policies, and interventions that have a historical consistency and political visibility.

Still, seeing the production of constraints, tensions, and limits as political and historical products does not necessarily imply that state officials, political leaders, and policymakers intentionally marginalize large segments of the population, including those on which political elites depend for their own political survival. In addition, seeing the state, even an authoritarian one, as indifferent to poverty is analytically unhelpful (Gupta 2012). However, I argue there is an intimate relation between the intentionality of political processes of mobilization and control and the ways development initiatives are informed by certain under-standings of what poor people ought to be given and how they ought to behave. Small-scale entrepreneurship schemes in Addis Ababa were not primarily concerned with reshuffling the patterns of social differentiation and the unequal distribution of resources that have made poverty, marginality, and exclusion persist in the inner city. Moreover, government officials implementing these schemes understood mobility out of poverty as something that mainly con-cerned individuals and their aspirations and attitudes. This convergence be-tween intentional political concerns with mobilization and control and the underlying understandings of improvement as an exclusive matter of individual dispositions is what made development programs ineffective in producing trajec-tories of social mobility but extremely successful in making experiences of politi-cal subjugation and marginality the terms of poor people's membership in Ethiopian society.

Recognizing the centrality of politics as it pervades punishment in the streets and shapes experiences of marginality is key to this book's historical contextu-alization of the *act of living* as well as its critique of the formulas that pervade narratives on African success stories. Positive assessments of Ethiopia's develop-mental model, but also those of Rwanda, Angola, and to a certain degree Uganda, praised the ability of the political elites to bring the state and politics back into development practice, and argued that political commitment to policy and to build the capacity of the state can make the difference in delivering services, development, and trajectories of economic growth (Kelsall 2013; Booth and Golooba-Mutebi 2012; de Waal 2013; Devereux and Whyte 2010).

This chapter shows how the politics of the state and the ruling party in Ethiopia enabled the delivery of development but at the cost of deepening experiences of marginality, subjugation, and oppression. By bringing "politics" back in, Ethiopia and fellow African success stories have offered alternative institutional arrange-ments to the "depoliticizing" effects of development discourses and practices that James Ferguson (1994) so effectively discussed in his analysis of the "anti-politics" machine in Lesotho. However, "politics" should not be taken at face value. We need to scrutinize the work of "politics" in development. In Ethiopia, the ways that development served the political concerns of the ruling party with control, surveillance, and mobilization made it a "politics machine," a central cog of a wider apparatus of oppression, repression, and subjugation. This, I argue in the conclusion of this chapter, created a toxic nexus between the delivery of devel-opment and the pursuit of a form of governance that cultivates the state's ability to assert itself through the accomplishment of its own actions and a self-given right to dispose of people for the realization of its visions.

Do Not Cross the Red Line

Engaging in politics has always been a dangerous business, as my informants understood from a very young age. At the end of the 1970s, when Haile had turned eleven and was on the verge of entering street life, those streets were embroiled in the political conflict between the military junta and the civilian left (see Bahru Zewde 2009; Donham 1999; Lefort 1983; Markakis and Nega Ayele 1986). Parts of the street economy characterized by a certain level of organization witnessed a politicization of conflicts that, until then, had revolved mainly around the control of particular illegal businesses (see chapter 2). In Merkato, Addis Ababa's main marketplace, clashes between two gangs, the China Group and the Genghis Group, over the extortion of local merchants were gradually subsumed into the violent struggle between the squads of the EPRP (Ethiopian People's Revolutionary Party), which opposed the Derg, and those of the Meison (All Ethiopian Socialist Movement), which initially supported the military regime (Yeraswork Admassie, Addis Ababa University, personal communication, 2010).

By the time the Red Terror was over, many young people in Arada had been killed (Tronvoll, Schaefer, and Girmachew Alemu Aneme 2009). However, the Red Terror did not definitively eliminate street life. Petty crime persisted throughout, coexisting with moments of political conflict (Andargatchew Tesfaye 1988). Already by the mid-1980s, organized robbery groups and group street fights reappeared on the streets of the capital (see chapter 2). As a veteran of street life explained, in the latter years of Derg rule, politics did not concern street thugs; disengaging from politics was a fundamental tactic to shield oneself from state repression and pursue one's activities on the streets. This did not mean that offenders like Getachew Bongar, the well-known gangster of the 1980s and a mythical figure for my informants (see chapter 2), were not prosecuted. "He was jailed during the Derg, many times! He got in and he got out," a former soldier of the Derg and a resident of the inner city told me. Staying away from politics did not grant Getachew and many others impunity; however, it did moderate their punishment. More specifically, it enabled them to be involved in illegal activities on the streets that would have led to far more severe sentences had politics been involved.

This game of engagement and disengagement continued to unfold on the streets of inner city Addis Ababa after the fall of the socialist regime in 1991. Politics remained an enduring experience of punishment, repression, and control, while "crime" was the ambiguous terrain of tactics and margins of probability where a new generation of hustlers, Ibrahim included, found ways of living through marginality and social exclusion.

As many ordinary residents of the inner city agreed, when the new government was established it knew nothing about the city, let alone the logic of the street economy. The EPRDF had work to do to ground itself in the city, especially as the population of Addis Ababa received its victory with a certain ambiguity. The demise of the Derg had put an end to fifteen years of brutal authoritarianism; however, the rural history of the EPRDF and the privileged links that its leading faction, the TPLF, had with the peasantry of northern Ethiopia were seen by the urban population as worlds apart from their grievances and expectations (Tronvoll 2012, 277). For its part, the ruling party viewed the capital with suspicion as intrinsically linked to the remnants of the previous regime.

This mix of mutual mistrust and the government's lack of institutional knowledge, together with persisting poverty and scarcity in the city, made the streets a complex terrain where the expression of dissent against the new rulers intertwined with the resurgence of street violence and crime. Already in the months immediately following the arrival of the TPLF in 1991, gangs of young men took to the streets, looting properties and throwing stones at foreign embassies (Henze 2007, 311). Later and throughout the early 1990s, the activities of organized robbery groups and group street fights, both petty turf wars and struggles for the control of minibus businesses, shaped the experiences and practices of street life (see chapter 2).

The immediate response of the government was to wage campaigns of repression and law enforcement, targeting the groups and individuals believed to be behind the street violence. One of the tough men who were hit by these campaigns was Mesfin Redi, the street child who had become a dangerous thief and snatcher and who was remembered and celebrated as a sort of Robin Hood (see chapter 2). In the last years of his life, Mesfin's main business had been to rob the city's new elites, the Tigrayans and Eritreans, who had come to Addis Ababa following the TPLF. Mesfin was creating too much trouble, my informants remembered, and for this reason, I was told, a government security officer shot him dead in the early 1990s.

These early campaigns of law enforcement were meant to show that the new government was in charge and that it had the capacity to punish and repress. The killing of thugs like Mesfin Redi and the imprisonment of some of the most feared gangsters in other parts of the city made the point clear. Yet these campaigns had limited impact on street life as a whole. Government campaigns had, to some extent, a limited focus. The execution and imprisonment campaign concentrated on the most visible personalities of the streets, without intervening against the incoherent army of low-key hustlers and thieves who continued to consider the street economy a viable way of getting by.

Petty crime thus persisted. However, by the late 1990s, the Ethiopian government had begun to make progress in managing and controlling street life. One important step in this direction occurred when the government curbed the group street fights over the control of minibus stops and parking areas by formalizing and regulating the territories that each group of touts controlled. Building on this initial achievement, the government's massive campaign to enroll street hustlers and thugs for the war against Eritrea (1998–2000) bore witness to the ruling party's increased institutional capacity at the bottom of urban society. As my informants remembered, enrollment was not forced conscription. Government officials relied on a carrot-and-stick approach that served both a concern with sending people to the front and an interest in keeping the capital in line during wartime. Two options were offered: go to the front and have your criminal record cleared, or stay at home and risk jail.

"Is it better to spend a life in prison or to become a soldier?" Haile asked me, reenacting the thought process that eventually convinced him to join the army. "Prison life is not good, even dying is better!" he concluded. Others in Haile's circle, including Mikias and Samson from the *yemot midib*, made the same decision, mixing their fear of life imprisonment with the hope that joining the army would give them a job and an opportunity to change their lives. "One hundred twenty-seven big buses came from Addis Ababa," Haile remembered, estimating the number of people who joined the front from the capital. Ibrahim chose not to board one of the buses—like many others, he stayed at home. He was aware he could have ended up in prison, but argued that had he gone to the front, he could have ended up dead. With their opposite decisions, however, Haile and Ibrahim depended on the smartness they had cultivated while getting by on the streets, hoping it could help them either on the front or while dealing with the threatening machinery of state repression at home.

The war ended in 2000 with a stalemate and cost tens of thousands of lives on both sides (Tekeste Negash and Tronvoll 2000). Most conscripts were sent home, though some were offered the chance to stay in the army, gaining the employment they had hoped for. Haile felt he could have been one of them, but an injury during a training session cut short his military career. He was soon back to his former life, hustling on the streets. Meanwhile, Ibrahim had managed to stay out of prison, at least during the years his friend Haile was away fighting. Having managed to enroll young people for the front, the government did not follow up on its threat to imprison draft dodgers. While crime persisted, hustlers like Ibrahim lay low, realizing that disorder such as group street fights would not be tolerated in wartime.

A couple of years after the war was over, however, the city witnessed a reemergence of violent street fights and a mushrooming of dissent and malcontent on the streets and in the ballot box—as well as in the inner ranks of the ruling party. Immediately after the end of the war, disagreements over the conduct of the

Ethiopian-Eritrean conflict triggered an intense power struggle within the EPRDF (Milkias 2003; Vaughan and Tronvoll 2003). Then, after the 2000 general election, the EPRDF lost four parliamentary seats in Addis Ababa, one of which had previously been held by a key adviser to Meles Zenawi.

Meanwhile, ten years after the liberalization of the economy, the persistent lack of opportunities for social mobility became a reason for deep frustration among the generation of young people who had grown up in the early 1990s, immediately before and after the downfall of the socialist regime. The failure of the government to deal with the social problems of the youth, together with its repressive treatment of public protest, fostered the mushrooming of dissent and unrest in the city. In April 2001, student demonstrations at Addis Ababa University calling for more freedom on the campus were brutally repressed, leading to riots and protests throughout the city (Balsivik 2007, 143–156). Thirty-one people died,[2] and looting caused damage valued at "hundreds of millions of birr."[3] Two years later, in 2003, a wave of street violence erupted. The number of young people who had turned to the street economy to find ways of getting by had continued to increase, triggering a fierce competition for respect as well as for the control of niches of the street economy (see chapter 2). The police magazine *Policena Irmejaw* reported that over five months of street groups fights, sixty-three people were badly injured and two were killed.[4]

Meles Zenawi and his faction endured this wave of unrest. Dissidents were purged, and a campaign of political reform and renewal was launched (*tehadso*) with the aim of creating a tight chain of command while emphasizing the importance of delivering development to the local population (Vaughan 2011; Vaughan and Tronvoll 2003). This process had a clear impact on Addis Ababa and its inner city. The whole administrative structure of the city government was reorganized and simplified. Measures were taken to boost the general development of the city as well as the livelihoods of the urban poor, such as the construction of the first "condominium houses" and the promotion of the container shops initiative, which gave Ibrahim a taste of what being a businessman was like (see chapter 3). Together with these development measures, the government also focused its attention on the youth. In 2004, it released for the first time a Youth Policy (Ministry of Youth, Sports and Culture 2004) as a general framework for further interventions to be promoted, conceptualized, and funded. The same year, the government issued a proclamation against "dangerous vagrants" (*adegegna bozene*)—the Vagrancy Proclamation Act (Federal Negaritgazeta of the Federal

---

2. "Police Say 31 People Killed in Last Week's Riot," *Ethiopian Herald*, April 24, 2001, p. 1.
3. "Editorial, behind the Riot," *Ethiopian Herald*, April 29, 2001, p. 2.
4. "Ye Gulbetegna Findatawoch Ketema Eyehonech New Ye Addis Ababa Ketema Newariwoch Kibirachin Yetebek Yelalu," *Policena Irmejaw*, Magabit 2 1994 EC (March 11, 2002), pp. 1–7.

Democratic Republic of Ethiopia 2004, 2533)—that provided the ruling party with a legal tool to tackle unrest in the future and that, as we will see, came to significantly shape its politics toward the streets.

Four years after the launch of this campaign of reforms, the EPRDF leadership believed that it had not only strengthened its position within the party and in Ethiopian urban society but also reversed the history of mutual distrust that had characterized relations between the rulers of the country and the population of the capital. Confident that the 2005 general election would result in electoral success and concerned with proving its democratic credentials to the international community, the ruling party relaxed its control of the political system and allowed opposition parties to campaign in Addis Ababa.

The outcome of the 2005 elections and the riots and demonstrations that followed revealed that the EPRDF had not succeeded in gaining the support of the capital. The day after the election, on May 16, it was clear that the Coalition for Unity and Democracy, the main opposition party, had captured all the parliamentary seats for Addis Ababa, as well as the city government. Counting was still going on in other regions of the country, and the National Electoral Board of Ethiopia (NEBE) planned to release the official results a month later. That same day, the then minister of information acknowledged the success of the opposition parties in Addis Ababa, but declared that the EPRDF had won the election on the basis of votes from rural areas. This statement, a subsequent ban on public demonstrations, and the NEBE's announcement of a delay in the official declaration of the electoral results triggered street protests in support of the opposition and against an election that many believed had been rigged (Abbink 2006). The ruling party responded energetically. It labeled protesters "dangerous vagrants" and "unemployed youth" and waged a pervasive and systematic repression campaign. The police were joined by the Special Forces, the Agazi, to shut down demonstrations. City neighborhoods were raided to arrest those whom informers and members of the local government office had tapped as troublemakers. By the time calm was restored in late November, two hundred people had died in the clashes and thirty thousand people had been detained in Addis Ababa and other major towns.

Rehabilitating the Marginalized

The 2005 riots brought politics into street life and the street economy in a way comparable only to the end of the 1970s, when gangs and gangsters took sides in political confrontations between the military junta and the civilian left. In a similar way, though in a less dramatic fashion, 2005 bore witness to an emerging alliance between the street and the opposition parties, breaking decades of political disengagement, as one of my informants recalled: "Everybody in the *tajj bet* [*arakie* drinking houses] and *khat bet* [*khat* chewing houses] was talking about politics." That year, opposition supporters were seen "going to secret places, talking to the Arada," campaigning on the streets, and reaching out to individuals, capitalizing on the fact that many people on the streets hoped to gain a position in government institutions if the opposition took power: "There were many people . . . thugs, who want to enter in the government, like policemen and so on. But they did not want to do it with this government. They wanted to go in with the new government."

To break this alliance, the EPRDF first repressed protesters. Then, after calm was restored, it worked to recapture the marginalized youth who had participated in the 2005 riots and demonstrations. As we will see, what followed significantly changed the lives of my informants and the meanings and practices of street life.

Paradoxically, the notions of "dangerous vagrants" and "unemployed youth" that the government used to criminalize dissent in 2005 also helped the ruling party rethink its approaches to the streets and shift political allegiances. The government mobilized these notions to make a clear distinction between the predicaments of marginalized youth and the political interests of the opposition. Unlike the opposition parties, which the ruling party depicted as mainly interested in toppling the legitimate government (Tronvoll 2012), "dangerous vagrants" and "unemployed youth" were portrayed as individuals troubled by social and economic problems—in particular, unemployment—that the government could effectively address.

With the financial support of international development organizations, in particular the German Technical Cooperation (GTZ [now GIZ]), the government moved to implement a range of employment programs. The 2005 Construction Sector Capacity Building Program sought to involve young people in government-supported cobblestone road construction projects (Federal TVET Agency 2014). A year later, in 2006, a wider scheme was launched to promote microfinance and small-scale entrepreneurship in a variety of sectors, such as textiles and clothing, metal- and woodworking, food preparation, municipal services, and urban agriculture (Ministry of Works and Urban Development 2006, 98–101). To fund the scheme, the government allocated over 5 billion Ethiopian birr (roughly US$300 million). The Micro Credit and Small-Scale Enterprises Agency was established to implement the program, with branch offices at different levels of the state administration. At the grass roots, local government offices were asked to act as the first line for establishing small-scale enterprises and assisting them in the search for funding and the provision of training and business facilities. Mass associations, which the ruling party revived in the aftermath of the 2005 riots, were actively involved in gathering and selecting prospective participants for the government schemes (Di Nunzio 2014a, 2015a).[5]

Efforts to provide employment were instrumental to the EPRDF's political plan to win the support of the youth. At the same time, they were also part of the ruling party's wider commitment to deliver development at the bottom of urban society and enhance the participation of young people in the country's economic growth. Programs were envisioned not just as a way to provide a means of getting by but also as a way to promote more substantial results through behavioral change: young people were to become entrepreneurs, creators of their own employment.

Policymakers in Ethiopia were not alone in conceptualizing poverty reduction measures in these terms. There is a wider policy debate in which promoting entrepreneurship is considered an effective means of tackling poverty, one that enables poor people to develop the skills and capabilities that will eventually allow them to help themselves out of poverty (Bateman 2010; Elyachair 2002; Rankin 2001; Rajak and Dolan 2016; Rogaly 1996; Roy 2010; Schwittay 2011; Prahalad 2006). According to this logic, by becoming entrepreneurs, poor people can be not only makers of their destiny but also active market actors. With their business ventures and creativity, newly created entrepreneurs are supposed to multiply opportunities for capital investment, acting as vectors of the expansion of the market into unexplored and economically underexploited domains of everyday life (de Soto 1989, 2002; Foucault 2008; Rose 1999; Weidner 2009).

The Ethiopian ruling party regarded this vision of poor people emancipating themselves and actively contributing to the economic growth of the country as something truly patriotic. And, interestingly, it looked at entrepreneurship through its own ideological lens. As I mentioned in the introduction, the EPRDF's original ideology was poles apart from notions of liberalism and individualism. Informed by Marxist-Leninist ideas of democratic centralism and proletarian

---

5. Youth and women's mass associations were initially established during the socialist regime. They were designed to mobilize the general population around regime activities and involved sections of the population normally excluded from the ordinary administrative structures of peasants' associations and *kebelles* (Clapham 1988). When the EPRDF took over, the Derg's women's and youth associations were disbanded and replaced with the mass organizations that were already active in the EPRDF (Vaughan 2011). However, the political roles of the mass associations faded; in 1997, the EPRDF formally disassociated youth and women's associations from the party, though an informal link continued to exist (Vaughan and Tronvoll 2003). In the months that followed the 2005 elections, old mass associations were revived and reempowered, and two new kinds of organizations were established: the Leagues and the Forums. The Leagues are mass associations directly linked to the ruling party. They formally work as political wings of the EPRDF and expressly aim to spread support for the ruling party among young people and women. The Forums, by contrast, are supported by the government administrations and their aim is social: their duty mainly consists of bridging the gap between communities and the government by running meetings and passing on information about government policies (Di Nunzio 2014a).

democracy, the EPRDF leadership promoted a society in which the individual is conceptualized as entirely part of the whole, committed to the common good and collective development of the country (Vaughan 2011).

Within this ideological frame, entrepreneurship programs were promoted to encourage such a collectivist and development-oriented ethos. As Demissie, the secretary of the local branch of the EPRDF in a *kebelle* in my field site, argued, government development initiatives were not aimed at providing opportunities for enrichment to single individuals. The ruling party and the government were concerned with the creation of "groups" and "cooperatives." Small-scale enterprises were considered to be ideologically valuable tools for development because they enabled the organization of "groups" and "cooperatives" that, through their collectively managed business ventures, embodied the development spirit praised and preached in the revolutionary democratic visions of the EPRDF. Indeed, walking around one of the bazaars that the local government office organized to showcase the activities of cooperatives and groups it had helped establish, Teshome, a government official elected through the ruling party to manage a Youth Office in inner city Addis Ababa, synthesized the ideological underpinnings of the promotion of small-scale enterprises: "In Ethiopia we follow a revolutionary democracy rather than a liberal democracy. This means that we emphasize the group over the individual. We want groups of millionaires rather than individual millionaires."

Discourses on entrepreneurship, behavioral change, and cooperatives informed the government's approach toward the streets. The notion of "dangerous vagrants" that had previously been used to criminalize marginalized youth was once again employed as government officials turned to the streets to implement development programs. The term "dangerous vagrants" drew on the long history of political repression described earlier in this chapter, which had seen actors in the street economy portrayed as the *lumpenproletariat* and unruly hooligans.[6] However, whereas historically these earlier notions had offered a generic picture of the activities and attitudes of street youth, the proclamation against dangerous vagrants issued a year before the 2005 election (Federal Negaritgazeta of the Federal Democratic Republic of Ethiopia 2004, 2533) provided a very detailed description of the economies of hustling and exchanges that take place on the

---

6. The Derg used the category of the *lumpenproletariat* to refer to that segment of urban society that was described as being composed of "vagabonds, criminals, beggars and coolies" to be employed, for instance, in agricultural development projects ("Lumpen Proletariat Here Begin New Life," *Ethiopian Herald*, December 18, 1977, p. 1). In 2001, young protesters were described as "hooligans," "criminals" ("Police Say 31 People Killed in Last Week's Riot," 1), and expressions of a "gangsterism" that, as a senior government official told the BBC, Ethiopia had never seen in its history ("University Reopens after Addis Riots," BBC News, April 24, 2001, http://news.bbc.co.uk/2/hi/africa/1293995.stm).

street.[7] It established the street youth as a political and juridical subject and a target of specific policies and interventions (cf. Mains 2012a).

In fact, the proclamation against dangerous vagrants was not designed to punish a particular crime, such as robbery, theft, or burglary. A dangerous vagrant, as police officers pointed out to me, is a particular kind of offender. As crime investigator Lieutenant S. explained to me, the difference between a thief (*leba*) and a dangerous vagrant (*adegegna bozene*) is that thieves are, to some extent, professionals. *Adegegna bozene*, on the other hand, are individuals who disturb "tranquility" and "order." A dangerous vagrant is an offender because he continues to commit crimes, Officer A., a community policing officer, told me, or because, as the proclamation itself states, he is "unemployed" and has committed an offense. "If you have a job, you are not an *adegegna bozene*," a young attorney posited. As a result, the response to the behavior of dangerous vagrants, Lieutenant S. and his colleagues argued, cannot just be punishment but must have a broader focus on "peace" and "rehabilitation."

On the streets after 2005, rehabilitation revolved around entrepreneurship and employment creation through a reorganization of the street economy into a formalized and regulated sector of the city's economy. In the inner city, for instance, the ruling party's strategies focused on areas of the street economy that were involved in the transport sector, like touting minibuses and collecting parking fees from drivers. These were licit businesses that provided a service, such as managing the flow of minibuses in a particular motor park or attending to cars, but until then had been organized in an unregulated and illegal manner.

If we look back on the history of street life and its relations with the Ethiopian state, we can see that there is something unprecedented in the government's move after 2005. In the past, individual thugs had been co-opted to work for government institutions, and many people in the inner city remembered "tough men" who became "bodyguards" during the socialist regime. But when large-scale political mobilization and repression took place on the streets, they often revolved around taking thugs away: to prison, to the front, and to detention camps. After the mid-2000s, however, state intervention took place *on the streets*. To use Timothy Mitchell's (2008, 2010) phrasing, government interventions sought to

---

7. The Vagrancy Proclamation Act defined the dangerous vagrant as an individual who "is found loitering or prowling at a place, at a time, or in a manner not usual for a law-abiding citizen . . . betting, gambling and playing other unlawful similar games involving money"; "intentionally alarms the public or people in the vicinity by intoxicating with alcohol or psychotropic or narcotic substance"; "disturbs the tranquility of residents in vicinity by participating in organized gang brawls"; "directly or indirectly receives or lets himself to be given money or other similar benefits by using his reputation for violent behaviour or brutality in his community or taking advantage of the fear he has caused to the community in vicinity due to such reputation" (Federal Negaritgazeta of the Federal Democratic Republic of Ethiopia 2004: 2533).

"remake the economy," or, rather, to "remake the street economy," into a terrain of interactions, relations, and transactions that was commensurable and compatible with the concerns that the government had with delivering growth and development.

Mobilizing the Marginalized

The process of remaking the street economy focused on both the organizational structure and the political allegiances of the street businesses concerned. For instance, before government intervention, the parking business was a fragmented street business largely dominated by the individual ventures of single hustlers, except in a few areas where small private companies were involved. Hence, streamlining this trade so as to embody that entrepreneurial and collectivist ethos that the ruling party aimed to foster required significant reorganizing and reframing: cooperatives were established and then assigned territories defined by the local government offices. As this business expanded and reached areas that were not previously involved in this trade, cooperatives of parking guys employed many people, like Ibrahim and his colleagues, who had previously found other ways of getting by. While new people entered the parking business, however, not everyone who had been involved in this trade before government intervention ended up working in the newly established cooperatives. Employees of preexisting private companies were regrouped in cooperatives, but some of the hustlers who had had small parking businesses lost their trade, as their individual ventures did not match with the new "collectivist" spirit—such as the old man I once saw wandering the streets who, until then, had made do by collecting money from rich people parking next to jewelers' shops in Arada.

Formalizing minibus touts did not present these challenges. Minibus touts had been historically organized into "groups" (see chapter 2), and, as mentioned earlier, the government had already worked to regulate the territories that each of these "groups" controlled in the late 1990s. Subsequent government interventions took the formalization of this business a step further, recognizing minibus touts as groups of "private investors" involved in the urban transport economy. While street fighting had been the means for maintaining a share of the market in the past (see chapter 2), after the mid-2000s, what mattered was the special relationship that minibus touts had with local government officials. A man in his twenties who worked in one such group made sense of the transformation thus: "We were *tara* [literally, "queue keepers"] with the stick, now we are with the *mahaber* [association or cooperative]."

The different strategies that the ruling party used for the minibus touts and the parking guys not only reflect the different histories and organizational structures of the two businesses but also were motivated by different political concerns. With the minibus touts, government officials were concerned with strengthening an existing relation that had not been "politically" and institutionally formalized. When the government had regulated the territories that each group of touts controlled in the late 1990s, this had not led to their political mobilization. It was only after the 2005 riots that the alliance between the ruling party and the minibus touts was forged. On June 8, 2005, after police repression of a student demonstration against the May elections had resulted in the death of a twenty-two-year-old woman,[8] taxi and minibus drivers staged a three-day strike that virtually paralyzed the city. In response, the Addis Ababa Transport Authority told taxi drivers to resume their services within two days, on penalty of having their licenses withdrawn.[9] The minibus touts played an important role, first as promoters of the strike action, and later as enforcers of the government order. Those among my informants who helped me draw up a history of this street business said that the leaders of the minibus touts were urged by local government officials to stop the strike from going further. In the years after the 2005 riots, the formalization of minibus touts as groups of private investors consolidated this alliance, bringing the business under the influence of the EPRDF.

Meanwhile, the establishment of the cooperatives of parking guys throughout the city did not revolve around forging an alliance with a highly fragmented niche of the street economy. The parking initiative was part of the government's entrepreneurship schemes and is better understood as a component of the wider concern of the ruling party to expand its reach at the bottom of urban society. As policy documents show, entrepreneurship schemes were designed to be implemented pervasively and systematically. When this initiative was launched in 2006, the government announced a target of 1.2 million beneficiaries (Ministry of Works and Urban Development 2006, 91), which became 3.0 million in the 2010–2015 Five Year Growth and Transformation Plan (Ministry of Finance and Economic Development 2010, 28). These numbers might seem pure exaggeration, especially when economists and statisticians (Jerven 2015), not just anthropologists (Comaroff and Comaroff 2006), urge us to be careful with government statistics. However, even though we might remain skeptical about government estimates, the implementation of entrepreneurship schemes, like many other development

---

8. "Ethiopia's Agonizing Suspense. How the 'White Revolution' Turned Bloody," *Fortune*, June 12, 2005, pp. 2, 21.

9. "Authority Orders Immediate Resumption of Taxi Services, Vows to Take Alternative Measures," *Ethiopian Herald*, June 9, 2005, p. 2.

programs, had a significant impact. Whether or not they reached the intended target, these initiatives required the strengthening of an institutional framework that enabled government officials at the grass roots to expand the number of people who were directly or indirectly linked to the ruling party for their survival and thus were expected to support the EPRDF when needed. Politics clearly framed the activities of the parking guys; as one of them reckoned: "You know, our job depends on the outcomes of the next elections."

This strategy paid off eventually. In inner city Addis Ababa, participants in small-scale enterprises, including the cooperatives of parking guys, were among those who filled the political rallies in the months immediately preceding and following the 2010 general election, which saw the overwhelming victory of the ruling party, with only one member of the opposition party entering Parliament. Five years later, in 2015, despite the political uncertainty that followed the death of Meles Zenawi in 2012, the ruling party confirmed that result, winning the totality of parliamentary seats in the country.

Marginalizing the Marginalized

Elections were won. Yet, the schemes that the ruling party had implemented to mobilize and rehabilitate the marginalized had contradictory outcomes: government entrepreneurship schemes worked for those who were already in the businesses concerned but failed to create new social opportunities for those most in need of government support. These entrepreneurship programs not only had a limited capacity to deliver expected outcomes but also actually reproduced existing patterns of social differentiation. Those who were already successful thrived, and those who had lived in a condition of social exclusion and marginality continued to do so.

For instance, touting minibuses had been a profitable street business long before government intervention. Being recognized as groups of private investors significantly benefited their business, enabling them to consolidate control of their respective areas and take advantage of the expansion of the city's private transport sector. Over the years that I conducted research in Addis Ababa, the number of minibuses grew, while the fees that minibus drivers pay to the "queue-keepers" (*tara askabari*), as minibus touts are known in Addis Ababa, doubled or even tripled.

Others also benefited from government intervention—namely, those who could rely on preexisting skills, resources, and networks before joining the entrepreneurship programs, and could then expand their business with government support. One of these was Rashid. Rashid was in his late twenties, a carpenter, and an active member of the Youth Forum, which was established in Addis Ababa with the support of the city government after the 2005 postelection violence to bridge the gap between the youth and government institutions (Di Nunzio 2014a). His "cooperative" was established in 2007. "We had work, we were just looking for a place. Through the Youth Forum, we organized a *mahaber* [association] and they gave us this place." In the years that followed, Rashid and his colleagues applied for a loan of 25,000 birr (US$1,525). They used the money to produce furniture for a construction project assigned to them by the government. When I asked him how the business was going, he replied: "When we are not given work in government projects, we do it by ourselves. We sell to a showroom in the city. I got a good experience in this. I have made some connections with rich people."

Alongside these successes were many who had been failed by government development programs, including enterprises whose members, unlike Rashid, were new to the business concerned and hence needed training, resources, and business networks to succeed. Among these was Khazin's cooperative. Like Rashid, Khazin was a member of the Youth Forum. When I met him in 2010, he was nineteen. He along with other members of the Youth Forum had been selected by the *kebelle* officials to participate in a microfinance and entrepreneurship program to produce ecological and low-fuel stoves, funded by an Italian NGO, COOPI (Cooperazione Internazionale). After the training ended, Khazin and his colleagues began working on their stove business. When I met him a couple of months later, however, things were not going well. Initially, fifteen people had been involved, but after a few months they were down to ten. The others had gone to work as shoeshine boys or were selling chewing gum and cigarettes on the streets and earning 30–40 birr (US$1.80–$2.40) a day, which was much more than Khazin and his colleagues were earning. "In the last days, we made 50 birr [US$3], this means 2.5 birr a day for us. This is not even enough to pay for the coffee that I am now drinking with you." I met Khazin several times in the following months. Things had not improved: "COOPI lied to us, we don't have money to go on. They even tried to make some market linkage, but it did not work out. Then a guy from GTZ came and told us that he wanted to buy our *injera* stoves for exporting them outside. He did not come again." Eventually Khazin's enterprise closed down.

There were also cooperatives that lasted more than a few months but provided low salaries and low-quality work. As a comparative study on micro- and small-scale enterprises has shown, joining these kinds of cooperatives was the most common experience of those involved in government entrepreneurship programs (Tegegne Gebre-Egziahbier and Meheret Ayenew 2010). Haile's and Ibrahim's cooperatives fell into this broad category. Haile first worked in a cooperative producing concrete blocks for government housing projects and then as a car attendant in the cooperative of parking guys. Ibrahim began at the government cobblestone site before landing in the parking business. These employment opportunities were not life-changing experiences. And this is even clearer if we consider that on top of their long-term engagement with street life, Ibrahim and Haile were not new to labor. The kind of employment that the government offered to them was not an improvement on their prior work experiences.

In the late 1980s, after serving his first long sentence in prison in his early twenties, Haile worked as a day laborer, pushing a *barella* (the Italian and Amharic word for "barrow") for a small company building a housing cooperative during the Derg. He soon left this job because it paid badly and did not deliver on his expectations. When the socialist regime collapsed, he crossed the border into Kenya in search of a better life (see chapter 3). Roughly fifteen years later, Haile's job in the cooperative producing concrete blocks did not represent a significant improvement. But Haile could not get out of this job as easily as the first time, when he was in his early twenties. Now he was in his late thirties and, on top of this, had to look after his young son. Haile had his son with a woman he had met while in military training in the Amhara region before going to the front, when he was looking forward to a career in the military. Working in the cooperative was not a good replacement for an army career. Haile's salary, along with his wife's job as a cook, allowed them to rent a one-bedroom house that Haile himself felt was worse than the house where he had grown up in the inner city and where Haile often sent his son to spend the day. Then, after five years, the enterprise of concrete blocks closed down. The government stopped providing contracts, and the enterprise had not made enough capital to move to another business. Haile was left with nothing and turned to his old friend Ibrahim for help. He joined the cooperative of parking guys, first as an employee and then as a member. He again received a regular salary, but he was no better off than before.

Ibrahim had a much longer work history than Haile. In his twenties, a couple of years after the end of the *yemot midib*, he joined one of the city's construction sites. He was determined to change and learn more, he remembered. The engineer running the site soon noticed him and gave him an opportunity to move up in the trade, learning on the job how to become a *ferraio*, a steel bar bender and steel fixer. He soon became very good at it, working for a few months at the site, until he was accused of stealing and fired. This did not end his career as a specialized construction worker. Another opportunity arose a few months later, proving to him that some of his fellow workers knew that he had been framed and fired unjustly. The foreman, an older man whom Ibrahim had met while working as *ferraio*, took him to another construction site, far from Addis Ababa, in the Afar region near the Djibouti border. Ibrahim worked there for a while, until a man threatened him with a rifle after Ibrahim had intervened to stop the man from beating his wife. After a few years, he once again found work on a construction site, this time as a night guard, working with his neighbor Teferi, who had got the job for himself and Ibrahim through a relative. Ibrahim recounted to me the story of working at the site while sitting with Teferi, who nodded in approval as Ibrahim remembered those days. Teferi gave Ibrahim *khat* to keep him awake. This made Ibrahim an efficient guard, and the number of thefts at the site soon went down. The work lasted for a while, until one memorable night. Teferi and Ibrahim were walking together through the site. Ibrahim heard a sound, *tu-tu tu-tu*, reminding him of the cry of an owl, and felt a shiver down his spine. He was scared. That was a sign, Ibrahim thought retrospectively. He started running, pushing Teferi out of the site. A big explosion followed. "You saved my life," Teferi told Ibrahim.

When Ibrahim joined the government programs, the jobs he was offered were no different—or even worse, since they did not provide the possibilities of career advancement that his work as *ferraio* could have opened to him. Squaring stones in a government cobblestone site, for instance, was like working as a day laborer. He was initially paid a salary of 30 birr (US$2.78) a day. Then the government changed the payment arrangements, paying stoneworkers a fixed rate of 1.80 birr (US$0.16) for each stone they squared. With this new arrangement, if Ibrahim worked fast enough, he could have earned a bit more than 30 birr a day, but for him, like many others among his friends who eventually moved to the cooperative of parking guys, those few extra birr were not worth the unfavorable working conditions. The cooperative of parking guys offered better working conditions, but the monthly salary earned by issuing parking tickets every half hour remained low: 400–800 birr (US$24–$48) a month in 2010 and 1,000–1,500 birr (US$50–$75) in 2014. This was higher than what waiters in inner city restaurants and bars earned, but lower than what day laborers in the city's construction sites earned.

The Place of the Poor

The outcomes of entrepreneurship programs in the inner city reveal a fundamental difference between being entrepreneurial and actually becoming a businessman. In a way, Ibrahim and Haile were entrepreneurial individuals, as revealed by the multiplicity of the activities they have engaged with throughout their lives. But low wages and low-quality labor—together with the fact that development programs ended up reinforcing, not challenging, existing forms of social differentiation—did not make them businesspeople. Access to the inner city's and city's business committees continued to be governed by the logic of exclusion and social differentiation, which we explored in the previous chapter.

When I talked to government officials, I soon realized that the shortcomings of entrepreneurship programs were visible and evident to them. Civil servants at the ministerial level were aware that a broader approach to poverty was needed, but did not question the value of entrepreneurship schemes as a tool of poverty reduction. That "success stories" existed suggested to government officials that entrepreneurship programs worked for those who were worthy of government support, while those who failed, they argued, were to blame for their lack of self-determination and spirit of entrepreneurship. For instance, after I spoke of the failures and contradictory successes of the small-scale enterprises in my field site, a civil servant in the Micro Credit and Small Scale Enterprises Agency at the city level responded: "Yes, I know, this is not good, is it? These guys [the youth] don't have a vision." Other government officials gave similar interpretations. When I went to the city Youth Office, government officials argued that many young people are simply not interested in working hard. What young people want, one of the civil servants I interviewed argued, is immediate profit; they are easily frustrated because "intensive work is needed to run these enterprises."

These explanations added a layer to the discourses on unemployed youth that the government used to criminalize political dissent in 2005. In that context, unemployment was seen as not only the reason why young people engaged with dissent but also the cause of their criminal and unruly behavior. Repeating an old trope, the "unemployed youth" were believed to be agents of disorder and unrest because lack of employment had made them lack discipline (cf. Waller 2006). Five years later, when I interviewed government officials, the officials blamed the "working youth" involved in government programs for the persistence of their own condition of marginality: they remained poor because of their laziness and alleged lack of self-determination. In other words, the unemployed youth and the working youth were described as being fundamentally similar. The former lacked discipline, and the latter were lazy and indecisive.

The resilience of these patronizing views suggests that these arguments were not just ways of making sense of dissent or the outcomes of small-scale enterprise schemes. They were rooted in a wider discourse about the place that the urban poor would and should occupy in society. In this view, social inequalities are understood as inevitable, while the position individuals occupy in society is seen as the result of individual actions, choices, and behaviors. The role of state institutions is thus more to enable worthy individuals to deal with inequalities and less to tackle the structural reasons for social inequalities, since to remain in poverty is a consequence of one's own "failures."

This view of poverty and inequality demonstrates a convergence of the narratives of the ruling party with a liberal and more individualistic understanding of social inequality (see McNay 2009; Foucault 2008) that the ruling party, with its commitment to a collectivist ideology, should have, in principle, opposed. However, this discourse on poverty and inequality was not just expressed by government officials who endorsed those views but also inscribed in the ruling party's ideological documents. For instance, the ideological statute of the Fourth General Assembly of the EPRDF stated the government's approach to "failures" and "successes" by comparing the fate of unproductive entrepreneurs with the successful commitments and achievements of development-oriented investors: "Any constructive development investor gets adequate and full support from the government and those who take advantage will prosper, and others will lose unhesitatingly. The system created in a way those who show productive results obtain progress, and those who do not show, will receive nothing" (EPRDF 2006, 39).

Likewise, when talking about cobblestone work, Teshome, the *kebelle* political cadre who told me about "groups of millionaires," argued that giving bad jobs to marginalized subjects is both fair to the young who persist with unproductive habits and necessary for broader development: "Many of these guys are drug addicts. They want the job and easy money. They work in the morning and they spend it at the *khat bet*. . . . As long as they are loyal and they work hard it is fine. They are addicted but the stones they are squaring are useful for the development of our country."

Fearing the "Politics Machine"

My informants did not see themselves as "drug addicts" working for the "development of the country." By being and becoming *Arada*, they had built a sense of respect and self-worth through an appreciation of their abilities to live smartly and toughly through marginality and exclusion. But why did they join these programs if these schemes did not work and if the government officials implementing them held such stigmatizing views? And how did the ruling party manage to win overwhelming electoral victories despite the failure of its development programs?

Against the odds, entrepreneurship schemes still provided my informants with a regular salary that they could combine with their incomes from brokering petty transactions. True, they could have worked as day laborers at a construction site, and their salaries would have been slightly higher than their wages as parking guys. But hard labor, together with the lack of labor rights or safety measures on construction sites, hardly represented the opportunity for the kind of life change my informants had long hoped for (Di Nunzio 2015b).

The second reason is that the memory of the 2005 postelection violence, and the ruling party's initiatives that followed, produced a fear of politics. This fear was hardly new. The protagonists of this book had previously experienced the repressive machinery of the state, and, for this reason, generations of thugs had learned to stay away from politics. However, the 2005 riots and demonstrations marked a rupture in this long history of political disengagement. The thugs joined politics and sided with the opposition. The memories of repression that followed were still very vivid in the inner city. Special Forces raiding the neighborhoods, the deaths of two hundred people, and the detention of thousands showed that the ruling party had an unprecedented institutional capacity to punish dissenters on a large scale (cf. Toggia 2008).

When calm was restored, there was an apparent opportunity for thugs and hustlers to revert to doing what their predecessors had done: to disengage from politics and return to the streets. Yet, my informants felt they could not do this, since politics continued to seem pervasive on the streets and in inner city neighborhoods. And when politics was involved, my informants had learned, going to prison not only appeared more likely; it entailed more severe sentences. In these circumstances, their decision to join government programs was motivated by not only their quest for a means of getting by but also the perception that joining the ranks of the ruling party's mobilized youth was a way of shielding themselves from the machinery of state repression. The political mobilization of street life reversed the understanding that "disengaging from politics"—as thugs did during the Derg—was an essential tactic to avoid repression. Engaging with politics was now key. It certainly did not grant hustlers and thugs impunity, but it seemed to offer the hope that if caught committing minor offenses they might receive mild sentences.

Whether or not this calculation was valid, my informants were right on one fundamental point. Politics was indeed pervasive in the inner city. As we have seen, the ruling party reorganized and politically mobilized important sections of the street economy. Moreover, development programs enabled the ruling party to increase the number of people who were directly or indirectly dependent on the local bureaucracy for their survival and thus expected to support the EPRDF. Politics had thus become pervasive because these interventions were soon recognized as serving the ruling party's concern with staying in power and limiting dissent and unrest on the streets. Contrary to James Ferguson's (1994) analysis of the depoliticizing effects of developmental narratives in Lesotho, development performed "extremely sensitive political operations involving the entrenchment and expansion of institutional state power" *visibly* and not "almost invisibly" (256). Development is, in Ethiopia, a "politics machine."

Nevertheless, this nexus between political mobilization and development alone did not produce my informants' fear of politics, or even of punishment and imprisonment. Rather, it was that the ruling party mobilized the most loyal members of this expanding political community to act as agents of surveillance and control. In 2006 while promoting entrepreneurship schemes, the ruling party was also establishing Peace and Security Committees in each *kebelle* of the city. These committees were versions of an older institution that had existed in the early 1990s in both urban and rural areas to help resolve local conflicts (Vaughan and Tronvoll 2003; Andargatchew Tesfaye 2004, 28; Hagmann 2007). The new "committees" kept their old focus on conflict resolution, but also became actively involved in gathering information about crime and potential unrest, working with the police and the *kebelle* Justice Office to maintain peace in the city's neighborhoods (Di Nunzio 2014b).

As party loyalists were predominantly believed to have been selected as members of these committees while ordinary citizens joined government programs, the perception that sympathizers of the ruling party and potential informers were everywhere gained traction for my informants. This is what politicized the streets, as a terrain perceived to be inhabited by the logic of political loyalty as well as the threats of being charged with more severe "political" sentences. Loyal members of the ruling party were seen to be more dangerous than policemen— the latter were professionals, and, more importantly, my informants felt they could find ways of negotiating the terms of their interactions. Individual policemen, as we will see in chapter 5, could sometimes be brought in and be extremely helpful in completing a street deal. Affiliates of the ruling party, however, were seen as guided by different motives, such as political loyalty or their quest for career advancement. Thus, they were potentially harmful, as people in the inner city had experienced in 2005 when local informers, often members of the ruling party and the local government office, played a key role in raids, pointing out people to be taken to detention camps.

During a time of peace, surely there were ways of navigating the ruling party's machinery of surveillance and control by, for instance, interacting cautiously with individuals who were commonly believed to be *joro* (ears) and *akataris* (spies) because of their loyalty to the ruling party. At the same time, however, my informants continued to worry whether even their friends, neighbors, and acquaintances had become "informers," and refrained from doing anything that could draw the government's attention. As one put it: "There are a lot of *akatary* [spies]." Another of my informants echoed, "They will catch you immediately." This climate of mistrust and suspicion amplified the effects of the government apparatus of political control and surveillance, reinforcing the fear of politics that encompassed my informants' everyday lives and enabled the ruling party to firmly ground itself at the bottom of urban society.

The Double Nexus

To borrow the language of philosophy, the political history of street life in inner city Addis Ababa bears witness to the intertwining of the interests of the "sovereign" to strengthen its rule with a "biopolitical" concern with making people's actions commensurable with the realization of growth and development. Looking at the history of street life and following Michel Foucault (2008), we might interpret these "biopolitical" concerns as a result of the emergence of new technologies of government grounded in shifting understandings of the role of the state and of why and how society is to be governed. Echoing Giorgio Agamben (1998, 2005), we might then see the political concern of the ruling party with mobilizing and controlling the lives and the bodies of ordinary citizens as a function of the strengthening of the rule of the sovereign and of its ability to assert itself above and outside the law. And, finally, drawing on Hannah Arendt (1958), we might contend that remaking the street economy as a functional and commensurable terrain of economic and social practice is a manifestation of a tyrannical politics of utility—and of the ways individuals are made into simple gears of a machine that sustains them while denying them their ability to debate, discuss, and contest.

The history described in this chapter includes elements from each of these interpretations. The implementation of development programs reflected the ways political elites at the top of the Ethiopian state understood their acts of governing the streets. The EPRDF has not seen delivering development, growth, or even a certain vision of "modernity" as simply a way of strengthening its power. Development has been seen as an emancipatory project, or as a *kebelle* official and part-time journalist in the inner city put it, a way of envisioning and pursuing a dream: "If you have a dream, people will follow you and trust you. We are poor and you have to make people dream. Otherwise, if you don't have a plan, you would go nowhere."

The making of this developmental dream has been praised by scholars of the developmental state and developmental patrimonialism in Africa who are concerned with identifying the political and institutional arrangements that enable political elites to "get capitalism started" (Kelsall 2013; Booth and Golooba-Mutebi 2012). Within this framework, the political centralism of the Ethiopian ruling party and its commitment to seeing development as a long-term trajectory—the dream, as the *kebelle* official put it—have been considered as key for the creation of the political and social arrangements needed to stimulate the country's economic growth. However, as Will Jones, Ricardo Soares de Oliveira, and Harry Verhoeven (2013) pointed out, this formula of development has resulted in the making of "illiberal" projects of state building in Ethiopia as well as Rwanda, Angola, and Sudan that, while enabling political elites to pursue their "wildest" developmental dreams, have fallen short of addressing underlying political and social tensions in the populace.

As we saw in chapter 3, my informants saw the making of this dream from afar, as persisting patterns of social differentiation constrained their ability to pursue trajectories of social mobility and improvement. This chapter completes the picture, showing how development programs ended up reinforcing, rather than challenging, patterns of social differentiation and exclusion. Growth and development have been visible in the inner city not only through their shortcomings but also through the expansion of the ruling party's apparatus of political control and surveillance. This granted the political elites overwhelming electoral victories, enabling them to benefit from the political stability that external observers and investors so appreciate. The strategies that the ruling party used to mobilize and control the general population thus, in philosophical terms, strengthened the rule of the "sovereign," enabling it to assert itself, not as being above the law as Agamben (1998, 2005) might argue, but as the leader, holder, and owner of the making of the developmental dream.

By developing a view of the street, we can make sense of the impacts of this "double nexus" between development and economic growth, political stability and authoritarianism that lay behind the making of Ethiopia as an African success story. The implementation of entrepreneurship programs and the ruling party's promotion of a collectivist entrepreneurial ethos had a limited effect in terms of rendering the actions and the everyday lives of people at the bottom of urban society commensurable with the realization of development, economic growth, and the market economy, as a purely Foucauldian analysis might suggest. Development programs failed. Yet, as Hannah Arendt (1958) might contend, these initiatives succeeded in codifying the terms of my informants' membership in society. Simply put, they carved out a space at the bottom of urban society within which the poor could sustain their lives and from which they were asked to contribute to the overall development of the country in a simple but problematic way: by being compliant, thereby enabling the political stability that allowed the "sovereign" to pursue its dream.

Poor people at the bottom of urban society were thus not redundant subjects that are allowed to die or even be killed (cf. Agamben 1998, 2005). My informants were, instead, subjects to be integrated, and this integration was funded with billions of Ethiopian birr. This, as we have seen, was a very particular form of integration: they had been integrated, but without the ability to fully negotiate the conditions of their integration. My informants had joined a sort of "inverted social contract" (Foucault 2008, 202), the terms of which they could not change and out of which they could never drop. Such integration enabled the making of wider economic and political projects, even though the urban poor themselves were not those who primarily benefitted. In this "inverted social contract" the poor provided services that the government did not need to pay for, as the parking guys did, or exchanged their hard labor for inadequate pay for construction of needed infrastructure, as stoneworkers and day laborers did. And when formalized, the taxes they paid from their low salaries contributed once more to the funding of the developmental dream.

KEEP ON HUSTLIN'

Living with Others

Haile, Ibrahim, and many others on the streets of the inner city complied with the ruling party's politics of mobilization and control out of both opportunism and fear. The perception that the ruling party's apparatus was pervasive and that it would strike if one crossed the "red line" of political opposition made state repression and control effective. At the same time, my interlocutors did not fully give up room for maneuvering. Paradoxically, by remaining within the red line, they could continue to cultivate street smartness, combining their long-term engagement with a street life of hustling with their new integration in the ruling party's structure of mobilization, surveillance, and low-wage employment.

As the anthropologist Michael Jackson (2011) might put it, this is a "life within limits," one that, while not bearing the seeds of revolt, resistance, and opposition per se (Ortner 1995; cf. de Certeau 1984), reveals that the experiences of the marginalized are not reducible to the forms of subjugation and oppression that frame their existence. By living within limits, my interlocutors certainly did not question the status quo. Yet they exercised a nested, or rather, a "conditioned," form of agency (Butler 1997, 14) that fueled a proliferation of practices, actions, and discourses documented in the second half of this book.

Later in the book I explore how, while never crossing the red line, Haile, Ibrahim, and many others on the street elaborated a fierce critique of development and economic growth and grounded their quest for change in an embrace of the potentialities of the uncertain. In this chapter I explore the *act of living* in the ordinary and the everyday experience of getting by and hustling on the streets.

I show how hustling was grounded in a recognition of living within limits—namely, that poverty was something to navigate but difficult to challenge and question. By living within limits, hustlers did not just make do. They understood their experience of enduring marginality as shared with a wider range of others. This sense of being acted upon by a shared predicament did not result in the emergence of a collective consciousness leading to collective action. Rather, it developed into an everyday sense of morality or, as Michael Lambek (2010) puts it, ordinary ethics, through which my interlocutors justified their own actions and comprehended the hustling of others.

What happened on the streets was a complex and often precarious synthesis between the political strategies of the ruling party and the exercise of reflexivity by those who inhabited the street economy to stay within the red line and make sense of what would be tacitly tolerated and what would be actively repressed. Petty thieving persisted, as it had in the past, even through moments of political conflict, especially because it was low key, situational, and fundamentally disengaged from politics. Similarly, street fighting continued to shape experiences of street life, yet, as I witnessed several times, mainly as bar brawls and occasional fights, not as a terrain where organized groups could launch street enterprises as in the 1970s and early 1990s (see chapter 2). Professional and organized street enterprises existed in the inner city, but their survival fundamentally depended on their links with actors outside, not inside, the street economy, such as the thriving group of fences discussed in chapter 3, which worked in cahoots with wealthy members of the inner city business community.

In these changed circumstances, Haile and Ibrahim were no longer members of an organized group committing illicit activities such as the *yemot midib* of their youth. They were members of a street group, but in the form of a government-supported cooperative of parking guys. On the side, they continued to be actively involved in the street economy of hustling. The two had long quit thieving but were still part of an incoherent army of people who turned to the streets to look for a *mella*, a way of getting by. These included day-to-day hustlers running errands or brokering petty transactions, individuals looking for someone to treat them to a meal or a couple of drinks, street tourist guides showing foreigners around for a fee, female players engaged in transactional sex, and wage laborers trying to top up meager salaries, as well as private guards and individual police officers who acted as both law enforcers and part-time hustlers to make an extra buck.

The cumulative effect of this large number of people turning to the streets to make do generated a "platform providing for and reproducing life in the city" (Simone 2004b, 410). As the urbanist Abdoumaliq Simone might put it, the conjunction of the heterogeneous attempts that residents made to eke out a living transformed them into the grids and knots of a human infrastructure (Simone 2004a, 2004b) that enabled economic exchanges and the provision of services, from retrieving stolen goods to the sale of secondhand mobile phones to transactional sex.

These interactions do not just make the city work and persist. They shape the sociality of the everyday. So far I have characterized the experience of marginality as caught in the tension between my interlocutors' attempts to be something other than their constraints, on the one hand, and the persistence of their subjugation and oppression, on the other. In chapters 1 and 2, I showed how Haile, Ibrahim, and many others in the inner city navigated this tension by cultivating practices and performances of street smartness. In this chapter I show how the *act of living* is not experienced in solitude. The philosopher Michel de Certeau (1984) taught us to appreciate how the weak are able to rework and act on the circumstances produced by powerful others with their "tactics" and ruses. Here I complement de Certeau's writing by showing how the weak do not experience marginality only by relating to those more powerful than themselves. Marginality is lived and navigated also in interactions with those others who are equally, or even more, marginalized. This experience of relatedness with the fellow marginalized not only enables livelihoods but also shapes understandings of one's position in society.

Hustling is a particular experience of living with and relating to others. While making do, men and women in the Addis Ababa street economy tested, cultivated, and asserted their capacity to act. Being able to hustle successfully and effectively was a reason for pride and self-worth. However, such feelings of self-worth are not cultivated exclusively by recognizing one's capacity to act. Success in hustling also depends on one's ability to relate to others and, often, to outsmart them. While we can easily understand why hustlers might target more powerful others—and ethnographers are prone to celebrate how the weak may trick the powerful—hustling is not always mutually beneficial when those involved share experiences of marginality. Differently from what Daniel Mains (2012a) and Sasha Newell (2012) argued in their ethnographies of Jimma in southern Ethiopia and Abidjan in Ivory Coast, respectively, street life and the street economy in inner city Addis Ababa do not make a "moral economy" of distribution and mutuality (Thompson 1971; Scott 1979) where individuals' attempts to get by coincide with normative and cultural expectations of bonding and sharing among people of the same condition. Hustling is embedded in a skillful ability to elude or, alternatively, take advantage of expectations of sharing and relatedness, grounded in the crude recognition that, at the end of the day, people have to look out for themselves if they want to get by and survive.

Hustling is not a synonym for social Darwinism, however. An individual's efforts to make do contrast with the awareness that one's condition of marginality is shared with those others who outsmart or are outsmarted. Henrik Vigh described how young combatants in Guinea Bissau in the early 1990s saw opposing troops in the country's civil war as "brothers," as "coming from a similar place," and as "having similar possibilities" (2006, 83). Similarly, hustlers in inner city Addis Ababa justified their own hustling and recognized the actions of others in their own concerns and preoccupations as reflecting a common fate and a similar range of possibilities. This awareness of a shared predicament transformed hustlers into moral subjects (Das 2007; Fassin 2012; Lambek 2010), struggling between the individual demands of making do and the collective experience of marginality and exclusion.

As we will see, provisional and occasional moments of collaboration, the enjoyment of moments of friendship and comradeship, and the play of games of love and intimacy were pervaded by the moral tension between making do and living with others. Love, in particular, amplified this tension, as hustling became the paradigm of gender relations on the streets. In chapter 2, I discussed gendered experiences of marginality as revolving around performances of toughness and how respect was achieved by relating to other men. Here, by comparing the experiences of male hustlers and female players, I document how the sociality of hustling and street life shaped experiences of marginality across gender lines. Women were not invisible on the streets, and women could claim to be *Arada* because of their smartness and urban sophistication. Like hustlers, players embodied and performed a particular version of inner city smartness, one revolving around the skillful navigation of the city's nightlife, a vigilance toward scroungers and abusive men, and the opportunities that relating to well-off men could open for them in terms of social mobility or international migration (see also Cole 2010; Brennan 2004).

Hustling, both in moments of friendship and in the economies of transactional sex, made sociality loaded with the preoccupations of making do, and characterized getting by as the experience of living with others. This connection between sociality and making do potentially either eased or exacerbated challenges and hardships. Hustling could take place through the enjoyment of a genuine act of sharing, but sharing might also conceal the predatory character of the street economy. These tensions shaped my informants' *act of living* on the streets and molded how they understood and navigated poverty as something difficult to question both individually and collectively. Indeed, as we will see in the conclusion of this chapter, my interlocutors had a single word to describe those tensions: *bammilo*.

I Know People

"Everybody is a cheater," Ibrahim told me, making sense of the fact that everybody he knew was somehow involved in "business." Living in the inner city I came to discover what Ibrahim meant. Some successful shop owners changed dollars on the black market. Others fenced stolen goods. An unemployed university graduate used his contacts with relatives abroad to run his own "Western Union," as he put it, delivering remittances anywhere in the city. Meanwhile, people stuck in jobs they did not like hoped to make good money through quick and profitable street deals—like a night guard I knew who found himself involved in trying to sell nuggets that he told me he thought were platinum. He had made contact with young people with street smarts who lived around his workplace and could help him find a buyer. This was hot stuff, and he could not sell it legally. He really hoped he could make it: "I will leave this shitty job and I will have a good life," he told me.

These dealings sometimes involved even more unusual goods. I was once approached on a street corner by a man who told me that he had seen me around. "I understand you are doing research and you speak Amharic," he said. Then he asked me if I was interested in buying dinosaur bones. I refused his offer but wanted to know a bit more about his business, recalling my undergraduate training in the archaeology of Ethiopia. That, the man told me, was a discovery he kept for himself; only he knew where to find such things, and he wanted to keep it a secret. To be sure, one wonders whether these exceptional objects, dinosaur bones and platinum nuggets, were ever actually part of the economies of inner city streets or whether the allure of fast money they encouraged was part of a well-designed scam. What was sure, however, was that a couple of months after the guard told me about his hopes for a better life, he disappeared from his workplace. His contacts remained on the street, looking for business, and I was told that the guard had also dealt in other small businesses, mainly selling some of the stuff he was supposed to guard. Nobody knew if he had been caught or if he had actually made good money and left for a better life away from the inner city.

Mobile phones predominated among the goods traded on the streets. In the beginning these were basic Nokia phones. When I started my research in 2009, smartphones and iPhones were initially so rare that I was once stopped by a man who dealt in secondhand phones and occasionally stolen goods. He held out an iPhone and asked me, "How much does an iPhone cost?" "Someone," he said, had given it to him and he wanted to sell it. I told him that I did not know, but the price was surely more than a hundred dollars. He replied, "But why don't you bring some iPhones from England and we will make some business together." By mid-2013, smartphones produced in China for the African and Asian markets, and widely believed to be of poor quality, flowed into Ethiopia. By this time, still stuck with my old Nokia, I was no longer regarded as a potential business partner but a customer. I was often asked if I was interested in buying an iPhone or a cheaper smartphone. I stayed loyal to my stuffy old phone. For me, a brand new iPhone was hot stuff, not unlike the bones of a dinosaur!

Ibrahim was also in the business of secondhand mobile phones, but he preferred dealing directly with sellers and buyers so he could get fees from both. Talking about a *mella*, a street deal he had just made, he explained to me how he sold a mobile phone belonging to one of his acquaintances: "He told me he did not have money. I knew he had a mobile. I suggested he sell it, then, we would buy another one that is cheaper. I called a guy. We dealt with the price, a mobile that would cost 1,000 for 800 birr. I complained. He [the buyer] told me on the phone, 'Well, the battery is good, it is expensive, it is 200 birr.' This was a way of saying that he would have paid me 200 birr [fee]. The [guy, the seller] sold the mobile and I got 200 birr from the buyer and 100 from the [guy, the seller]. Then, again, we bought another mobile, I got 100 birr from this. This is a *mella*. You have to know how to do it."

Mobile phones as well as cameras and laptops travelled through networks on the street. Some of them were stolen; others were just secondhand. Street smarts and the knowledge of the "geography of shady activity," in Sudhir Venkatesh's words (2006, 163), not only enabled one to act as a fence or a broker, as Ibrahim did. Indeed, returning stolen goods to the legitimate owner could also get a "hustler" a fee. This was the only kind of *mella* my informants were involved in, which I felt comfortable following.

One of Ibrahim's associates for this kind of *mella* was Mikias. When I met Mikias for the first time he was in his late thirties. Ibrahim and Haile had mentioned him when they recounted the stories of *yemot midib*. Mikias was a joker, a very joyful person, but also a very skillful hustler. He did not have a stable job, and he found ways of getting by, often by combining many sources of income. His mother lived in Italy and she sometimes sent him money. He lived in a government house with his brother, and rented out one of the rooms to Netsanet, a middle-aged woman and experienced sex worker, who lived with her nephew and her nephew's daughter. The money that he made through the occasional remittances and the few hundred birr a month from Netsanet's rent were not enough to make do, Mikias told me. And as I got to know him, I realized that a significant part of Mikias's "income" came from his ability to navigate the web of transactions, exchanges, and interactions taking place on the streets.

In the morning, Mikias usually made some extra money by brokering petty dealings, helping a friend or a neighbor. I followed him in one of his morning *mellas*. Liya was one of his old friends. She grew up in the neighborhood and came from a very poor family. She had married up, however, and now lived in a nice house in the suburbs. But her brother, Tewodros, was still living in the inner city and was a troubled kid, Mikias reckoned. Tewodros stole to get by and had been in prison many times for minor offenses. When he saw his sister's brand new phone, he took it and sold it to a fence. Liya soon realized her brother had taken the phone and, fed up with Tewodros's lifestyle, turned to the police. Tewodros was caught and was sent to a common police cell. However, Liya did not get her phone back, so she asked her old friend Mikias for help. Mikias brought Ibrahim along. Ibrahim went to what he called the "pushers" of the neighborhoods—namely, shop owners who fence stolen goods—and then to the *mancu*, the mobile snatchers, that he knew were working in the area. He did not find much; Tewodros was known to not be a smart hustler and many stayed away from him. "This kind of guys are not *duriye* [thugs] or *Arada*. They are just rats," Mikias complained. "How could you steal from your own family! What you should do is to steal outside to bring it in the family, not taking from it." The only thing to do was to ask Tewodros himself. Ibrahim went to the police station to talk to him. He did not get any useful information, but he managed to speak to a policeman who told him about Tewodros's case. When Ibrahim came out, he reported to me and Mikias what he had found out: "Fuck, the investigator told me that they want to give him two years. Tewodros is always in the *tabia* [police cell]. The *tabia* is his house, he is always there." Then turning to me, he said, "I am getting away from this, the police are stepping in." They called it off, and Mikias got only 30 birr for his help instead of the 200 birr Liya had promised if he got her phone back.

If Mikias and Ibrahim did not manage to get a good fee for assisting Liya, they succeeded on another occasion. Aster was a young university student who had grown up with the young men in the cooperative of parking guys. When her iPhone and laptop disappeared, she turned to her old friends. With the help of a photograph Aster had taken of the laptop when it was new, Mikias and Ibrahim tracked down the thief and the buyer. It turned out that Aster's cousin was the thief and that the buyer was drinking in one of the Arada bars. When I bumped into Ibrahim, Mikias, and a few other parking guys, they had already gone to see Aster's cousin. Supported by a group of guys at her side, Aster insulted the thief, who was easily persuaded to give up the money he had earned from the sale of the laptop. I witnessed what happened when the group approached the buyer in the bar. At first, the buyer did not want to make a deal. When an undercover policeman had been brought in, however, he quickly agreed. Having a policeman did not necessarily disrupt the *mella*; the policeman, like everyone else, was there for a small fee. And, to be sure, settling what after all was a family dispute can be seen as "community policing."

The deal was on. The buyer took the whole group into another bar where he kept the laptop and the iPhone. By that time, Aster's brother had joined in. "You need to go by yourself now," Ibrahim told Aster, instructing her to follow the buyer. After a few minutes, she came out smiling with her laptop and iPhone. Those who helped her now expected a fee. Within seconds, Aster's brother was surrounded by the helpers, including the undercover policeman. In a quick succession of movements, Aster's brother handed a few birr to those within reach around him. Ibrahim got his fee. He had made his extra bucks for the day.

What I observed firsthand was only one of the broader economy of transactions and exchanges taking place on the street. The street economy is a massive service economy that branches out in many different directions. A hustler in Arada, for instance, told me that he sometimes bought drugs for rich people: "I know where I could go and buy it, even cocaine. Since they [rich people] are afraid, I go there instead." Another helped people get fake medical certificates to obtain a visa to Cuba. His customers believed that getting into Cuba would be an easier way of reaching the United States: from Cuba to Ecuador, then Mexico, and finally the promised land. These businesses were conducted in secret, and researchers and external observers are hardly welcome, unless they are interested in the "services" provided. Yet, it is clear that, just as in Liya's and Aster's deals, the independent variable behind these businesses and exchanges is the ability of the hustler, the fixer, and the part-time broker to connect people and navigate the relations between them.

In these circumstances, success is highly contingent and uncertain. Liya's deal did not work out because of Tewodros's lack of connections in the inner city economy and the fact that the policemen had decided to pursue a more repressive approach owing to Tewodros's criminal record and Liya's contacting them in the first place. A series of coincidences was instrumental in the success of Aster's *mella*: the thief had turned to an Arada fence known to Aster's friends, her photo of the laptop helped track down the buyer and the thief, and the intervention of the undercover policeman with his "interested" act of community policing sped up the deal.

Following the making of a street deal reveals that what makes a *mella* successful is the kind of people a hustler knows and how he relates to them. Getting by is not an individual endeavor, just as smartness is not the trait of a particular kind of personality my informants sought to embody. Making do and smartness are embedded in social relations. When asked how he managed to get by on his everyday dealings, Mikias explained to me: "I know many people through my family and even when I was in prison. I got to know a lot of people from many areas in Addis Ababa. If I need something or know someone who is looking for something, I know where I should go and ask."

Keep on Hustlin'

Mikias and Ibrahim found their *mellas* by inhabiting and navigating the wider networks they were part of. There were other hustlers who could not do so; these were the street tourist guides, who targeted "outsiders" and "foreigners" (*faran-jocc*) whom they had never met and with whom they shared very little. For this reason, street tourist guides saw themselves as the ultimate hustlers since their *mella* depended entirely on their skills, their wide range of "pickup lines," and moves they employed to approach an *ingda*, literally a "guest."

The street tourist guides constituted a particular niche of the street economy mainly occupied by former street children or young people who left their home regions (often tourist destinations, such as Lalibela, Gondar, Bahr Dar, Arba Minch, and Harar) to find better opportunities in the capital city. Some of them made their way to Addis Ababa using their earnings from working as street tourist guides in their home cities. Others followed a tourist or "sponsor" who promised to support them in Addis Ababa or pay their college fees in the capital. For those who ended up hustling tourists on the street, things had not worked out as they expected.

Among them was Fasil. He was born in Lalibela, northern Ethiopia, in the late 1980s. When I met him in late 2009, he had already spent seven years on the streets of Arada. He first approached thinking me a tourist and, hence, a potential target. Fasil told me that he had previously worked for a French photographer and he wondered if I knew his friend. I told him that I had never heard of his friend. Later I realized that this did not really matter, since talking about his photographer friend was a pickup line that Fasil often employed to approach tourists. I explained to Fasil that I was not in Addis Ababa for sightseeing. I was doing research and planned to stay in the inner city for a while. When he heard I was interested in researching the lives of young people in the city, Fasil proposed to bring me along on one of his strolls around the inner city, looking for tourists. After a couple of days, we were on the streets "hustling together," as he and other street tourist guides put it.

First, Fasil told me, you have to spend a lot of time on the street, checking the spots tourists might pass by, like a street corner near a tourist agency, an airline ticket office, or a hotel in the inner city. In one of these spots we bumped into Wolde, another street tourist guide, who joined us. Wolde was born in Nazreth, 100 kilometers southeast of Addis Ababa, and he was in his early twenties. Fasil was not very happy to have Wolde with us. Wolde was not very experienced, and Fasil felt that he might screw things up if we met a tourist. I realized what Fasil meant when I saw Wolde scaring a tourist off by yelling at him, "You, you *faranjii* [foreigner], come here!" This, Fasil complained, is not the right way.

A trick of the trade is to be polite and impress the tourist with your stories and pickup lines.

We decided to go to a café to rest for a bit, and there we saw a tourist reading a guidebook. Fasil asked the tourist if I could have a look at the book and then introduced himself. When Fasil found out the tourist was from France, he brought out his story of how he had helped a French photographer make a documentary on Ethiopia. This was meant to prove that he was trustworthy and had met foreigners in the past. Fasil's classic pickup line worked. He had successfully drawn the attention of the tourist, who agreed to go for a short walk. As we left the café, Fasil began telling him the history of Addis Ababa and pointed out the buildings that the Italians built during the colonial occupation. The tourist seemed unimpressed and made a few critical remarks about life and poverty in Addis Ababa, pointing out how widespread prostitution was and that he had seen many young people wasting time and money chewing *khat*. I blathered something in disagreement with the tourist's patronizing remarks. But Fasil kept calm, avoiding argument. He said that he agreed with what the tourist had just said about prostitution, but he politely pointed out to the French man that he was mistaken in considering *khat* a hard drug. "It is more like drinking a very strong coffee," Fasil contended. I nodded in agreement with what Fasil said, to the amusement of the tourist, who was visibly surprised to hear that I had actually tasted *khat*.

We went to Churchill Avenue, a beautiful long road that extends from Addis Ababa City Hall to the Chemin de Fer, the train station built by the French in the 1920s, which offers a spectacular view of the city. The French tourist spoke English with many French words mixed in, but Fasil was able to follow him. While Fasil was busy talking with the tourist, Wolde, who had kept quiet until then, turned to teach me some new words in Amharic. After a few minutes, Fasil said out loud, to communicate to me and Wolde: "*gujbet!*" In Amharic, *gujbet* literally means "inflation." In late 2009, this was the word of the moment and constantly appeared in the speeches of Meles Zenawi, the then prime minister and chairman of the ruling EPRDF, to describe the state of the economy. The word made it into the street and came to describe someone who is broke. The French tourist was a *gujbet*; hence, Fasil thought there was no point in spending more time showing him around.

Fasil and Wolde then decided to walk the tourist back to his hotel. I had to leave for an appointment at the university. "Don't worry," Fasil told me in Amharic when I told him goodbye, "we are going to ask for some money anyway." When I met Fasil a couple of hours later, he told me that he did not ask for money from the tourist but Wolde did. It was the wrong thing to do, Fasil felt. There is a right way of asking for money. Perhaps the French guy would have returned and once Fasil had shown him around for half a day or so he would have asked for something. "Wolde is a fucking *gujbet*. He does not know how to do this job!" Fasil cried out.

In the eyes of Fasil and his circles, showing tourists around for a fee is without doubt a "job." Being a guide requires social skills and a certain form of work ethic, as Fasil's remarks on the right way of asking for money suggest. Hotel managers, tour agencies, and the bureau for tourism and heritage might disagree, questioning whether street tourist guides actually deliver a service to tourists and contribute to expanding the tourist economy in which the country is now significantly investing. Street tourist guides are not affiliated with offices or tourist agencies; they pick up tourists on the street. Yet Fasil insisted that being a guide is a job, that this hustling is part of the tourist economy. Some restaurants and hotels charge tourists higher prices than locals. Street tourist guides do not do anything different, he reckoned.

Still, street tourist guides faced certain challenges and periodically experienced police harassment. As Fasil and his friends understood, this was a direct consequence of the fact that street tourist guides were not easy to organize in cooperatives and hence could not be part of the ruling party's mobilization structures. While I was in Addis Ababa in 2009, the local government tried to establish cooperatives of street tourist guides, but failed to do since the majority of street tourist guides were not formally Addis Ababa residents and could not be involved in the city's development programs. Additionally, while the prices of hotels and official tour guides were fixed, when dealing with street tourist guides, tourists might behave like *gujbet*. "You walk a tourist all around a city the whole day long and then they give you just 30 birr. It is not fair. The *Lonely Planet* was published eight years ago and it says that the price for guide is 15 birr. But now things have changed, the price for a tourist guide is now 200 birr a day!" Fasil complained.

In these circumstances, what you have to do, Fasil reckoned, is to "keep on hustlin', keep on hustlin'," as he told me, intoning the words of a hip-hop song while he was moving around, back and forth, looking for a tourist to show around. The stake of his hustling could be very high indeed. If he met a tourist who was loaded and generous, he could make good money. "I could even make 2,000 birr in a day," Fasil said. This is the reason why Fasil, like many other street tourist guides, kept on hustling, chasing tourists. Even if the tourist was not loaded but was generous and understanding, a lower fee, a good meal together, a couple of drinks, and perhaps a bag of *khat* would be considered a fair fee for a couple of hours of sightseeing.

Between Sharing and Hustling

That Fasil and many others on the street considered being treated to a meal as fair compensation shows that hustling is not just about the more or less professionalized phatic labor of hustlers working for a fee. Getting by is also embedded in a wider sociality that wittingly or unwittingly includes anyone inhabiting the streets, tourists and researchers included. This is a form of sociality and relatedness that is fundamentally ambiguous: it is lived and experienced through interactions that can be simultaneously acts of sharing and hustling.

Being treated to a full plate of *injera* (Ethiopian pancake) or a couple of beers, for instance, was an act of sharing and friendship that my informants enjoyed, both for the conviviality and as a way of getting by in the immediate. Mikias eked out a living by running errands and brokering transactions in the morning with hosting his friends throughout the afternoon until the early evening. When I spent time at Mikias's place, sharing was the rule. This was an important aspect of his everyday life and a key tactic for survival. At lunch, when Mikias went home, there was always someone with money present who could treat the others to a meal. Alternatively, a collection around the room easily raised the money for a good plate of *injera*. In the afternoon, the parking guys who had finished the morning shift usually came to Mikias's. There, they chewed *khat* and usually pooled their money to buy it. This meant that the more people were in the room, the more leaves of *khat* were chewed. Similarly, when Fasil was short of money and no tourists were around, he hit up his circle of friends and fellow street tourist guides for some money or a meal to share.

Being treated to a meal could potentially also be an intentional act of deceiving and hustling. Friends and tourists might not always be willing to pay for a meal or hand out money. Hence, "hustling" and "cheating" could be a way of tricking people into "sharing." For instance, one of the tricks that street tourist guides employed to make "stingy" tourists fork out extra money was to take them to restaurants and bars where the bill for an overpriced cola or a very expensive beer and a simple meal also included, without the foreigners' knowledge, a fee for the guides, the waiters, and, sometimes, the managers of the place. On a broader level, relationships that are commonly considered to be characterized by sharing and commonality, such as friendship, might also involve elements of cheating, as friends hustled or even stole from each other. As I mentioned in chapter 2, Ibrahim remembered that guys in the *yemot midib* robbed each other. As the cases of Liya's brother and Aster's cousin earlier in this chapter reveal, stealing sometimes occurred even among close relatives.

As experienced by many people in my field site, tourists and myself included, there was a fine line between acts of sharing and hustling. The oscillation toward one or the other depended on the kind of relationship or interaction that linked together the people involved in that particular transaction. Referring to a similar microeconomy, Mains (2012a) argued that unemployed youth in Jimma (southern Ethiopia) engaged in what, borrowing from Mauss (1990), he described as a "gift economy," both to get by and to accumulate resources that were shared with friends and peers to expand and strengthen relationships. Echoing Strathern (1988), Piot (1999), and Newell's work on the street economy in Abidjan (2012), Mains argued that investing in relationships was key for these young people because it enabled them to affirm themselves, strengthen social relationships, and, potentially, gain a position of prestige.[1]

The street economy in Arada, however, presented dynamics and logics different from those Mains and Newell explored in southern Ethiopia and in Abidjan. In fact, as I spent time with my informants and found myself participating in exchanges and transactions, mainly by treating people to meals and drinks, I soon realized that sharing resources did not straightforwardly correspond to increased status and prestige, or to an enhanced capacity to expand and strengthen relationships.[2] Moreover, as the cases of Mikias and Fasil show, while strengthening relationships was crucial, it was the ability to skillfully navigate these relations that enabled my informants to get by (cf. Vigh 2006). Echoing Piot's (1999) examination of exchange among Kabre farmers in northern Togo, I prefer not to look at sharing as something that is valuable and valued per se. I contend that the social significance that people recognize in the circumstances and performance of a particular transaction or act of sharing enables them to strengthen and navigate relationships.

Paraphrasing David Graeber's (2001) efforts to define an anthropological theory of value, I argue that the ways, moments, and performance of an act of sharing not only define the value of an exchange; they signify the capacity of doing possessed by those involved. This, Graeber stated, has an effect that goes beyond the transaction and exchange. Individuals acquire a certain kind of fame and recognition as their capacity to do is witnessed by others through exchanges,

---

1. Interestingly, Mains (2012a) contended that the ability to share wealth with friends and peers, often by way of meals, drinks, or bundles of *khat*, was not equally distributed among unemployed youth. This was because the capacity to accumulate resources was contingent on the quality and quantity of networks that these young people had access to, for instance, through the "wealth-in-people" and the material wealth of their parents, relatives, and their parents' friends and neighbors, or through the kinds of activities they could easily get involved in because of where they lived. In a context where some of the unemployed were more successful than others in accumulating resources and, thus, in expanding and strengthening relationships through sharing, Mains reckoned, multiple forms of social inequality were produced and reproduced, intertwining existing patterns of social differentiation and unequal capacities to exercise control over relationships.

2. Mains (2012a) referred to the fact that acts of sharing among his informants were also characterized by negotiations and conflict over the value of the goods, suggesting that in Jimma, there was not necessarily a direct correspondence between sharing and strengthened relationships.

transactions, and interactions. This constitutes the symbolic capital, as Bourdieu (1977) would say, on which people ground their ability to not only directly act on others but also convince others how they should behave toward them (Graeber 2001, 91–115).

To better understand how this interpretation applies to the street economy in inner city Addis Ababa, it is worth reminding ourselves how economies of respect and people's performances and embodiment of smartness and toughness have historically characterized the street economy in the inner city (see chapter 2). While learning how to navigate this economy, my informants developed a range of social skills that enabled them to act on others and effectively make a *mella*. As Ibrahim put it, talking about his job as a part-time broker of secondhand mobile phones, "This is a *mella*. You have to know how to do it." As people navigated the street economy and proved their skills and abilities on the streets, they gained a reputation of being either foolish or smart. This reputation was crucial for hustlers and affected the ways people related to them while operating on the streets. When doing the *mella*, the appreciation of one's and others' *Arada-ness* and smartness often significantly contributed to steering the transaction toward either an act of sharing or one of intentional deceiving and cheating. My informants argued that "sharing" usually pervaded the interactions and transactions between those who mutually considered themselves to be *Arada*, whereas hustling characterized the actions of *Aradas* but usually targeted those who were not felt to be *Arada*. Mikias told me: "We are all *Arada* here, you cannot cheat us! We know about things and if you are a good person or not. . . . If I want, I can take money from people, I know how to do it. . . . Remember, *being Arada* is getting things in the easiest ways. . . . This is very important."

Similarly, Jonas, a man in his forties who liked painting and writing stories but survived by doing odd jobs for friends, neighbors, and acquaintances, made a similar point:

> One is the *mella* [that you do] when you share what you have with your friends. The other *mella* is when you cheat people and you take money without *fikir* [love].
>
> *Is it a trick?* [I asked]
>
> Yes it is. . . . You could trick a *farra* [literally, a "country bumpkin"; an unsophisticated, naive individual], but an *Arada* would know that it is a trick.

Jonas's distinction between *farra* and *Arada* is an example of a form of the situated morality encompassing hustling and street life. In Jonas's view, as well as in Mikias's words, smartness was a site of justice, a criterion according to which people got what they deserved depending on their skills, abilities, and capacities.

We can see how problematic this is, as it justifies hustling as a predatorial enforcement of a paradoxical and ambiguous idea of fairness and equity (see chapters 7 and 8). At the same time, Jonas used "love" to distinguish an act of sharing from an act of hustling. By doing so, he seemed to suggest that a *mella* was considered to be an act of sharing to the extent to which it was embedded in a relationship of friendship and companionship. Or rather, borrowing from Arada's street slang, sharing was a *mood*, one interlinked with the enjoyment of moments of conviviality.

In this understanding, stinginess and giving away money with the aim of being liked and praised were equally considered as not very smart things to do. Seeing someone as unwilling to share or suspecting them of using acts of sharing as an instrumental tool to strengthen position or show off wealth were considered good justifications for hustling them. Tourists were hustled and cheated if they were not smart enough to understand that they should have shared their money with—or at least treated to a meal, a couple of drinks, or a bag of *khat*—the street guide who was showing them around. At the same time, as Ibrahim told me, a very common *mella* was to sweet-talk a person who happened to be flush with cash into giving money away, whether as small handouts or by paying the bill at a restaurant or a drinking house.

Of course, there were exceptions to this logic. A street hustler might end up endorsing a vision of society and the street economy with a sort of social Darwinist undertone, suggesting that those who are hustled have no one to blame but themselves and their lack of street smarts. Yet it is also true that my informants, as well as many others on the streets, were active moral subjects and elaborated their range of distinctions on which they grounded acts of sharing and hustling. Ibrahim, for instance, believed that those who were genuinely and truly "innocent," as he put it, did not deserve to be hustled and cheated. Likewise, Fasil employed his idea of work ethics to distinguish between those who were truly *gujbet* (broke), those who were genuine and understanding, and those who should be hustled because of their stinginess and their pretended smartness.

Moreover, others might themselves accept being hustled. Gambling, for instance, is without doubt a way of making money, and it has both losers and winners. "Cheating" or "bluffing" might be considered part of the skill set of a winner. Gambling is illegal in Ethiopia, but gambling houses exist here and there in the inner city, often at the back of a bar or a small shop where people mainly play card games. I was told that thousands of birr might be made or lost after a couple of hands. Meanwhile, on the streets, young people in particular played for lower stakes. I met a young man who was very skillful at pool and tricked people into betting that they would win. He would initially pretend that he could not play, letting his opponent win a couple of times. Then, when the stakes had risen, he would win over and over again. The trick was to boost the confidence of his opponents at the beginning and thus entice them to gamble in the following games, which they would lose. Card games, mainly rummy-style games, were common among those with whom I spent most of my time. Mikias's house was not just a place where people shared a meal and a bundle of *khat*. In the early evenings, when the afternoon shift of parking guys joined the others there, the whole group played cards and gambled until late. Those who won and those who lost were not always the same. Yet one individual always got some money. This was Mikias, as the gambling rules dictated that the owner of the house takes a 20 percent cut of the win.

Mikias's ability to make money from the gambling of others (whether they won or lost), Fasil's attempts to be treated to a meal, the street tourist guides' capacity to turn moments of conviviality into petty confidence tricks, and Ibrahim's sweet-talking a rich man or a friend loaded with cash are all revealing. They show that acts of sharing and hustling are not only tuned toward strengthening social relationships and achieving positions of prestige, as interpretations of the street economy as a "gift economy" suggest (Mains 2012a; Newell 2012). Certainly, sharing is a way of bonding by diffusing one's gains across one's network of friends and peers (Newell 2012, 96). Yet the tensions between hustling and sharing show that people are concerned not only with strengthening relationships but also with skillfully navigating them as a way of getting by. Friendships, companionship, and love, as we will see in the next section, are experienced on shaky ground since, at the end of the day, people have to look out for themselves if they want to get by. In these circumstances, the tensions between hustling and sharing and the awareness that an exchange between friends could involve cheating inspired a form of radical realism. This enabled my informants to not only deeply enjoy acts of genuine sharing when they happened but also nurture and cultivate their capacity to hustle (and avoid being hustled) by knowing when to share, when there was an opportunity to make some extra bucks, or when others were trying to rip you off.

Love Is a Game

Love is the ultimate expression of sharing. And love, as Jonas argued, is what distinguishes sharing from hustling. Yet love, as in the experience of *being in love*, is, as we all know, a complex matter. In chapter 8 I explore how Ibrahim, Haile, and some of their friends dealt with their long-term relationships. In everyday life on the streets, especially in its nightlife, love is not necessarily and exclusively about affection. Love is a game. And *playing* is the notion that my informants used to describe how women and men interacted in the game of love and sex in the inner city. This game of love was imbued by the tension between sharing and hustling.

Players could be men or women, though in significantly different ways. In the words of my male informants, a male player embodied an ideal of masculinity. When a man played it meant that he behaved smartly in his way of fascinating and charming women. Nimble dancing, fancy clothing, and bravery in street fighting were believed to be what was needed to impress girls. Money is part of the game, both as something traded and as something discussed. As Wolde, the street tourist guide we met earlier, told me, "Girlfriends are expensive." *Don't you think that love is important?* I asked him. "Money is important too, otherwise your girlfriend could run to another person who could help her," he replied.

In these circumstances, where material help and economic support were expected in long-term relationships, playing took place in the here and now and opened opportunities for love and enjoyment in the immediate. "We cannot have a girlfriend. We just find a girl and we fuck. We fuck and forget," Fasil said. As de Certeau (1984) might put it, playing is a "tactical" form of love. Money is still involved. But if one is broke, tactics are needed to play the game. As Mikias argued, this kind of love is for smart people: "I went to a club and I met this girl. I really like her. I know she was a player and I told her, 'you know, there is a Somali who wants to sleep with you. He has a lot of money.' She came with me to a *bergo* [a cheap hotel]. I opened the door and I told her, 'I am the Somali!' She laughed and we slept together." *Did you pay then?* I asked. "I did not pay. This is *being Arada!*"

From the perspective of female players, the game of love was slightly different. "Players" were those who "played" with love. Some of these women were "dancers" or young women who knew they could make money by flirting with occasional lovers and with friends they knew were loaded with cash on that particular night. Others were players because they "played" with foreigners. As Denise Brennan (2004), John Chernoff (2003), and Jennifer Cole (2010) have discussed in their work on young women engaged in transactional sex, the play of love does not always correspond to prostitution and sex work. Yet it remains part of a broader continuum of practices of intergender relations where money and sex are often exchanged.

Transactional sex and sex work have a long history in Ethiopia and, unlike other social realities of the street economy, have been examined in their different historical and sociological varieties. Richard Pankhurst (1974) points out that already in the sixteenth century, courtesans and the king's mistresses enjoyed social consideration, deference, and respect for their beauty. In Addis Ababa, the blossoming of drinking houses in its early history was characterized by an expansion of prostitution mainly involving the women who ran these places. Later, starting from the late 1920s and 1930s, the opening of bars and clubs shaped the emergence of a more commercialized form of sex work. As commercial sex continued to expand, as Laketch Dirasse (1991) and Bethlehem Tekola (2005) have explained in their studies of the 1970s and the early 2000s, respectively, prostitution in Addis Ababa has been characterized by a significant heterogeneity of life trajectories and arrangements concerning residence, economic independence, and workplace. This heterogeneity also affected commercial and transactional sex in my field site.

On the main roads in Arada, "street girls" stood waiting for customers to take them somewhere else. On the side roads, house-based sex workers received their customers. Some hired a room for the night. Others waited for clients in their own home. Meanwhile, not only players but also bar ladies populated Arada's clubs and hotels. "Bar ladies" is a collective category for a variety of arrangements between sex workers and the owners of clubs and bars concerning, for instance, the commission sex workers received for the beers their customers consumed, or the amount per session sex workers paid to the owners. Finally, in some Arada drinking houses, experienced sex workers, often with the help of younger peers, served drinks and occasionally slept with their customers.

Among the older and more experienced sex workers, there were women who could claim to have known quasi-mythical figures of the history of the inner city, such as Mary Armede, who is commonly considered the best-known example of a woman who was an *Arada*. In the 1950s and 1960s, Mary Armede was a famous player of the *krar*, the Ethiopian lyre. She was a sex worker, but of a particular kind. She ran her own "dancehall" where many young women spent the night. Haile considered Mary the "source" of ideas and performances of *being Arada*. She was a master of fashion. She was the first in the city to wear a miniskirt and have her hair permed. And many people told me that when Miriam Makeba, the South African singer and anti-apartheid activist, came to Addis Ababa, she visited Mary Armede to listen to her music and have her hair permed. Whether Mary Armede was a madam is hard to say. As people remembered, many girls danced and worked in her house, and Mary chose the person she herself wanted to sleep with.

The legacy of Mary Armede extended beyond her music. Her life, Haile told me, was closely linked to that of Getachew Bongar. Getachew had been a close friend of Mary's son, Tamrat, who died at a young age a few years after Mary's own death. Like many others in the inner city, Getachew was fascinated by Mary's performances and sophistication and learned from her what *being Arada* meant. That Haile and many others believed that Getachew's *Arada-ness* came from Mary Armede was not only proof of her role in molding Getachew's heroism. It reveals how women, sex workers in particular, were believed to have significantly shaped what *being* and *becoming Arada* meant in inner city Addis Ababa. Sex workers I talked to claimed to embody such ideas of *Arada-ness* because of the relative social independence that their trade offered them and the fact that street smarts are needed to endure the challenges they had encountered throughout their lives. Sex workers themselves can be cheated and hustled, and getting smart and *being Arada* were key to navigating such an environment.

Whereas sex workers embodied smartness while being engaged in commercial sex, players embodied ideas of *Arada-ness* in the ways they were able to navigate the game of love. As with Fasil's sharing and hustling, playing could become a form of "sharing" between a smart woman and a smart man or a mere "exchange" between a customer and a sex worker. The difference between the two was often subtle. But it was in this subtle distinction that players made sense of and narrated their engagement with transactional sex. Some of the young women who spent time at Mikias's house and whom Ibrahim called the "teenagers" (they were in their late teens and early twenties) turned to Arada nightclubs to enjoy themselves and occasionally find lovers to play with who could treat them for the night. This was a game of flirting and did not always include sex. At the same time, sex could be just for a night or open up more long-term relationships that could allow a player to eke out a living through a "boyfriend" with resources or access prestigious goods and forms of leisure through more or less stable lover(s). For young female players, love was a game that enabled them to find ways of getting by in the present and of imagining and pursuing potential trajectories of social mobility (cf. Cole 2010).

Sara was one of the players who looked at the game of love as a gateway to a better future. She had grown up in Addis Ababa and lived with her mother, who worked as a cleaner in a church. When I met Sara, she was in her mid-twenties and was studying part time for a vocational degree in marketing at one of the city's private colleges. In the afternoons and evenings she often hung out in one of the Arada hotels where many budget tourists came to stay. When I asked her why she spent so much time in the lobby of that hotel, she said, "I like foreigners. Foreigners treat you." Ethiopian men, she said, were problematic. Some wanted to sleep with her without helping her out. Although she admitted that she would like to marry a *habesha* (Ethiopian), she also reckoned that this was not a good choice because Ethiopian men often slept with other women. However, foreigners, she told me in another conversation, were also tricky, and finding a good foreigner (*faranjii*) to marry was difficult: "Many *faranjii* are cheaters, they come here and they just want to have sex." Despite this, however, Sara was convinced that marrying a foreigner would open up better social opportunities than those currently available to her. "I have to find a husband, anyway," she explained. A friend of hers had improved her life when she married a *faranjii*: "She changed her life, she is rich, she has a good house and now she is living there." Over the years, other friends managed to go abroad, suggesting to Sara that this was a viable and possible trajectory of social mobility.

As I got to know Sara better, I was struck by her confidence and determination. "I don't drink, I don't chew [*khat*], I study and I go to the gym," she told me. This disciplined way of life shaped how Sara experienced her engagement in transactional sex. "Love is sacrifice," she told me. "Sacrifice" was the ability to stay focused in order to achieve one's goal. Being focused provided Sara with a way of thinking of her existence beyond the present horizon of her everyday life, and hence of imagining the likelihood of a trajectory of social mobility.

Foreigners and wealthy men did not always honor the promises they made to players like Sara, who, like street tourist guides and part-time brokers, needed to rely on their hustling to get by. For Sara and many other players, enjoyment, survival, and the quest for better opportunities were all part of a continuum of meanings and practices that shaped the game of love. While inner city men played with notions of smartness, cultivating ideas of masculinity through their experiences of tactical love, for young women, the game of love was not just a way of enjoying a night. Love was a tactic, but of a different kind. It was a way of getting by or even mediating between the necessities of the immediate and the imagination of a prosperous future. This reminds us of the predicament marginalized subjects face in their lives: while hustling is a way of getting things done, the fact that people turn to hustling in the first place bears witness to the broader political economy of exclusion that shapes their existence. Love is a game, but as Sara made clear, it is also "sacrifice"—that is, the painful experience of dealing with the immediate necessities that made *being a player* a viable way of getting by for the sake of a happier and more loving future.

The Hustler's Predicament

The tensions and logics of living a "life within limits" in inner city Addis Ababa do not just revolve around the multiple identities and roles people play while hustling to get by. These tensions and logics go deeper, bearing witness to the predicaments my informants faced as they relied on street life to endure their condition of marginality, exclusion, and subjugation. As in the past, by getting by on the streets, skillfully navigating relations and transactions to make a buck, my informants found ways of acting on the circumstances of their lives, nurturing that sense of *being Arada* that they deeply valued and appreciated. At the same time, engaging with the street economy was a particular experience of living with others. By continuing to engage with the economies of hustling and getting by,

Haile, Ibrahim, Sara, and many others on the streets found themselves operating in a domain of action that, while it reinforced their sense of smartness and sometimes led to genuine solidarity, was imbued by an ambiguous morality, as transactions on the streets turned out to be predatorial and at the expense of others.

In street Amharic, a *mella* is a way of getting by. *Bammilo* is the slang term that hustlers used when their hustling failed or when their con was unmasked or when they were simply trying to persuade reluctant others to hand out some money. When people said "*bammilo, mella naw*," literally, "*bammilo*, it is a *mella*," they meant, "Yes, I know it is not good, but I am doing this for a living; please give me something." The use of *bammilo* is an invitation to recognize the crude banality of poverty while pointing out the moral tensions of experiencing marginality while living with and hustling others. The recognition of hustling as inevitably tied up with the necessity of getting by was, my interlocutors felt, the ultimate foundation of the hustlers' and players' predicament. Fasil described his trade and the logic that underpinned it thus: "Sometimes I want to kill myself. There are months when there is no job and you don't know how to survive. Hustling is tiring. You always have to be smart, always on the street finding the right way of finding money. It is surviving. What we do with the tourists is this. If they ask for a pack of cigarettes we cheat them. We tell them it is 12 birr, instead it is 10 birr. This is how it works and this is the way we survive. . . . Some tourists think we are animals. But we are not!"

In these circumstances, street smartness and *being Arada* are indeed both the individual capacity to act and act on others and the recognition of the fact that one's action is situated in a social reality that is lived and experienced while relating to others. The street economy and *being Arada* thus do not exclusively revolve around sharing, bonding with others, and strengthening social relationships. The street is a terrain where people try to navigate relationships to make a living through hustling and cheating. The sociality and situated morality underpinning these activities can be disruptive. At the same time, being aware that others might be equally overwhelmed by hardship and that hustling and cheating are sometimes needed if you do not have money can produce a certain form of solidarity, which serves as not only a justification for one's own actions but also for the conduct of others.

"It is always like this, hustling," Fasil told me, sitting on a chair outside one of the bars in Arada, after one of his friends called him a "beggar," alleging that he was not sharing the money he had made from a tourist. "We always hustle, this is the life on the street," Fasil repeated to me and himself, trying to calm himself down and be understanding toward his insulting friend. Likewise, Wolde was not punished by his fellow street tourist guides after spending the 100 or 200 birr that he and two other guides had made from a tourist. I was told that Wolde had squandered the money, drinking by himself. As John Chernoff wrote, "Poverty is hot like a fever," and poor people "are aware of what they need to make their lives easier: anything cool" (2003, 49). After a long discussion, his friends recognized and somehow understood Wolde's attempt to cool things off with a full night of solitary binge drinking.

Across gender lines, players navigated economies of love and intimacy to get by while also seeking those opportunities of social mobility and international migration through relations. Sara relied on her sense of sacrifice to imagine a way of combining her daily hustling with her aspirations for a good life somewhere else. Like hustlers, players had to skillfully navigate economies of hustling and sharing, yet in a context where what was either potentially shared or hustled were intimacy and the player's body. In this game, as Mikias's boast of getting free sex through a ruse of knowing a rich Somali shows, hustlers cultivated dreams of masculine prowess by seeking to employ smartness in the relation with players and sex workers.

For players, however, hustling had higher stakes. The everyday experiences of living with similarly marginalized others and the wider history of exclusion and subjugation explored in previous chapters intertwined at a deeper level in the experiences of players and women in the inner city. Therefore, for players such as Sara, hustling and smartness had a particular gendered meaning. Smartness was not just the ability to steer the direction toward hustling or sharing. It was the capacity to either disengage from a specific interaction of hustling and sharing or turn that moment of intimacy into a long-term opportunity of social improvement, and potentially transcend the immediate necessities of getting by.

For some male hustlers, this game of hustling and intimacy was not inevitably predatorial. Just as in the case of the *duriye Arada*, the thug *Arada* we explored in chapter 2, being a male *Arada* did not mean being out of control. For some, smartness consisted of one's ability to recognize that experiences of scarcity, abjection, and exclusion were shared across gender lines and that players and sex workers were not to be hustled, bothered, or cheated. Unfortunately, as chapter 8 will show, this was not shared by all hustlers, showing how the moral space of togetherness, in which hustling and sharing, friendship and collaboration, intimacy, getting by and opportunity took place, is radically contingent on a disposition to identify a shared predicament.

However, as I show in the next chapter, the experience of being acted upon as a condition of enduring poverty and exclusion did not only result in a crude realism and moral ambiguities. Firmly grounded in an understanding of poverty as something that is difficult to question and challenge, my informants also elaborated an idea of enjoyment that was tuned to the appreciation of their capacity to redefine questions of what a poor person could do and look like in the face of exclusion and marginality.

LIFE IS A PARADISE

An Enjoyable Existence

About poverty in Ethiopia, historian John Iliffe wrote: "Ethiopians did not criticise poverty, but nor did they idealise it. They saw it with the weary realism of those who lived with it every day and had no thought that it might be prevented" (1987, 29). Notions and practices of *being Arada* played with a similar awareness that poverty is unquestionable and undeniable. As we saw in chapter 2, the heroism of the thug *Arada* revolved around the ability to live through poverty smartly, bravely, and with toughness, while poverty itself was an unchallengeable, unavoidable frame of existence. We learned in the previous chapter that hustling and cheating operated on the same logic. They were grounded in the banality of poverty and gained their legitimation through a crude realism that "you do what you got to do" to get by. Yet my informants did not live a gloomy existence: hustling was also fun. As Ibrahim explained, it was fun because you go back and forth, you see and do things. Even more fun was dancing and flirting in the game of love. And it was fun to eat, drink, chew *khat*, and dress up. Enjoyment was an important part of my informants' everyday lives.

However, enjoyment cannot be seen as an undefined experience of pleasure. Friedman (1994), for instance, argued that consumption is enjoyed because its goal is the "achievement of fulfilment by the creation of a life space" (121). Consumption is "an aspect of a more general strategy or set of strategies for the establishment and maintenance of selfhood" (122). Similarly, having fun implies the appreciation of particular recreational activities. This appreciation occurs through a frame of reference in relation to which people experience a sense of satisfaction. What my informants found amusing and enjoyable was exactly what made *being* and *becoming Arada* appealing: the capacity of redefining what a poor person could do and be in the face of exclusion and marginality.

With this understanding of enjoyment, I aim to provide a particular interpretation of what MacGaffey and Bazenguissa-Ganga (2000) describe as the relation between "shining" and "surviving." Part of the scholarship on youth has tended to identify a certain degree of resistance in youth identities and practices of leisure and enjoyment, perhaps in partial reaction to criminalizing and patronizing discourses (Abbink and van Kessel 2005; Amit-Talai and Wulff 1995; Maira and Soep 2005; Nilan and Feixa 2006; Honwana and de Boeck 2005; Skleton and Valentine 1998; Hall and Jefferson 2006). This literature suggests that when young people "shine"— for instance, by engaging in leisure—they produce alternative and parallel realities from which to contest the political and social order that relegates them to conditions of mere survival. In doing this, young people create new meanings and experiences that might potentially transform themselves and society in general.

Taking a different perspective, Weiss (2009) examined how the exercise of imagination and fantasy in young people's engagement with the "gangsta style" in Arusha (Tanzania) was a way of inhabiting experiences of oppression and exclusion. Similarly, I do not see shining and surviving as being in opposition. Shining shaped how my informants survived and endured marginality and exclusion. When they shone, my informants did not inhabit alternative realities. When my informants had fun, they did not see their enjoyment as transformative. Poverty, exclusion, and marginality remained unchallenged. With their quests for enjoyment and satisfaction, they dwelled in a tension inherent in a life within limits, between the logic of marginality and exclusion that imposed constraints on their action, on the one hand, and their attempts to live a meaningful and enjoyable existence (cf. Michael Jackson 1989, 2005), on the other. The *act of living* can indeed be enjoyed.

To explore this tension, the chapter focuses on dressing up, posing as gangsta rappers, and consuming *khat*. These were not the only activities my informants enjoyed, but they reveal most eloquently how scarcity, exclusion, and subjugation populated the streets of Arada yet gave space to the performances of style, excess, and exaggeration that my informants deeply enjoyed.

Cool Guys, Freaks, Loiterers, the Thugs, and the Exploded

In the early 1970s, the style of *jolly jacketism*—that, is bell-bottoms, straight jackets, and Afro-style hair—was all the rage in the clubs, bars, and streets of Addis Ababa, remembered Ato (Mr) Dereje Tekle, a resident and acute observer of

Arada. As the socialist Derg regime took over, the ideological struggle against antirevolutionary attitudes in society resulted in more sober fashion. Clothes imported from the socialist bloc—in particular, the khakis that Mao Zedong, Kim Il-Sung, and Mengistu Haile Mariam wore—shaped fashion and style in Addis Ababa. At the same time, though Western clothing was formally banned as antirevolutionary, it remained popular. Defiant teenagers, Ato Dereje recalled, wore T-shirts with "USA" printed across them underneath their jackets and showed them to their friends as acts of bravery.

With the fall of the socialist regime and the opening of the free market, new goods, style, and media flowed into urban Ethiopia. In the mid-1990s, Michael Jackson–style jackets imbued their wearers with coolness. Though Haile was my most important source for the oral history of the street, he rarely mentioned his own fashionable youth to me. It was Ibrahim who told me about Haile's Michael Jackson style, rating him as among the coolest guys in the neighborhood during that time. However, Ibrahim admitted, Haile wore counterfeits. The authentic ones were still very expensive, and in Ibrahim and Haile's circle, only Noah, the manager of the video house where the *yemot midib* met for the first time, could afford them.

When I first started my fieldwork in October 2009, a variety of fashion, forms of consumption, and leisure characterized the performance of style in Arada. Two categories of style were among the most identifiable and distinguishable: the freaks and the cool guys. "Freaks" was the term that my informants used to describe the exuberant fashion and style of the young men, usually in their late teens and early twenties, who wore hip-hop-style baggy trousers and sweatshirts and of the young women of the same age who dressed in tight pants and shirts with an R&B style. Smoking marijuana, heavy drinking, and social ease were also believed to be among the features and activities of leisure of the freaks. If I wanted to find freaks, young people who lived around my house told me, I had to go to two or three clubs in Arada where DJs played hip-hop music from the afternoon until late at night. One of these clubs was hidden behind a tall fence because, as some of my informants told me, even though smoking marijuana was formally forbidden, it was tacitly allowed in there. "Cool guys," or *chewa*, formed another category of style in Arada. *Chewa*, in Amharic, is a well-behaved person. The English term "cool guys" was used to describe an idea of fashion and lifestyle that was poles apart from the exuberance of the freaks. Cool guys engaged in more sober leisure; they dressed in casual, but still fashionable, clothes, frequented cafés and restaurants, and, importantly, avoided heavy drinking, chewing *khat*, smoking marijuana, and staying out late.

The cool guys and the freaks did not differ just in their performances of style. The performances of the cool guys diverged from those of the freaks because they were embedded in a different repertoire of "desires," aspirations, and expected or actual social trajectories. Cool guys were usually older than the freaks, and some of the young men and women who defined themselves as cool or *chewa* admitted that they had been freaks in their late teens and early twenties. On the other hand, not all the freaks turned into cool guys, just as not all the cool guys had been freaks. Age was a cleavage between cool guys and freaks, but it was not the only or most relevant one. Being a cool guy, in fact, was usually economically and symbolically grounded in a particular social trajectory to which only some young adults in their mid-twenties had access. Cool guys were usually university students, recent graduates, young white-collar workers, and young men and women waiting for office jobs. Being well behaved and cool thus embodied the engagement of these young men and women in an expected trajectory of social mobility, or rather, with an ideal of a productive experience of time in the present, inspired by a "healthy" balance between enjoyment and work as a formula for social success.

Cafés are interesting public spaces to fully appreciate the performances of style and leisure of the cool guys. They are relatively expensive, usually extremely busy in the evenings, and often patronized by very well-dressed young men and women. Being well dressed is, of course, not mandatory, and waiters do not refuse to serve customers because of their style; but the casual style of the cool guys is desirable and expected. The cafés were the public stage where young workers and university students engaged in a form of leisure that stressed their disengagement from stigmatized forms of enjoyment, such as chewing *khat* or smoking marijuana, and emphasized a commitment to respectable, responsible, and productive ways of living.

By flirting with the performances of the gangsta rappers, R&B dancers, and hip-hop artists, freaks were situated in another social and cultural space of the city from which cool guys, with their café culture, firmly disengaged—namely, the street life and the economies of the streets. However, this allegiance of the freaks with the street does not mean that those who wore hip-hop-style baggy trousers were inevitably hustlers and that street hustlers were inevitably freaks. For instance, Ibrahim and Haile rarely wore baggy trousers. While freaks engaged with the imageries of the gangsta rapper and the street hustler, their performances were part of a wider repertoire of ideas and categories of street life and street style. This includes the *bozene* (literally, "loiterer"), *fendata* (one who is on the verge of exploding), and, as we have already seen in chapter 2, the *duriye* (thug). The term *bozene*, for instance, sometimes described people who were far from being well dressed but usually referred to young people who lingered at particular spots on the street or in chewing houses (*khat bet*). I myself was addressed as *bozene* by some of my neighbors who frequently saw me lounging on the street with my informants. The term *fendata* was often associated with a particular hairstyle—

long hair on top and short hair on the sides—but mainly alluded to the unruly and rebellious teenagers frequently involved in street fighting or, more specifically, to the young snatchers and thieves who were commonly believed to be dangerous and difficult to deal with. Finally, *duriye* was a term that mothers used to scold naughty boys, but also a wide category that, as we learned in chapter 2, embodied the broader repertoire of histories, stories, characters, and practices of street toughness and bravery that the protagonists claimed for themselves. Ibrahim was certainly too old to be a freak, but he did not have a problem with calling himself a *duriye*.

Chewing *khat* was another pillar of street style. *Khat* has a long history in Ethiopia, extending back to the fourteenth century (Ezekiel Gebissa 2003, 2010). It has historically played an important role in the religious and social lives of Ethiopian Muslims, whereas it has been largely stigmatized by Orthodox Christians. This stigma persists today across both religious and class lines; however, heavy *khat* consumption has become increasingly common among young men in urban areas, including Orthodox Christians (Mains 2012a). *Khat* is rarely consumed publicly on the street. Minibus drivers usually chew inside their vans, parked on side roads, during their afternoon breaks. Many people chew alongside other regular and occasional customers in the very busy *khat bet* and video parlors (*video bet*), or at home with friends, such as at Mikias's place, where Ibrahim, Haile, and other parking guys usually went to chew *khat*. All these locations are away from the public gaze. While people are chewing, doors and windows are closed, creating a sense of hiddenness or even invisibility for those inside. Within those places, chewing *khat* was accompanied by conviviality, with people chatting with their friends, making jokes, and sharing ideas, memories, and experiences. As *Rajimu*, a very tall (*rajim*) street tourist guide and a regular customer of a *khat bet* in my field site, said, "You first like the *khat* and its effect. After, you usually end up liking what happens in the *khat bet*." Kitabu, a close friend of *Rajimu*'s and a street tourist guide himself, threw a bundle of chewed stems on the floor and added, "This is freedom, you do what you want and you enjoy it."

Kitabu's gesture describes what he meant about freedom and enjoying freedom even more expressively than his actual words. In a *khat bet*, people came as they could and behaved as they wanted because, from the perspective of my informants, they were free to perform and enjoy the repertoire of practices with which they were confident. Whereas in cafés or restaurants, people had to behave differently, conforming with the expected respectable conduct and fashion of the cool guys. I understood how different *khat bet* and cafés or restaurants were when I once treated Haile to a meal at a restaurant in Arada. He seemed lost, like a fish out of water. His sense of inadequacy suggested to me that my informants did not frequent cafés and restaurants not only because they could not afford it, but also because these sites required a repertoire of styles, signs, postures, and gestures, what Bourdieu (1984) described as "cultural capital," which they were not able or even willing to master.

The sociality of the *khat bet* and video parlors is rooted in a game of display and concealment that, as we will see later, also encompassed the performances of style of the gangsta. Being located away from the public gaze, the *khat* spaces granted a certain sense of freedom and ease. Like Kitabu, the anthropological literature on resistance has often associated hiddenness with freedom. Scott (1985) *in primis* talked about the "hidden transcripts" to describe the weapons that the weak employed to smooth, negotiate, and even oppose and resist the terms of their own oppression. On the other hand, the very condition of being "hidden" or "invisible" bears witness to the fact that those experiences of freedom and easiness contain and embody the terms of the very forms of exclusion, criminalization, and stigmatization that directly and indirectly make poverty hidden.

In fact, when *khat bet* enter the discourses of government institutions, politicians, NGOs, and journalists, they are usually described as unhealthy and dangerous, populated by thugs, good-for-nothings, and criminals. This stigmatizing commentary on chewing *khat* revolves around two kinds of concerns and narratives on the state of urban society. The first taps into a moralizing and patronizing discourse on laziness and lack of self-determination as the reasons for poverty and social marginality (see chapter 4). From the perspective of government institutions, NGOs, and policymakers, chewing *khat* is the biggest obstacle to young people's productive engagement with the development of the country. The second is the political anxiety of government officials and the ruling party's cadres about their inability to control what actually happens in the *khat bet*. During the 2005 elections, for instance, *khat bet* were key political spaces where people discussed politics and where the opposition parties built up support among the most marginalized sections of urban society (see chapter 4). The 2005 demonstrations, many among my informants ironically argued, were a "*khat* revolution." The government, for its part, claimed that dangerous vagrants and criminals hid out in *khat bet*, which encouraged unhealthy, antisocial, and criminal attitudes and behaviors. Since the 2005 postelection violence, while selling *khat* is permitted, managing a public space where people can chew *khat* is illegal. My neighbor, a young man in his late teens, explained the rationale behind this repressive measure: "[In a *khat bet*] you are not only with your friends, but you could meet new people and this is dangerous for the government."

In this context of political criminalization and social differentiation, the respectability of the cool guys and their performances of respectable leisure versus, on the other hand, the "unruliness" of the entangled repertoire of street style in the performances of the freaks, *bozene*, *fendata*, and *duriye* recalls the distinction made between "gentlemen" and "thugs" in the 1960s and mid-1970s. As I showed in chapter 1, thugs and gentlemen constituted the categories that people in Arada used to narrate their own version of history and then map these narrations of the past and present onto what they perceived to be the current social topographies of the city. Today's categories of cool guys, freaks, *bozene*, *fendata*, and *duriye* constituted similar ways of defining and experiencing social difference.

Indeed, as in the past, *being Arada* did not necessarily coincide with a particular style—such as the hip-hop trousers of the freaks and the worn clothes of the *bozene*—or with a particular leisure activity, such as chewing *khat*, engaging in heavy drinking, or going to cafés. The notions and the practices of smartness and of *being Arada* encompassed all of these different styles, performances, and activities. In other words, *being Arada* was a metaidentity or metanarration through which my informants understood, appreciated, enjoyed, embodied, or alternatively, stigmatized and kept a distance from the styles and leisure activities that were performed *in* Arada. Expanding on this, I investigate how clothing and the consumption of *khat* were enjoyed through paradigms of smartness or, more precisely, how ideas of smartness and *Arada-ness* made enjoyment a way of dealing with and living through forms of marginalization, stigmatization, and criminalization.

Gangsta Style

On the wall of the office of the lieutenant investigator at the Arada police station, photographs of pickpockets, forgers, gold snatchers, and robbers were visibly displayed to all who came in to report an offense. Intrigued, I asked the lieutenant investigator about the photographs. Offenders, he said, must provide these themselves. Some brought a photograph from home. Others paid a photographer to have their picture taken. The backgrounds of the photographs are thus not the walls of the police station but home furniture or a photographer's studio. Some of the young men in the photographs look scared, the kind of mugshot one would expect to see at a police station. But as I glanced through the photographs, I noticed that, along with a few timidly smiling faces, some people looked confident and boastful, posing with hip-hop and gangsta rapper gestures and postures.

The gestures and postures of the gangsta rapper have gained increased currency in the youth performances of style in Africa and beyond. Behrend (2002), for instance, wrote about Peter, a young man in Mombasa who had his picture taken while dressing and acting like a gangsta rapper. In Peter's experience, Behrend reckoned, performing the role of the gangsta was a way of embodying a horizon of social aspirations from which he felt excluded. Similarly, in his ethnography *Street Dreams and Hip Hop Barbershops*, Weiss (2009) examined young men's engagement with the imagery of the gangsta rapper in Arusha. Contrary to the emphasis on mimicry and emulation in studies of popular culture on the continent, Weiss built on Žižek's (1997) understanding of "exaggeration" and "excess." Exaggeration, the Slovenian philosopher argues, is an act of taking the Part and elevating it to the Principle of the Whole. In these conditions, "the subject emerges in the event of the 'exaggeration' when a part exceeds its limited place and explodes the constraints of balanced totality" (92). Hip-hop posing, Weiss contends, is an act of exaggeration that taps into the disjuncture that young men in Arusha feel between "the world they live in and the plentiful possibilities they aspire to" (2009, 37). By posing as gangsta rappers, young men took the Part (that is, a repertoire of hip-hop gestures and postures) and elevated it to the actual experience of the Whole (that is, the visions of affluence, abundance, and wealth that commercial hip-hop embodies globally, and that the young men in Arusha deeply desired and aspired to). In doing so, Weiss continues, they did not pose a challenge to the global order of wealth and affluence through mockery or resistance, but unsettled it in two complementary ways. First, by reducing the Whole to the partial reproduction of its forms and appearances, young men in Arusha experienced and dealt with that disjuncture between the socially imagined and their everyday experiences of marginalization. Second, by doing so, they did not actually manage to bridge that gap, but became aware of the impossibility of fully realizing those aspirations.

In Arada as in Arusha, the currency of the gangsta rapper in performances of style taps into experiences of exclusion and marginality. However, whereas Weiss emphasized the disjuncture between aspirations and actual social realizations, I focus on how enjoyment provided ways of dealing with social realizations in the here and now, rather than in comparison to an imagined horizon of aspirations and expectations. By embodying the gangsta rapper, my informants did not compare their condition of exclusion to the affluent world of hip-hop artists. Instead, they tuned their performances of style to inhabit and enjoy the imaginary affluence that the gangsta rapper represented.

In the mugshots at the police station, the gestures of the gangsta let offenders use a particular modality of presenting the self as a thief, a pickpocket, a snatcher at the margins of urban society. In the very moment when their image was made an example of criminality on the walls of the lieutenant inspector's office, offenders turned to the imagery of the gangsta, a man who, through his smartness in street life, builds his fortune. This exaggerated performance was, in a Goffma-nian (E. Goffman 1961) sense, a face-game. The exaggeration moved the "offender" out of the frame that the mugshots imposed on him and his image. The gangsta blew up the paradigms imposed on him by his criminal identification. The person portrayed in the photograph thus looks more like a crazy young boy who winks at the ideas of success and wealth that the gangsta rapper embodies than a petty criminal who commits offenses to survive. His "craziness" is not clinical, but as Žižek (1997) says, elevating the Part to the Principle of the Whole is a "crazy" process because it unsettles the "constraints of [a] balanced totality." In other words, behaving or posing as a gangsta did not make one a "ghetto gangster." By taking the Part and elevating it to the Whole, they unsettled and exceeded the frames of their social encounters at the police station.

However, embodying and performing the role of the gangsta rapper was not just a way of blowing up the frames of the criminalizing encounter. It could also be an active way of pursuing opportunities for income in the street economy. An example is *Prof John*, a street tourist guide. He was in his forties when I met him, and in the past he had been a hustler like many of the street tourist guides who trod the streets of Arada looking for tourists. When I met him, he had a website through which he found customers from abroad. His job earned him a considerable amount of money, but he was far from being a rich man, as I realized when I visited his small room in the northern part of Addis Ababa. With his income, however, *Prof John* was able to personify the role of a "big man" among the street tourist guides. His appeal and charm were drawn partly from the fact that he often helped out other street tourist guides with small handouts when they were in trouble, but also from his "scary" gangsta style. *Prof John*, in fact, really looked like the kind of street gangster one usually sees in the movies. He was a very big guy, with a flat nose and a very round face. He was always dressed in hip-hop clothes and talked and gestured like a gangsta.

Many believed that he was a "fake gangster" because, it was rumored, when fights or bar brawls happened, he always found a way out. However, *Prof John*'s performances of "gangsterism" were never directly challenged because they were enacted in relation to a particular modality of being on the street. He behaved like a big man with the street tourist guides, who related to him accordingly by acting as his henchmen when he was around. In return, they received a few bucks, a bundle of *khat*, a plate of *injera*, or even temporary work in his touring business. *Prof John*, for his part, also behaved like a tough street man with tourists and foreigners. With me, he often emphasized his potential and unpredictable dangerous nature: "Hey, pay attention, if you don't respect me, it will be dangerous for you." Or, on another occasion to persuade me to join him at a *khat bet*, he told me, "If you do not come here, I will kill you." By doing this, *Prof John* gained both the trust of his customers as a reliable bodyguard and their fearful respect. This turned out to be useful, as I myself experienced, in setting up con games—for instance, when he called me in the middle of the night to tell me that one of his friends wanted to kill me, saying that I was sleeping with his girlfriend. When I asked Ibrahim for advice on how to deal with *Prof John*'s phone call and false accusation, he explained to me that provoking fear was the first move in a successful con game, especially with naive foreigners who will pay to avoid trouble and admit to wrongdoing even if they have done nothing wrong.

Performing the gangsta rapper to set up con games was not the only function of this role in the street economy. In fact, the gangsta rapper was also an experience of enjoyment. This became clear when Ibrahim and I assisted at one of Mikias's performances of style and fashion. Throughout the time I had known Mikias, I could tell that he was much more fashion conscious than I or his old friends Haile and Ibrahim. But, Ibrahim reckoned, a hooded gangsta sweatshirt I brought for Mikias from England triggered a temporary metamorphosis in the latter's behavior. "Marco, after you brought him that hooded sweatshirt from England, Mikias now behaves even more crazily. He thinks he is still young. He thinks he is a teenager," Ibrahim commented after a crazy night out. It was Easter Monday night, after a full day of religious celebrations. The "teenagers," as Ibrahim called the young people who often spent time at Mikias's, some of them parking guys themselves, were coming and going between Mikias's house and the nightclubs nearby. That night, there were a lot of people at Mikias's and all were dancing. Mikias himself was ecstatic. He was dancing in the middle of his room and shouting "Whooo . . . Whooo" until late at night. "All the people who live around Mikias' house did not sleep the whole night. I hate those fucking teenagers . . . and also Mikias, who thinks he is like them," Ibrahim said.

Mikias's performances of style and excess and his "hooded sweatshirt" lasted for a little while. When I interviewed him in front of my video camera, Mikias wore his hooded sweatshirt. Posing and gesticulating like a gangsta rapper, he told me about the philosophy of enjoyment and fun of *being an Arada*: "Life is a paradise. . . . We drink always, we chew *khat* always . . . we eat, we sleep, we go with women . . . eh? *Trip trip, trip* always, *trip* day to day, day to day, without rest, fun always. . . . Why shouldn't I like life then?"

Trip in Arada street slang (*yeArada kwankwa*) describes fun. It implies moving through different activities and experiences, such as drinking, dancing, having sex, and so on. What is interesting here is the connection that Mikias, with his hooded sweatshirt and his celebration of life as a paradise, made between embodying the gestures of the gangsta rapper and experiencing fun. An examination of *les sapeurs* is helpful in understanding how "embodiment" becomes an experience of enjoyment. MacGaffey and Bazenguissa-Ganga (2000) defined *les sapeurs* as a "cult of appearance" that, by the 1970s, was widespread in Brazzaville and Kinshasa and an important part of the popular culture of the two Congos. This cult of appearance mainly consisted of dressing up in expensive clothes and accessories from major French, Italian, and Japanese *griffes*. With his style and performance of elegance, Gondola argued, the *sapeur* "does not dress like a CEO to imitate the CEO. He is a CEO" (1999, 32). Similarly, by wearing the hooded sweatshirt of the gangsta rapper, Mikias was not behaving like a gangsta; he *was* a gangsta. This experience of embodiment, incarnation, or even, as Gondola reckons, illusion is enjoyed because, as Friedman (1994) points out in reference to *les sapeurs*, dressing up like a rich man or even "living like a king" is not meant to be a strategy of distinction or constitute a "political statement of relative status." Rather, it is an "enjoyment of the highly valued luxuries associated with such status" (121).

Enjoyment is not an undefined experience of fun and pleasure, however. The existential frame through which individuals achieve satisfaction makes single experiences meaningful and enjoyable. In Arada what is fun and enjoyable includes not only consuming, performing, and wearing desirable goods but also the ways one gains access to them through smartness or bravery. Performances of style, fashion, and leisure per se did not make a person an *Arada*; rather, it was that his or her performances of style were located within the broader economy of practices of smartness that shaped meanings and experiences of street life. Haile, for instance, criticized the loud fashion of young people who thought they were smart just because they dressed up as gangsta rappers. He called them the *yelibs Arada*, "the *Arada* of the clothes," or rather, those who are *Arada* only for their ways of dressing. Mikias, for his part, questioned the *Arada-ness* of many young people who populated Arada nightlife. These were not true *Arada*, Mikias reckoned; they were *yeKidame Arada*, or "Saturday *Arada*": the ones who pretended to *be Arada* by getting drunk and wearing expensive clothes on Saturday nights. For both Haile and Mikias, clothing did not make a person *Arada*. Smart fashion had to be substantiated by actual smartness of action.

MacGaffey and Bazenguissa-Ganga (2000) investigated how some *sapeurs* turned their quests for style into a business, and pointed out that "stolen goods" are sold for more than what they sell for in the stores. The reason for this lies in the fact that stolen clothes "have acquired greater value because they have been stolen and there has been triumph over risk" (153). Even though money did not directly circulate in the performances of fashion in Arada, dressing up and behaving like, or even being, a gangsta rapper tapped into a repertoire of practices and exercises of smartness that made performances of styles valuable and enjoyable.

Zinabu matta in Amharic means "the rain has come," but in Arada slang it means a "clothes thief." "When the rain is coming, women bring their washing into their houses. They would do the same if these guys are around," Ibrahim explained. A *zinabu matta* and his thieving activities inhabit a particular interconnection between enjoyment and smartness. A *zinabu matta* will not wear the clothes he has stolen but will sell them and buy fancy new clothes and, hence, can afford a night out in the exclusive clubs of the wealthy southern neighborhood of Bole. Stealing clothes from poor families in Arada to buy clothes that the *zinabu matta* can display in a wealthy part of town is a modality of "reversing" poverty and wealth. This reversal is enjoyed by the *zinabu matta*, not only through his ability to conceal his social background under the guise of a well-dressed young man, but also by pursuing that appearance through an exercise of street smartness that targets poverty and inhabits imageries of wealth.

This game of concealment and display also pervaded the performances of style and fashion of some of my key informants, though in different ways. *Kayyo* (literally "red") was a young man in his late teens. He was very fashion conscious, with a shiny style, often wearing baggy hip-hop trousers and sweatshirts. As I spent more time appreciating his performances of style, I realized that *Kayyo* actually had very few clothes in his wardrobe. As de Certeau might put it (1984), his art and skill consisted of a *tactical* ability to combine trousers, sweatshirts, a nice hat, and a *keffiyeh* in a way that these pieces of clothing would always look shiny and new. This skillful game of showing and hiding allowed *Kayyo* to continue to engage with the imagery and style of the rich gangsta despite his scarce means.

Ibrahim also had style. I was extremely impressed when he stood up in the middle of Mikias's house to teach the robot dance to a young girl who was practicing R&B dancing before going to a club. He said: "I was the first one who dressed in a *Latino style* in my neighborhood." He described what he meant by buttoning up his shirt at the neck and unbuttoning the shirt at the belly. "Look, this is also a way of hiding the fact that the shirt that you have underneath is broken!" With this ironic statement, Ibrahim suggested an interesting way of looking at the connection among enjoyment, exaggeration, and smartness. Exaggeration—that is, performing the gestures and appearances of the gangsta or, rather, the Latino gangsta—is achieved through a bluff or even a trick. A trick is achieved and pursued in the here and now of social experiences (de Certeau 1984). A trick is an exaggeration, a game of reversals. Through tricks and reversals, the individuals discussed in this section, from Ibrahim and *Kayyo* to the "offenders" in the mugshots and the *zinabu matta*, embodied the wealth of the gangsta. Their exaggerations blew up the criminalizing and moralizing frames with which state institutions, NGOs, the inner city middle class, and even some cool guys looked down at street life. At the same time, their reversals tricked and bypassed the actual opportunities that my informants had to "shine," such as the expense of hip-hop clothes or the costly entrance fee to an exclusive club. This experience was deeply enjoyed, not only because it delivered an experience of abundance but mainly because it was pursued through a *trick*, the ultimate expression of the *Arada* street smartness that my informants valued and appreciated.

Getting High

The consumption of *khat* was an important aspect of the everyday lives of my informants, often taking up nearly half of each day, from early afternoon until late at night. One of the reasons for this is that getting high on *khat* takes time. In fact, as I myself experienced and as my informants said, the *merkana*—that is, the state of excitement and euphoria that *khat* produces—"comes" usually after a few hours of constant chewing. When *"merkana* comes," discussions become more animated. Plans for the future and memories of the past flow, and personal issues and problems seem to be resolved more easily. *Khat* makes the brain work faster. You can see things that you would not normally see. You consider aspects that you would not usually understand to be linked and interconnected.

Discussing the life of unemployed youth in Jimma (southern Ethiopia), Mains (2012a) argued that chewing *khat* is a way of passing time and, at the same time, reinstating hope. Similarly to a common way of understanding youth practices, Mains positioned chewing *khat* into the disjuncture between aspirations of social mobility and actual opportunities to fulfill those expectations. Expanding on the literature on "waiting" in youth practices (M. Ralph 2008; Jeffrey 2010), Mains argued that spending time chewing *khat* for hours enabled young people to deal with the excess of time that resulted from their being unemployed. Thus, providing a reinterpretation of Weiss's examination of "too much thinking" among young people in Arusha (2005, 2009), he suggested that while chewing *khat*, young people in Jimma dealt with *cinqet*, the stress and anxiety deriving from the mismatch between their expectations of progress and their actual inactivity. The *merkana*, he reckoned, triggered imaginations and aspirations that provided young people in Jimma with positive ways of looking at their future and their present, restoring in them a sense of hope.

I discuss anxiety and stress in chapter 8, where I examine how my informants elaborated their notions of destiny and chance. I also examine *cinqet* as a lived experience concerning the present and an encompassing experience of marginality and exclusion. Here, expanding on my analytical concern with enjoyment, I argue that the consumption of *khat*, as well as the stream of ideas and imaginations that *merkana* triggers, should be understood in its own terms. Seeing chewing *khat* simply as a coping mechanism clouds our understanding of how it is actually experienced and why people enjoy it. I understand chewing *khat*, spending time, and getting high as activities that mainly concern the present and the immediate moment of people's existence. Even when imaginations about the future are elaborated under the effects of *khat*, they are not to be seen as actual projections of possibility, but as ideas and thoughts that are enjoyed and "consumed" in the here and now.

Carrier's (2007) examination of *khat* use in Kenya shows that *merkana* consists of a particular kind of experience of excitement and euphoria that differs significantly from the "highs" of other drugs. *Khat* contains cathinone, which, like amphetamine, affects the central nervous system but with a much milder effect. The effects of *khat* "are strong enough to absorb the consumer into whatever he or she is doing at the time, but not so strong as to drastically alter one's conscious state. . . . By becoming so absorbed, the consumer is more able to persevere with either work or leisure: one can be happily active when chewing, or happily inactive" (5–6).

In other words, *khat* is far from being an escapist drug that leads the consumer somewhere and *somewhen* to contemplate alternative realities and possibilities. Instead, it triggers a sense of presentist euphoria that is experienced and enjoyed in relation to the very moment, place, and activity where, when, and while *khat* is chewed. This experience of presentist euphoria, Ibrahim and many among my informants admitted, could be addictive. Mikael, a man in his forties and a friend of Ibrahim and Mikias's, described *khat* as a "chain." However, as several studies have pointed out (Carrier 2007; Ezekiel Gebissa 2003), the chemical effects of *khat* do not cause dependency. What is addictive is that chewing *khat* and the *merkana* give a deep sense of satisfaction and fulfillment that people look for in their everyday lives. As Ibrahim explained, "When I chew, I think that what I have is enough." He continued, "You know, you want that feeling."

A consideration of the activities undertaken while chewing *khat* might help us appreciate what is behind the sense of addictive satisfaction and fulfillment Ibrahim alluded to. The process of chewing consists of a quintessential experience of consumption, literally, a binge. Tea and cola are usually drunk to sweeten the bitter taste. Peanuts are eaten. Cigarettes and *shisha* (hookah) are smoked. When night came and my informants were experiencing their *merkana*, they sometimes gambled, combining the euphoria of *khat* with the excitement of a possible win. Beers or spirits such as *arakie* (a kind of brandy), *tella* (local beer), or *taj* (honeywine) sometimes followed the *khat*. *Chebsi* was the term my informants used to describe the desire to drink after *merkana*, or that drinking was necessary to "kill" the *merkana* and be able to go to sleep.

A certain degree of overstimulation pervaded some of the environments where people went to consume *khat*, such as the *khat bet* or the busiest *video bet*. Posters of gangsta rappers and female R&B singers in sexy poses were sometimes posted on the walls, together with images of Jesus or Mary with the Holy Child. Stereos often played very loud music. When TVs were available, they showed hip-hop videos and Hollywood action movies; English or Amharic dramas or comedies were sometimes shown, but customers often opposed these genres because they clashed with the sense of overstimulation *khat* was supposed to induce. When Fasil (the street tourist guide we met in chapter 5) and I went to a *khat bet* that had been turned into a video parlor, a movie drama was on the screen, but nobody seemed very interested in what was happening. After a while, someone shouted to the manager: "*Musica, musica!*" In an instant, the tunes of well-known hip-hop singers resonated throughout the room, and images of gangsta rappers holding money (a lot of money), women, boobs, expensive cars, and shiny clothes appeared on the screen. People at the *khat bet* started following the music and commenting on the images. Fasil seemed hypnotized, chewing *khat*, eyes fixed on the screen. "It's all about the money!" he said; after that, another customer shouted: "Money! Money!" Then, after a video clip that was somewhere between hip-hop and soft porn, he said "*Ims, bizu ims!*" (pussy, a lot of pussy!).

Such experiences of abundance and overstimulation were, of course, far from being a sign of wealth but were a way of living through a condition of poverty and scarcity. My informants pursued excess by consuming goods that were very cheap and thus easily accessible, such as tea, coffee, and peanuts. Cigarettes were not usually bought in packs, but loose, usually just one or two. The qualities of *khat* that my informants chewed—that is, *guraghe*, *gelemso*, or even *Colombia*— were believed to be among those that not only gave a very strong *merkana* but also were the cheapest. *Wendo* or *Abo mismar*, the ones that gave the gentlest *merkana*, were among the most expensive. The entrance fee to a *video bet* was one birr in 2010 and three birr in 2014, remaining largely affordable despite the wider rise in the cost of living (see chapter 3). Beer was expensive, but *tella* and local spirits were cheaper. Through cheap abundance and overstimulation, reaching and experiencing the *merkana* was not just undefined excitement, euphoria, and pleasure that resulted from enjoying excess. As with the gestures of the gangsta rapper, the cheap abundance that my informants experienced while chewing *khat* reversed poverty with wealth, elevating the consumption of cheap goods to an experience of excess or even wealth. *Merkana* was enjoyed because it bore witness to the fact that a poor young man could also live like a king. The *merkana* witnessed the smartness of the poor man and his ability to enjoy and experience excess despite poverty and scarcity. What was enjoyed, what was even addictive, was not the excess and the abundance per se, but rather the sense of smartly living through poverty and achieving an abundance from which my informants were usually excluded. As Ibrahim put it, "You know, you want that feeling."

Enjoyment and Marginality

Exaggeration, reversals, excess, and games of concealment and display inter-twined, making enjoyment a modality of living through poverty, marginalization, exclusion, and criminalization. The enjoyment pursued and achieved through exaggeration is of a particular kind, however. As Žižek (1997) suggests, exag-geration not only reverses the Part with the Whole, or rather, poverty with wealth, but also and more importantly turns humiliation, loss, denial, and pain into pleasure. Reversing humiliation with enjoyment does not break those con-straints that produce pain and humiliation. Enjoyment in the spaces of a video parlor or a *khat bet* was not about resisting or reverting existing social and politi-cal hierarchies. Enjoyment reframed the experience of being acted upon by hu-miliation, pain, scarcity, and exclusion in the very moment of the here and now.

That enjoyment did not "ask for anything" (Bakhtin 1984, 7) does not mean, however, that the protagonists and coprotagonists of this book accepted op-pression and marginality. While this chapter has drawn on Žižek's analysis of exaggeration, I disagree with his claim that exaggerations and reversals "make us accept the framework of the social relationship of domination" (1997, 48). Writing about the role of exaggeration and reversals in the postcolony, Achille Mbembe (1992) similarly argued that they reveal how dominant visions of power and privilege are internalized and accepted, not resisted and challenged. In this and the previous chapter, I have shown how my interlocutors' attempts to reframe the ways they lived through marginality via enjoyment and a sense of crude mo-rality were not about resistance. In subsequent chapters I argue that this lack of resistance did not feed into a straightforward acceptance of subjugation and op-pression as given, normal, and inevitable. The protagonists and coprotagonists of this book desired wealth and abundance, reflecting how (in this, Achille Mbembe is correct) symbols, signs, and discourses produced by authority populate the ordinary experiences and aspirations of the dominated. Yet even while desiring wealth, Haile, Ibrahim, and many others elaborated a harsh critique of privilege and power in Ethiopia's time of promise, as lacking moral authenticity, grounded in the ruling party's politics of opportunism and in the selfishness of the country's rich and superrich. As we will see, this critique was not just about words. It was the basis of a search for an alternative ground for action and hope.

THE TIME OF THE BUMPKINS

The Development Bluff

Enjoyment, morality, and the crude realism of hustling and getting by pervaded the way the protagonists and coprotagonists of this book established and evaluated their actions in the face of marginality and exclusion. This chapter shows how marginality was not just imposed or navigated but also discussed and openly criticized. By living within limits, my interlocutors nurtured and exercised their capacity to skillfully, bravely, and smartly live through poverty and exclusion. Yet they were far from content with living within limits. Poverty, exclusion, and marginality were unquestionable, but certainly not desirable.

Economic growth and development had offered Haile, Ibrahim, and many others in the inner city nothing to build on to meaningfully change their lives. Access to the inner city business community was fundamentally closed (see chapter 3), and development programs failed to provide opportunities for social improvement (see chapter 4). However, while their condition of marginality persisted, the construction of high-rise buildings and the increased availability of resources and goods triggered expectations and desires for social mobility and material success.

Haile and Ibrahim were fascinated by the promises of abundance that the city's economic growth offered. Yet, the persistence of their own marginality made them wonder about the actual foundation of this wealth, success, and power. They questioned the moral authenticity of wealth and politics, the pillars of their country's growth and development, as being grounded in the selfishness of businesspeople, the occult practice of the country's rich and superrich, and the fakeness of politics as a site of opportunism and deception. As the anthropologist Sasha Newell would put it (2012), the protagonists and coprotagonists of this book saw development and economic growth as a "bluff." Development was a bluff because it was recognized as the outcome of illicit and immoral practices. Businesspeople hustled and cheated, just as hustlers did. Rich people turned to sorcerers to unleash spirits and magic for personal enrichment. Business elites and top politicians rubbed shoulders to dodge taxes and accumulate wealth behind the facade of party politics and propaganda about the country's development and collective achievement.

This critical account was far from nuanced and was often grounded in rumors and perceptions (West and Sanders 2003; L. White 2000). Yet, the critique of the selfishness and greed of businesspeople was a powerful moral indictment of the logic of the "relatives with relatives and donkeys with ashes," which, as discussed in chapter 3, produced their condition of exclusion and abjection. Similarly, understanding wealth as embedded in occult practices was a way of making sense of its apparently inexplicable emergence in a country with extreme poverty. The images of businesspeople and politicians rubbing shoulders were grounded in the widely shared perception of intimate connections between politics and business in the country. Finally, seeing politics as fake was a way of questioning how the celebrations of Ethiopia's success remained incommensurable with how state policies and development programs only reinforced marginality and subjugation as the terms of poor people's membership in society.

The philosopher Achille Mbembe (1992) argued that the postcolony is a site of "illicit cohabitation" and "conviviality," making attitudes toward power and wealth, and not just aspirations and visions of success and improvement, widely shared between the ruled and the rulers. In a similar vein, Sasha Newell (2012) showed how Ivorian hustlers saw a sort of continuity between their hustling and possibilities of success. Inner city Addis Ababa presented a radically different reality. No doubt, Haile, Ibrahim, and many others in my field site wanted to be rich and powerful. However, the existence of a critique of power, wealth, and success reveals how my interlocutors saw a fundamental incommensurability between the spaces of their existence and the logics that delivered success, wealth, and power. Unlike the Ivorian hustlers described by Newell, my informants felt that they could not join the bluff of development and economic growth. Sure they were hustling, and bluffing is the domain of the hustler. But they also felt that they did not have the resources to play the "big" game of faking and cheating that they saw "rich people" playing. As Ibrahim put it, "We are *čebeta* [squeezed], we gamble with no money, we don't have opportunities, we don't have a past, a present or a future." There was a big divide between the "small" hustling of the survivors and the "big" cheating of the wealthy, and that divide could not be crossed. The red line of politics (see chapter 5) was combined with the "glass ceilings" that limited their hustling.

As we will see, the inability of hustlers to join the bluff of the wealthy and powerful resulted in a questioning of the actual smartness of street *Arada*. As an increasing number turned toward the visions of abundance and wealth that the city offered to elaborate ideas of desirable and achievable futures, my informants witnessed a wider questioning of their claims to smartness and *Arada-ness*. Many in the inner city began to argue that the *Arada* were no longer those who just lived smartly through poverty and scarcity; rather, they were those who were smart enough to get away from it. In this emerging conceptualization, the *Arada* were those who became rich, not those who remained poor. This questioning of the smartness of the *Arada* in the face of the bluffing of the powerful provided the reasons for questioning the underpinnings of Ethiopia's growth. My informants' critique of economic growth and development was an attempt to recapture a sense of self-worth through the recognition that the moral ambiguities of their hustling were nothing compared with what politicians and businessmen were believed to be accumulating behind the facade of development and politics.

In these circumstances, what my informants felt they could do was to call and recognize the "bluff," naming it as something "other." Characterizing power and wealth as "other" was not followed by a sort of "internalization," embodiment, or "mimesis" of that powerful "other," as Mbembe (1992), Newell (2012), and studies of the marginalized and oppressed in postcolonial Africa more generally have argued (Weiss 2002, 2009). Conversely, by recognizing the bluff as something other than themselves, my informants sought to exorcize, externalize, or, more simply, morally and existentially disengage from what they regarded as the source of their condition of social exclusion and political subjugation. Such moves, as James Scott (1985) might argue, did not neutralize and challenge the status quo. Yet they became sites for the elaboration of a critique that informed how the protagonists of this book morally positioned themselves in wider society and questioned the limits imposed on them by patterns of social differentiation and political authoritarianism.

By calling the bluff and morally distancing themselves from the forces producing their condition of oppression and subjugation, my interlocutors made themselves into what the anthropologists Penny Harvey and Hannah Knox (2015) described as an "impossible public." Impossible publics, Harvey and Knox argued, are characterized by a "'politics of refusal' enacted by those whose modes of arguments step outside the frame of established debate altogether" (172). The protagonists and coprotagonists of this book defined their position in society in a relation of incommensurability with the narratives and discourses that pervaded their country's development. However, their critique was not just oppositional; it

FIG. 7.1 Addis Ababa's construction boom © Marco Di Nunzio

also attempted to reimagine ways of engaging with those imaginaries of improvement that current logics of power, wealth, and success denied to them. As Harvey and Knox argued, an impossible public is not always and inevitably a "counterpublic" (cf. Fraser 1992; Warner 2002). Expressions of hostility, refusal, and aversion and claims of incommensurability also reflect an underlying search for being "otherwise engaged" with the desires and aspirations from which marginalized people remain excluded.

The anthropologist Elizabeth Povinelli (2011) argued that "the otherwise" is the expression of that sense of potentiality that philosophers from Aristotle to Giorgio Agamben (1998) have understood as the condition of an ability, a vision, an idea of being there potentially and possibly even without being realized in actuality. The otherwise, Povinelli wrote, is that incoherent repertoire of possibilities and alternatives that constantly "stares back at us without perhaps being able to speak to us" (10). My interlocutors' critique was a way of unlocking the possibility that life could be otherwise. It was an attempt to nullify, or at least mitigate, the effects of exclusion and subjugation on their sense of self and possibility and, hence, find alternative grounds for action and hope.

Elaborating a moral indictment of the sources of their predicament was central in the way my interlocutors sought to tame the tension of their *act of living*. Questioning the authenticity of power, wealth, and success enabled them to reinstate the possibility of being "for somewhere else and for something else" (Fanon [1952] 2008, 170) in the face of the endurance of their condition of subjugation and oppression. This chapter shows how reasserting the possibility of being something other than one's constraints entails a moment of destruction, critique, and refusal. The next chapter will then explore how my interlocutors built their life above the ruins of this critique, by seeking to reestablish grounds for action and hope through an appreciation of the potentialities of the unknown, the uncertain, and the open-ended.

No Country for Poor Men

I was sitting with Ibrahim and his friend and neighbor Mustafa in one of the many bars in Arada. It was an afternoon in early June 2010, the time of year when the rainy season is imminent. Ibrahim wanted me to meet Mustafa because he had seen many things in his life and could tell me something about everyday life in the inner city. Mustafa was in his forties. He had previously managed a small retail shop. He used to be rich, he nostalgically remembered, but lost everything when an employee fled with all the profits, leaving Mustafa with nothing.

On a shelf near our table was a small television. The volume was high and often drew our attention to what was happening on the screen. ETV (Ethiopian Television [now Ethiopian Broadcasting Corporation]) was broadcasting a speech by Meles Zenawi on the state of the economy. It was just two months after the EPRDF's overwhelming electoral victory in the 2010 General Election. I tried to break the ice to begin the interview. *So Mustafa, tell me something about Arada*, I said. He gave a quick look at the television and replied, "The *Arada*? The *Arada* have been eaten."

Ibrahim burst into loud laughter. Mustafa smiled, pleased with his own joke. I remained confused. It took me weeks to understand that Mustafa's cryptic remark described something many of my informants felt as they made sense of their life trajectories and of their position in society. Ultimately, Mustafa was describing that sense of having been left with nothing. Growth and development had delivered the endurance of marginality and subjugation, transforming a moment of promise into an experience of disempowerment, despair, and alienation. Wealth, power, and success were not for the street *Arada* to enjoy. In these circumstances, Ibrahim felt, respect had also gone: "Respect without money is nothing," he told me, making sense of the fact that if he had not managed to achieve something, the respect he had gained being a thug might eventually be for nothing. Because, as he told me on another occasion, "if you are *čista* [broke], nobody is going to respect you." In a similar vein, Wondimu, a former member of the Ashanti group (see chapter 2) and a parking guy at the time of my fieldwork, made sense of his long-term involvement in the street economy: "I was a gangster. In the past, people from other part of the city could not get in [our neighborhood]. We got the money from them and if they did not have it, we would just stab them. I did not get anything out of this. You see, 2PAC [the late American hip-hop artist] was a gangster and was rich, but it did not work out here."

For Wondimu, this was the end of history. "*Ahun tariq yellem*," he said, "there is no history going on." For him, history had ended, but not as Francis Fukuyama (1992) had it, because society had reached the highest point in its evolution. For him, it had ended because while narrations of the "developmental dream" celebrated success and economic growth, there was an imbalance between the strength of patterns of social differentiations and technologies of power in defining experiences of subjugation and the ever-decreasing ability of poor people to act on the circumstances of their lives.

Just a couple of weeks after the encounter with Mustafa, another conversation helped unpack his fascinating but cryptic reflections on the predicament of my informants in the inner city. It was late June and the rain had become more intense. We could not hang out on the streets as we usually did. Haile invited me to go with him to a *khat bet* in the inner city. He wanted me to meet other people, beyond the parking guys I was spending most of my time with. The *khat bet* Haile took me to was no different from the others in my field site, except that the majority of the customers here were minibus drivers and *tara askabari* (minibus touts). "We meet at work and, then, you know, we make appointments here, after work, to enjoy together," Daniel, a minibus tout, told me. Daniel was in his late twenties. When he was a child, he worked as a *listro* (shoeshine boy) until around 1998, when he took control of the minibus stop along with his friends. Before this, the area had been controlled by a group whose members left Ethiopia for Sudan, the Arab countries, and Italy. Daniel and his friends had to fight to get control of the minibus stop. Later, after the 2005 riots, the government decided to institutionalize the minibus touts (see chapter 4). They now had formal authorization and were organized into a cooperative with a defined area and work shifts.

Yibeltal was sitting with Daniel. They were the same age. In the past, Yibeltal had worked as a minibus tout but was now a driver. Daniel wanted to make the same move, as driving paid better than controlling the minibus stops. Yibeltal himself had once been a shoeshine boy, studying and working at the same time. He had given his money to his parents, keeping a little for himself. He remembered that the teachers were not so good in the schools. "Government schools are bad and teachers are *cold*," he said. He did not get good grades and dropped out.

After years as a shoeshine boy, he became a minibus conductor when some of his friends introduced him to the trade. Things got better when he, with Daniel and other friends, took control of the minibus stop. This gave him time and money to learn how to drive. Over the years he made contacts with minibus owners. As soon as he obtained his driver's license, he became a driver.

Haile introduced Yibeltal and Daniel to me as the "last generation of *Arada*"—"They do not know about the history, they just work," he said. Karremanz, a veteran of the minibus business, also joined the conversation and immediately remarked on the history of the trade: "The minibuses started in 1984. There was no such thing as a contract, just an agreement between the driver and owner." "It was history, I don't know much about this," Yibeltal said, almost as if to distance himself from what had happened in the past. "When they [Yibeltal and Daniel] started, things were already different," Haile commented.

Daniel, perhaps in response to the comments of these "old people," stated what *being Arada* meant to him: "Arada is drinking, chewing, going with women, fighting, dancing and the *farra* [literally, "country bumpkins"] were the ones who were not doing this life. The *farra* were the ones who were just working and saving. But you know what? We are the *farra*, we ended up having nothing, while those guys have a business. They are the *Arada* now." "If you have money, you don't have just to spend it as we do. You have to keep on going around, working and making more money," Yibeltal said. "I don't know about the future but I know that what you have to do is to go step by step." "Now young people want to work," Yibeltal concluded.

The quick cut and thrust among Yibeltal, Daniel, Haile, and Karremanz was one of many discussions I heard about the true nature of the *Arada*. As we saw in chapter 1, middle-class gentlemen argued that the *Arada* were artists and intellectuals, denying to thugs and hustlers the status of *Arada*. In chapter 2, we heard Haile and Ibrahim making the link between ideas of the *Arada* and models of toughness and smartness. In chapter 5, we saw how street hustlers drew a distinction between those who were *Arada* and smart enough to share and enjoy acts of friendships and *farra* who did not know how to behave and ultimately became targets of hustling and cheating. Daniel used the same terminology but to make a different point. For him, having been an *Arada* had not paid off, while those who had taken care and worked hard ended up being successful. At the end of the day, those who felt they were the smartest people in town ended up as fools and were left with nothing.

This shift in local understandings of *Arada* and the nature of smartness was more than an evaluation of where individual thugs and hustlers ended up. Remarks about *Arada* and *farra* were embedded in a wider discourse about poverty and economic growth on which government officials themselves drew when they praised "success stories" and blamed poor young people's lack of self-determination for the failure of small-scale enterprises (see chapter 4). This discourse had wide currency, far beyond the perimeters of government offices and an animated discussion in a *khat bet.*

Stories of poor people who had become rich through hard work and entrepreneurialism circulated widely in the inner city, suggesting to many that success was indeed a possibility. Concurrently, newspaper editorials, civics textbooks, and the expanding literature on self-help and entrepreneurship that dominated street newsstands all talked about success and provided formulas for achieving it. Life-skills training provided by NGOs and talk shows arranged by youth organizations focused on the virtues and attitudes of successful businessmen to imagine ways of engaging with and gaining access to the benefits of economic growth. Local business experts provided advice to those who were willing to attend their lectures, like the Genius College school of entrepreneurship established by Werotaw Bezabih Assefa in the heart of the inner city. On the gate of the school was the inscription: "Development is not by chance [*idil*], it is a matter of choice [*mirča*]," and "A poor man is not a man without money. He is a man without a dream." When I interviewed Werotaw, he presented himself as intending to be the richest man in Ethiopia so as to prove his determination to pursue his goals. His writings encouraged his readers to develop and achieve their dreams. Failure and blaming others were the first stumbling blocks to overcome. In the introduction to his book *Entrepreneurship: An Engine for Sustainable Growth, Development, Prosperity and Good Governance,* Werotaw emphasizes: "Blaming others for our personal failure is what non-achieving people often do. Failure doesn't require explanation. The world doesn't have time to listen to failure explanations. It has a lot of success stories to listen to" (Werotaw Bezabih Assefa 2010, 2).

Even though the majority of my informants and neighbors in the inner city could not afford to pay between 650 and 1,350 birr to attend one of Werotaw's courses, or were not so daring as to see themselves as the future richest men in Ethiopia, these narratives were effectively molding their aspirations for the future. Khazin, the young would-be entrepreneur whom we met in chapter 4, for instance, continued to cultivate his dream of becoming a businessman despite the failure of his cooperatives. Like him, the individuals from the "success stories" whom an NGO officer invited me to interview spoke of opening a small company and running their own businesses.

From this point of view, Daniel and Yibeltal's questioning of the smartness of the street *Arada* was more about embracing the ideal of the poor man who had become rich than about blaming thugs and hustlers for their failures. As we saw in chapter 6, street life fascinated young people in the inner city as a paradigm of enjoyment and coolness. Even if they did not manage to become rich, people like

Haile and Ibrahim continued to enjoy some form of recognition and respect in the inner city because of their past as a skillful hustler and a brave fighter, respectively. At the same time, though respected and celebrated, Daniel and Yibeltal, like many others in my field site, did not want to be street *Arada* for the rest of their lives. By reversing the distinction between *Arada* and *farra* and endorsing business-minded visions of success, they were trying to break with a "past" of smartness and bravery that had delivered nothing but the persistence of social exclusion and poverty.

The Time of the Bumpkins

While celebrating the deeds of the new *Arada*, a sense of frustration also imbued Daniel's words when he described himself as a *farra* in a context where *Arada* are rich and successful. In their conversations about *Arada* and *farra*, both Daniel and Yibeltal expressed worries that many young people in the inner city felt about the increasing disjuncture between a widening sense of the possible and actual opportunities to achieve aspirations. Disappointment and disillusionment spread in the inner city as quickly as expectations of success. This is even more revealing if we consider that Daniel and Yibeltal had achieved relative social improvement. They were engaged in a growing niche of the street economy, the business of minibus touts and the expanding private urban transport sector. Yet their opportunities to move up remained limited.

Like many other minibus touts and drivers, Daniel and Yibeltal believed that a first step in changing their lives was to collect enough money to buy a minibus. This was considered a feasible plan. They could then use their personal knowledge of the sector to find a good, hardworking, and trusted driver. Owning a minibus would give them a monthly income comparable to what Daniel earned as a queue-keeper, but which could be combined with another job. However, this plan was difficult to implement. Buying a secondhand minibus cost at least 130,000–160,000 birr (US$6,800–$8,500) in 2013 and 220,000 birr (US$10,500) in 2015. Even with a good salary of a few thousand birr a month, an individual would struggle to accumulate this amount.

A deep frustration emerged even more clearly in the words of Ibrahim and Haile. They, like many in this book, were worse off than Daniel and Yibeltal. They were older and were stuck in jobs that did not provide any prospects of social improvement. Besides, unlike Daniel and Yibeltal, they had witnessed firsthand the challenges hustlers encountered when they sought to become businessmen (see chapters 3 and 4). From Haile and Ibrahim, however, we can easily see that remarks about the *Arada* who had been eaten and the *farra* who had become *Arada* not only gave a voice to a sort of bland criticism emerging from deep frustration and disillusionment. By mobilizing the *Arada* and *farra* terminology to account for trajectories of economic success, people in my field site were, wittingly or unwittingly, also engaging in a very specific evaluation of the actions and trajectories of the city's and inner city's businesspeople.

As we saw in chapter 5, notions of *Arada* and *farra* were not only generic definitions of smartness and foolishness; they clearly distinguished between those who knew how to navigate the economies of transactions and interactions on the streets and those who did not know when was the moment to share, when there was an opportunity to make a few extra bucks, or when others were trying to rip them off. By using these categories, my informants were making a specific argument on the reasons why city and inner city businesspeople were both *farra* and *Arada*.

Businesspeople were *Arada*, not just because they worked hard but because, as Ibrahim himself admitted, they were good at cheating and hustling: "You see that shop? . . . [The owner] is fucking crazy, but he made money! He had a small retail shop. . . . He made some money and opened another small shop where he used to sell clothes and leather clothes. He burnt it and he got the money for the insurance. With the money that he got, he opened [another] shop . . . where he sells nice and expensive clothes. And you know what? [He] did it again. He burnt another shop he had opened meanwhile. Now, he has three shops. He is crazy!"

However, businesspeople were also *farra*, Ibrahim argued. What enabled them to become rich was ultimately a fundamental disengagement from the sociality of sharing and enjoyment that had long defined ideas and practices of *Arada-ness*: "People around here do not share anymore. When they get the money they just go away. . . . In the past, if you did not share with others, people did not like you. Now, if you have made your money and you just have for you, you are an *Arada*."

In chapter 3, I showed how connections and relations made the difference in opening opportunities for economic success, and in particular, a career as a businessman. Haile, Ibrahim, and many others were denied access to valuable resources and connections because business networks and communities operated in an exclusive fashion. Those who were able to pursue imagined trajectories of social improvement by taking advantage of their networks wittingly or unwittingly contributed to excluding or at least limiting the trajectories of others who did not belong to those networks. In this regard, the narrative of the *Arada* and *farra* was a critical commentary of the logic of the "relatives with relatives and donkey with ashes" explored in chapter 3. While the proverb voiced a sense of inevitability, the *Arada* and *farra* discourse emphasized that mere selfishness—not simply that "birds of a feather flock together"—limited access to opportunities of social improvement and that relations were made to become agents of exclusion.

Having said that, these remarks on the trajectories of businesspeople as selfish and cheaters did not always accurately describe the trajectories of individual businessmen. They were imbued with a romanticized vision of the street *Arada* who, as we saw in chapter 5, were themselves problematically embedded in a moral endorsement of the predatorial economy of hustling and cheating. As Ibrahim's comparison between "the past" and "now" reveals, his words were informed by a nostalgic celebration of the past, when people shared what they had with others and when "everything was cheap," as Haile put it, echoing Ibrahim. True, the cost of living in Addis Ababa had risen remarkably. And to some extent, many among my neighbors in the inner city would have agreed with Haile's assertion: "When you buy something for you, you don't have money for others." But as we saw earlier in the book, the past was not necessarily as idyllic as Haile and Ibrahim described when, as the former "remembered": "If we were in a [drinking] place, people were rushing to pay the bill for them and their friends."

Yet discussions of *Arada* and *farra* delivered something very specific: a moral assessment, or even an indictment, of the ethos of city and inner city businesspeople. This was a critique of the selfishness and greed of the new rich. This was a discourse on the city's new wealth as the outcome of skillful hustling and cheating, which the hustlers regarded as more harmful than their own sometimes predatory acts. Rich people's hustling was not embedded in the collective experience of scarcity and poverty that, in the eyes of my informants, justified even the most predatory street hustlers (see chapter 6). Rich people's cheating was different. It was tuned to an individualist accumulation of resources at the expense of others. If put in the position of a businessperson, a street hustler might do the same. But this eventually does not matter; as we saw in chapter 3, hustlers hardly felt they could become businessmen. Biased, openly nostalgic, partially informed, morally relativist, and possibly moved by a certain dose of envy, the narrative around *Arada* and *farra* was key to the ways my informants made sense of the sources of their exclusion. It was a counternarrative to the logic of the "relatives with relatives and donkey with ashes" that did not just exclude my informants; it limited their actual ability to pursue trajectories of social improvement.

Occult Economies

If selfishness accounted for the trajectories of personal enrichment of businesspeople in the inner city, it could not explain the wealth embodied in the highrise buildings in the business districts. Selfishness alone could not have produced

FIG. 7.2   A real estate venture in Addis Ababa © Marco Di Nunzio

the scale of the abundance those in the inner city saw materializing in the city's landscape. This was a level of wealth that my interlocutors could hardly imagine and quantify, and deemed to be fundamentally inexplicable in a country and city that have experienced poverty and abjection for decades or even centuries. I sought to comprehend the scale of this wealth by looking at the costs given in brochures for new real estate developments in the suburbs and in the business districts. Prices ranged from US$140,000–$430,000 for a villa in the suburbs, from US$150,000–$600,000 for an apartment or penthouse in a Chinese-built real estate development in the eastern part of the city that had already sold a large number of its units, and down to the more modestly priced US$30,000–$70,000 for an apartment in a building developed by a local contractor.

Hearing those figures, Haile told me, there was something else than mere self-ishness: "If you are rich, there is something behind you," moving his hands as if he were writing a question mark in the air. Haile's argument was that rich people mainly owed their wealth to their special relationship with either a *tanqway* or a *debtera*. *Tanqway* literally means "sorcerer" and is a generic term used to describe and stigmatize the activities of fortune-tellers and spirit mediums. *Debteras* are men with considerable religious knowledge, commonly linked to the Orthodox

Church, who are believed to engage in magic and deal with spirits, sometimes to heal their patients, sometimes to deceive (Mercier 1997, 44), and sometimes to serve their clients' desires.

Haile was not alone in his belief. Ibrahim and Mikias and many others presented similar accounts of the city's wealth. Gizachew and Fatima, for instance, like other "local businessmen" running small-scale commercial ventures, claimed that some rich people had prospered because of *tanqway*. Others were skeptical about this nexus between wealth, magic, and witchcraft but were ready to argue that whether magic worked or not, many people in the city turned to a *tanqway* or a *debtera* to fulfill their desires.

A few weeks after Haile described his views on the dubious origins of the wealth of Ethiopia's rich individuals, Asres, a former schoolteacher and book dealer, helped me map out the nuances of the discourses on wealth and magic. I met Asres for the first time when Haile and Ibrahim took me to the St. Giorghis church. "He was the school teacher of all of us in the *sefer* [neighborhood]," Ibrahim said when we saw him sitting on the church's steps.

"I did so many jobs. Then I became a book dealer because I read a lot of books," Asres said about himself. When prompted, he described his understanding of the work of *debtera* and *tanqway*: "*Tanqway* and *debtera* used to be priests, then they moved away from the Church. . . . Here, in Ethiopia people prefer to become rich through sorcery rather than working hard. . . . Ten per cent of the rich people become so by cheating [stealing, fraud] and cheating the government [corruption], ten per cent become rich by working hard and eighty per cent become so through a *tanqway*."

He proceeded to describe his take on the history of the *tanqway*:

> In the past if you wanted to go to a *tanqway*, you had to go to the rural areas. Now, *tanqway* have opened their offices in Addis Ababa.
> *Why?* [I asked]
> The Derg killed many sorcerers. Now, in capitalism, things are favourable for the *tanqway*.
> *Why?*
> In the rural area, people know each other and sometimes there is more than one *tanqway* in the village. One would work against the other and they would end up killing each other. Addis Ababa is a big city and there are so many people and there are plenty of customers. . . .
> *But why did they move to Addis Ababa?*
> Because after the Derg, people want to go to the *tanqway* and they understood this.

Why?

After the Derg, people want money and they need money. Everybody wants to be rich.

Asres might have erred in his description of the work of *tanqway* and *debtera*, as well as the nature of rich people's wealth. However, as Harald Aspen (2001) pointed out in his work on Ethiopia's northern highlands, the classifications of "spirits," magic, divination, and "witchcraft" in Ethiopia are often blurred. Laymen frequently have only vague ideas about the differences and content of terms, and even spiritual experts disagree. Nevertheless, such references to witchcraft and magic significantly affected how many people in my field site described the society they inhabited and made sense of their position in it.

The fact that people resort to witchcraft to understand the accumulation of wealth is not new to anthropologists. Drawing on literature going back to Evans Pritchard (1937), Jean Comaroff and John Comaroff (1999) argued that references to witchcraft, magic, and the occult often appear in situations of rapid social transformation, voicing both the "magical allure of making money from nothing" (Andrews 1997, cited in Comaroff and Comaroff 1999, 281) and the despair of those who are excluded from this fast, quasi-magical accumulation of wealth.

This twofold dimension of the discourses on witchcraft and wealth appeared in the words and experiences of my informants and neighbors in the inner city. That the riches of the high-rise buildings, luxury hotels, and shopping malls appeared in a relatively short time and seemingly from nothing fueled my informants' suspicions of the occult nature of the city's new wealth. Fast money is what people were believed to go for when they turned to *tanqway*, as an inner city woman in her forties told me: "The people who go to the *tanqway* are the ones who have *čaqquli* [those who are in a hurry]." The apparent speed of the accumulation of wealth clashed with the persistence of my informants' condition of poverty, and discourses on witchcraft, magic, and the occult enabled them to explain what they saw as fundamentally inexplicable. While rich people were seen to be quickly accumulating more and more wealth, high-rise buildings and luxury shopping malls remained far from what Haile, Ibrahim, Mikias, and many others felt they could actually achieve in a lifetime.

If the concerns behind my informants' references to witchcraft resonate with those in other ethnographic contexts within and beyond the African continent, the reasons why they understood wealth as the outcome of an involvement with the occult was specific and embedded in local understandings of the "visible" and "invisible" world, where spirits and magic are believed to operate. Unlike, say, Mbembe's findings in Cameroon (2001), my informants did not regard the visible and the invisible as mirroring each other. The invisible remained hidden, and the relations between what was visible and invisible were mediated by the specialist knowledge of the *tanqway* and the *debtera*. However, relating to the invisible was not only a matter of knowledge. The motives behind people's engagement with the invisible were often subjects of moral judgment. The invisible was a highly ambivalent domain: it was the domain of God and his inscrutable will, but also of spirits and human beings seeking to force, through magic, the course of events in order to satisfy their own desires.

If we dig into the literature and listen to my informants, we appreciate that local understandings of the invisible and the visible are embedded in the long-term influence of Islam and Orthodox Christianity on religiosity. For many among my informants, spirits were fundamentally "evil," and developing a relationship with them was a betrayal of one's allegiance to God, or even, potentially, a questioning of the oneness of God. This does not mean that religious experts like *debtera* were of no use. Their knowledge of spirits could be of some help, but only to exorcise spirits, not to forge an alliance with them (see also Mercier 1997).

This is, of course, only one version of the local understandings of the invisible and the work of spirits and spiritual experts that I encountered. For instance, while my informants emphasized that turning to the *tanqway* meant going away from God, a significant number of people sought help from a *tanqway* or a *bale-wuqabe*, an individual who has a special relationship with a spirit (*wuqabe*) and can ask it for assistance. For them, resorting to a *bale-wuqabe* was not a betrayal of their allegiance to God; it was no different from asking for the help of a saint to intercede with God. As an old woman put it, a *wuqabe* can make God listen.

Notably, making God listen was not done only to gain wealth and success. The old woman who spoke about *bale-wuqabe* was sitting with other women, including former and current sex workers. Many of them were clients and followers of a *bale-wuqabe*, reflecting how forging a relationship with spirits or those who are possessed by them has historically been a site for dealing with affliction and suffering, especially for marginalized women, in Ethiopia and in neighboring countries (Leiris 1958; Boddy 1989).

Haile, Ibrahim, Mikias, and many others among my informants knew that not only rich people but also poor people who remained poor resorted to *bale-wuqabe*. Moreover, their own disinclination to turn to a *tanqway* did not mean that they did not want to be rich or were not afflicted by a deep sense of despair like the women above. Refusing to engage with a *tanqway* was a way of counterbalancing their own "sins" (*hatiat*) with those committed by others—mainly, by rich people. In other words, my informants' straightforward stigmatization of those who resorted to a *tanqway* and their stated unequivocal allegiance to God were part of their wider attempts to define themselves as moral subjects who deserved His attention and help, even though as hustlers, thugs, and thieves they had committed deeds of which God would hardly approve.

Using witchcraft and the occult to describe the state of the society my informants lived in had, however, another implication. Sex workers established a moral ground for their wish for a better life through a syncretic understanding of the world of the spirits and the work of God. Former hustlers and thugs, like many others in the inner city, elaborated a sense of morality embedded, as Judith Butler might say (1997), in acts of denial and renunciation. By arguing that wealth was a product of witchcraft and by claiming a moral stand through their disengagement from the occult, they wittingly or unwittingly accepted their condition as those who were cut out of opportunities for social improvement. However, differently from what Butler argued, renunciation and denial were not celebrated as fundamental components of their sense of self and morality. My informants did not give up their desires. As we saw in chapter 6, smartness and enjoyment remained a valuable and meaningful way of living through marginality and exclusion because they enabled my informants to access a certain form of street abundance that they deeply enjoyed. Hence, in their critique of the occult sources of the city's wealth, as they saw them, my informants sought to shift the blame for their condition of marginality and social exclusion onto those rich people whose selfishness and immoral use of invisible forces actively limited poor people's access to opportunities for social improvement.

The Politics of the Fake

Politics and political affiliation with the ruling party was believed to be another key to unlocking opportunities for wealth and personal enrichment in Ethiopia. In the imaginations of many among my interlocutors, top politicians were hiding large amounts of wealth while the country's tycoons owed their success, properties, and luxurious lives to their intimate connections with the country's political elites. Recognizing the links between political connections with the country's leadership and wealth accumulation gave my interlocutors an explanation for otherwise inexplicable personal enrichment while reemphasizing the immorality of Ethiopia's rich and superrich.

This recognition did not just mold understandings of the underpinnings of wealth in Ethiopia. It also shaped understandings of politics. Politics was not the *political*, to put it in Hannah Arendt's (1958) terms—namely, a space for active disagreement and open-ended negotiation. In the experiences of my interlocutors, politics fulfilled a specific function: it imposed a regime of control and surveillance that effectively silenced dissent and unrest at the bottom while enabling political elites and affiliated businesspeople to accumulate large amounts of wealth and power at the top.

The regime of control of power and wealth this achieved, however, was not as effective as my informants were ready to argue. Without doubt, the centrality of the ruling party in guiding and leading Ethiopia's development had resulted in a business community dominated by a few very powerful and well-connected actors. The TPLF's own endowment fund, EFFORT (Endowment Fund for the Rehabilitation of Tigray), was one of the largest business conglomerates in the country, with a total value of over US$520 million in 2010 (Vaughan and Mesfin Gebremichael 2011). However, while the connection between politics and wealth in Ethiopia was widely recognized, the actual geographies of power and accumulation—how wealth is accumulated and by whom—remained difficult to discern and prove. Corruption cases provided a glimpse into the ways high-profile politicians, government officials, and businesspeople rubbed shoulders to dodge taxation or gain kickbacks from government contracts. Corruption scandals left the party's leadership untouched. However, the perception that such charges have been systematically used to eliminate political rivals within the ruling party and the business community (Paulos Milkias 2003) raised suspicions among ordinary citizens that much more was taking place behind the closed doors of party politics.

It is hard to gauge whether there were grounds for these suspicions. Nevertheless, their persistence produced understandings of power, politics, and wealth that shaped how people related to the state and its leadership. In particular, there was the perception that what people saw in documentaries on Ethiopia's achievements on television, read in government newspapers, and heard in the ruling party's meetings and rallies was not to be trusted. As with the occult economies discussed earlier, my interlocutors experienced politics through the relations between the visible and the invisible. What can be seen conceals that which cannot be seen: the visible creates a mystifying semblance that conceals what remains hidden and, importantly, really is. As one of my interlocutors put it: "Seeing is not believing."

Politics was thus seen as dressing the invisible in a mystifying set of narratives that concealed both what was experienced in the everyday, through the ordinary experiences of oppression, subjugation, and marginality discussed in chapter 4, and the hidden workings of power and wealth. My interlocutors were aware that they did not have the power to know what really went on behind the scenes, not because they lacked vision (cf. Newell 2012) but because they did not have access to the inner circles of the powerful. Nevertheless they recognized politics as "fake," as actively producing narratives, discourses, and expectations of improvement and collective development that their own condition of marginality and oppression taught them to distrust.

The recognition of politics as "fake" resonates with Achille Mbembe's description of the postcolony as a "regime of unreality" (1992, 8), namely in the ways power and the state institutionalize themselves through fantasies, projection, and deceptions that distort reality while celebrating power, the elites, their missions, and achievements. However, differently from what Achille Mbembe argued, my interlocutors did not internalize those fantasies and projections to reproduce them "in all the minor circumstances of daily life" (28). Fantasies, projections, and deceptions did not have the power to persuade. Instead, they had the power to be pervasive because they were embedded in the power of the sovereign to assert itself through the accomplishment of its own presence and its own acts. In other words, fantasies, projections, and deceptions were to be seen, heard, and read by my interlocutors not because they persuaded or achieved legitimation, but because they had the power to impose themselves as narratives, discourses, and signs defining what ought to be considered real and true.

In these circumstances, the only weapon that my interlocutors had was to simply not trust them or recognize them as "fake." But, for all their critique of the selfishness of the city's businesspeople and the occult wealth of the country's superrich, people in the inner city could not simple disengage from politics. My informants could claim a distance from the occult and immoral grounds of wealth because wealth did not populate their existence. Unlike wealth, politics, as we saw in chapter 4, was pervasive in their everyday lives. Disengaging was not, my informants felt, an option. Recognizing politics as "fake" was, in this regard, a way of navigating the imposition of politics and its narratives on their existence as well as a way of guarding a sense of self under the surface of what is *visible* to politics.

The experiences of the members of small-scale enterprises are paradigmatic in this regard. As "beneficiaries" of the ruling party's interventions, they were expected to support the party and campaign for it during elections. Participating in rallies and meetings, wearing EPRDF caps and watches, and singing party songs, however, were not necessarily expressions of support. For some, joining meetings and rallies was primarily a matter of appearances. After spending a few hours at the *kebelle* office, a member of a government-supported small-scale enterprise told me: "We were invited to join a meeting this morning but only some of us showed up. You know, it is not that important, but you have to show them that you are interested in what they say."

Another day, while shouting the name of the EPRDF and raising the arm on which he wore his EPRDF wristwatch to cheer on the speaker at an electoral campaign rally, he said in a whisper: "They are looking at me, I must do it; in this way, they will think I am one of them."

Being true to the "invisible" self under the facade of such performances of compliance and support was a matter of tuning one's performances to meet expectations without becoming directly complicit with the ruling party's structure of mobilization, surveillance, and control. My informants argued there was a difference between acting like a supporter and being an active member and part of the ruling party's politics of oppression and deception. A few days before the 2010 National Election, the man with the EPRDF wristwatch told me: "You know, in 2005, things were different. The election day was an *ammet bal* [a holiday or even Christmas]. Everybody was waiting for it. . . . Now we are *ruffiano*."

Ruffiano, in both Amharic and Italian, means "flatterer," "sycophant." *Ruffiano* were those like this man who played the role the ruling party expected him to play in order to keep his job in a government-supported small-scale enterprise. By defining himself as a *ruffiano*, he made sense of the transformation he himself had gone through. In 2005, he stayed away from the ruling party. Five years later, he was wearing EPRDF shirts and watches.

Ruffiano, however, were not all the same. Some, like the man above and others among my informants, only marginally benefited from performances of false compliance, obtaining low-paid poor-quality employment that only reinforced their condition of exclusion within a wider frame of political subjugation and control. Then, there were other *ruffiano* who were seen as gaining advantages from joining the ruling party's machinery and becoming active parts of the apparatus of control and mobilization. These were *ruffiano* who did not get just a means of getting by, but a salary and a career in the public sector or useful connections they could utilize to develop their own businesses. These individuals were described to me as having taken a "shortcut," bypassing others and pursuing improvement via active and direct involvement in the ruling party's politics.

Those who took the shortcut were often *kebelle* officials or loyal members of the ruling party who saw their advancement as the outcome of their active engagement in the administration of the community and the learning that comes with it. As Tesfay, the chairman of a youth office in inner city Addis Ababa put it: "You know, we work hard from Monday to Sunday without break, until late in the evening. The parking guys work only in the morning or in the afternoon, this is the same for the waiters. They get a small salary, but they also get tips." His colleague Habte, who, unlike Tesfay had business experience working in his family's small café, added: "With this experience at the *kebelle*, I learned so many things. I know that they are so many different kinds of people with which you have to deal with. I know how to behave and live with them. And I know the strategy and the aims of the ruling party. This surely help for my business in the future."

Some felt that direct involvement in the party's structure was big cheating and driven by mere selfishness. As a result, I observed, people like Tesfay and Habte were often regarded with contempt by their neighbors. The weight of suspicion in everyday interactions was an effective deterrent for many who might have been tempted by a career in the ruling party. Joining the ruling party was perceived to be significantly different from dissimulation. It meant selling oneself to the politics of the "fake" for personal advantage. Dissimulation, some believed, enabled people to gain extra means for survival while remaining loyal to an underlying and invisible dissent toward the party that continued to oppress them.

Performances of false compliance did not question power relationships in the inner city, however. Paradoxically, dissimulation strengthened the rule of the EPRDF at the bottom of urban society. Even though some of those involved in government programs did not support the ruling party, the fact that they behaved as they were expected to simply reproduced the rule of the EPRDF at the grassroots. Publicly acting as supporters of the ruling party in meetings and rallies contributed to a general perception of the pervasiveness of the ruling party's apparatus of control, surveillance, and mobilization in local communities.

While false compliance and dissimulation did not challenge the status quo, it had a deeper effect on politics. Acute *kebelle* officials like Teshome were aware of this. We met Teshome in chapter 4 while talking about the outcomes of entrepreneurship schemes in the inner city. I openly disagreed with his remarks about "drug addicts" and "cobblestones." Yet he was a skillful and dedicated administrator, and a careful observer of the context where he worked: "Look at our *kebelle*, EPRDF now counts 700 members but only a hundred people show up at the meetings, we sometimes cannot even trust our members. People are going to vote EPRDF because there is not strong opposition. It is not a matter of satisfaction [*fikir*, literally "love"]. It is a matter of lack of alternatives."

The lack of *fikir*, or, as we might put it, "consent," troubled *kebelle* officials like Teshome because it reminded them of the quality of the support that mobilization brought to the ruling party. This had very practical effects for the work of mobilization, even though the overall power of the ruling party was not questioned. In fact, Teshome and others among his colleagues were constantly worried that underlying antipathy toward the ruling party might affect the number of people who showed up for a meeting between residents and high government officials, or cause discrepancies between those who registered to vote and those who eventually showed up at the polls. The lack of *fikir* was thus a real danger for government officials because partial success in mobilization could be considered by their superiors as a sign of an inability to perform their political duties, and impede their movement up the ranks.

On a wider level, the lack of *fikir* and the pervasiveness of false compliance and dissimulation limited the capacity of the ruling party to achieve hegemony. Meetings and rallies, documentaries celebrating the history of the TPLF's guerrillas against the brutality of the Derg and the achievements of the EPRDF's government, billboards visualizing growth through Addis Ababa's high-rise buildings, and the new power plants across the country were not simply for the sake of deception. They reflected a genuine concern of the ruling party to convince the population of the good that its government was doing for the country. What spoiled this effort, however, was that acts of government at the bottom of urban society revolved around building an apparatus of political surveillance, control, and mobilization that made the ruling party, and its political and business leadership, the exclusive leader, holder, owner, and designer of the country's developmental dream. The persistence of dissent and antipathy was about the shortcomings of the development projects as well as the fact that the EPRDF's political leadership was accused of seizing the political and economic potential of the country.

For my interlocutors, dissimulation hid discontent and made domination recognizable behind its facade. By disguising this discontent, they mitigated the violence of political authoritarianism. By creating a distance between their performances of false compliance and what they believed was their "true self," they turned politics into a moral space with logics similar to those they saw in their hustling. For them, joining small-scale enterprises and the ranks of the mobilized population to have an extra means for getting by in a condition of enduring poverty and with the hope of shielding oneself from severe sentences was not to be blamed. Politics, like hustling, was *bammilo* (see chapter 5)—something you do to make do. It was an attempt to live through conditions of marginality, and not in contradiction with the claims that many made to themselves and others that in their hearts they strongly opposed the ruling party and its structures of oppression and mobilization. However, taking the shortcut, as some *ruffiano* were alleged to have done, was another matter. That was a conscious moral choice that some of my interlocutors actively despised. As a young woman and resident of the inner city told me: "It depends on your *hilinna* [literally, "conscience"]." It depends on whether you want to live believing in what you see or by seeing what you believe in.

Otherwise Engaged

Following Luc Boltanski and Eve Chiapello (2005), we might argue my informants' critique of inner city businesspeople, the city's wealth, and the ruling party's politics was an "artistic critique," in which the transformation of society was a "source of *disenchantment* and *inauthenticity*," as well as "*opportunism* and *egoism*" proving "destructive of social bonds and collective solidarity, especially of minimal solidarity between rich and poor" (37). Critiques of this kind are often nostalgic for either an imagined past or a utopian future (cf. Piot 2010). They are products of aesthetic contemplations or, as in the case of my informants, of moralistic quasi-philological disquisitions aimed at differentiating those who are smart (*Arada*) from those who are fools (*farra*).

Boltanski and Chiapello (2005) have argued that artistic critiques are often highly ineffective in bringing social change and are key in laying out the platforms and paradigms through which capitalism reforms its mechanisms of capital accumulation, deepening its penetration into everyday life and achieving legitimation. If we look at urban Ethiopia, processes of reform and readjustment have to some extent taken place. The government responded to the quest for employment underlying the riots of 2005 and made it a central site for the expansion of its apparatus of political control. In a similar way, Abiy Ahmed's plans for a more thorough liberalization of the economy followed an intense period of protests in the country demanding more political rights and economic opportunities. Nevertheless, critiques are not just absorbed during reforms and readjustments; they remain, emphasizing distance and malcontent. In the years that followed the 2005 riots and demonstrations, my informants confronted the pervasiveness of surveillance and the climate of suspicion it fostered, the failure of developmental programs, the normativity of discourses on entrepreneurship, the enduring of forms of social differentiation, the ambiguous celebration of individual success, and the tendency in the public discourse to blame poor people for their poverty, and they tried to distance themselves from it through their artistic, moralizing critique.

Whether this kind of critique can fuel a radical rethinking of political, economic, and social hierarchies is unclear. As James Ferguson (2006) argued, development programs' tendency to focus on purely technocratic understandings of growth and their sense of necessity might suggest that government and international development organizations are incapable of understanding and addressing claims and demands from below. However, the hustlers' artistic critique has been fertile terrain for the ways my informants sought to mitigate the effects of political authoritarianism and social exclusion on their sense of smartness and self-worth. Distancing themselves from prefigured visions of success and the immorality of the occult economies was not just about destruction and refusal. It was the first step toward being able to see the possibility of their life being otherwise and to imagine alternative paradigms for action and hope. The next chapter will show how a critique of what is there to be known and be seen was followed by an appreciation of the potentialities of the unknown, the uncertain, and the open-ended as the grounds for my interlocutors' attempts of being "for somewhere else and for something else" (Fanon [1952] 2008, 170).

EMBRACING UNCERTAINTY

"A Pass for Something Else"

"Being a guide is a pass for something else," said Fasil. He hoped to move up in the tourism business: first, by getting a mobile phone and printing business cards to capitalize on his wider networks; second, by developing a website for potential customers outside his networks. If he was successful, he might be able to buy a car that he could rent out to tourists for a good fee. If this did not work out, Fasil (and many of his fellow street tourist guides) believed, tourists might become "sponsors" who would send him money on a regular basis, or business partners who would help fund a career in the tourist business. Tourists might even become lovers and girlfriends who could help him get a visa and a flight to Europe or the United States.

Fasil's sense of progress was informed by the perception that some street tourist guides had successfully taken these steps. *Prof John*, the tourist guide we met in chapter 6 who acted like a gangster, for instance, was making good money, though he remained a hustler. *Mon Ami*, who earned his nickname because he had learned some useful pickup lines in French, had married a middle-aged woman and now lived in Poland. Gebre, another friend and a former street tourist guide, had done even better. He was married to a younger woman and was living in much richer London.

Fasil himself had been close to achieving his dreams when he met a Swiss woman in her mid-twenties in late 2009. He met her in the inner city and traveled with her across the country. They were soon in a relationship that continued after she returned to Europe. Before her departure, she and Fasil discussed the possibility of getting him a visa to Switzerland. Afterward, she sent money to help him get by. However, as the months passed and the momentum faded, Fasil realized that his chances of going to Europe were diminishing, and the relationship ended. Fasil continued hustling in the inner city until a few months before I returned to Addis Ababa for the third time in late 2014. A good friend of his, known as *Dr Dre* for his massive presence resembling the famous American rapper, told me that Fasil and many others had decided to return to their home regions. They had left Addis Ababa, but not as they hoped.

By 2014, not many street tourist guides were left hustling in the inner city. *Dr Dre* was among those who remained. He was in his late twenties and had previously worked in a barbershop and occasionally turned to showing tourists around to make some extra bucks and look for an opportunity to go abroad. For a short period, he had given up his job at the barbershop to work full time as a street tourist guide. He soon returned to his previous job when he was unable to make a living showing tourists around. In late 2014, the barbershop closed down, leaving him with no alternatives. He returned to hustling on the streets. Yet he remained better off than his fellow street tourist guides and could rely on a sister who had a job that paid little but could make rent on the small room the two shared.

Wolde, the young and inexperienced hustler we met in chapter 5, was also still in Addis Ababa but was hardly better off than before. As his friends and fellow tourist guides left, he found picking up tourists by himself difficult. By the time I met him again in December 2014, he was begging and sleeping on the streets. Going abroad or making it "big" in the tourism business had slipped away from his horizon of possibilities, and going home was not an option. The journey back to a home 500 kilometers from Addis Ababa cost money, and Wolde did not know how he could get it.

The one who made it was Sara. She was now living in Germany with a man she met by skillfully playing the game of love. Others among her friends and peers had made similar journeys, bearing witness to how players had more opportunities to succeed in a niche that street tourist guides also occupied—that of attempting to marry a foreigner who would take them away from the inner city. The reasons for this are many. First, the flow of male tourists looking for "adventures" is significantly greater than the number of female tourists cruising for local partners. Second and more importantly, players occupied a restricted niche within the wider economy of transactional and commercial sex in the inner city. Their access to hotel lounges depended on their friendships with porters and waitresses. Moreover, players rarely spent time in hotels by themselves. They clustered together and young women became players, with the most experienced players "adopting" the less experienced ones and introducing them to the game of love.

Sara herself had been following another friend who also now lived abroad. And while Sara was looking for a foreigner to marry, she also taught a less experienced player how to behave with tourists. This very personal relationship that players had among themselves restricted access of other young women to the game, limiting competition.

Even so, Sara was among the lucky few. Hustling was rarely a "pass for something else" for women involved in "sex work," whether as bar ladies, home prostitutes, or street girls. The customers who turned to these women usually paid low fees and few could act as gateways to social mobility. Moreover, even though some sex workers established a relationship with their usual customers, the transactional nature of their encounters limited their capacity to transform themselves into "stable partners" even if they did meet wealthy men.

One such woman who did not make it was Netsanet, who rented a room in Mikias's compound. She was in her late forties and had long been engaged in commercial sex. In the past, she had run a small drinking house where she received customers. Her long experience in the trade had enabled her to find a way into the city's luxury hotels. Yet this did not make her a player. She was much older than Sara, and her usual customers were older men who were unwilling to embark on a relationship that might have opened up an opportunity for Netsanet to emigrate. Hers was a job more than a game.

Netsanet was not well off but did better than many women with past and present involvement in commercial sex in the inner city. Some of the women her age received customers in drinking houses. Meanwhile, younger women in the trade, mainly street girls and bar ladies, were significantly constrained by the low prices their customers were willing to pay. Stories of beating and customers walking out without paying were not rare. Some young women turned to their male friends and lovers for care and protection and to extort payment from their customers. These young men were pejoratively called in the inner city *wend shermuta*, literally "male whore," since they lived off their partners' earnings. Some of these young men were loving and understanding. Others abused the women on whom they depended. For these unfortunate women, their trajectories in the inner city were the expression of the condition of exclusion they shared with other sex workers and a more dramatic experience of gender-based domination.

The Stubbornness of Hope

Mikias's house was the stage of many of my conversations with my informants. It often allowed two generations to be involved: the "old thugs," represented by Haile, Ibrahim, and Mikias, with their stories of the *yemot midib*, and the "young" parking guys. Mikias's place was not big, but around ten or eleven people often spent their afternoons here. The first time I stepped inside, there was an old couch, his bed, a small cabinet, and an old desk in the room. There were few pictures on the wall: a magazine cover saying "women's place is in the home," a photo of Haile Selassie, and an image of the Virgin Mary. On the green painted walls, Mikias and his guests had written a few sentences. These were mostly in English: "If you talk behind my back, you are in the right position to kiss my ass," "We are equally wise and equally foolish before God," "Zoom Sad," and "Alcohol is the best enemy of Mikias, but Zoom tells him to love his enemy." I asked Mikias what Zoom was. Zoom, Mikias told me, was God. God is Zoom, because he zooms into the lives of people and when he sees what people do, Zoom is sad. "He will see you drinking and doing other things, but God is patient."

When I returned to Addis Ababa in 2013 after two years away and stepped into Mikias's place, what I saw deeply saddened me. All the furniture was gone; just two old mattresses remained, on which the guests were sitting. Mikias himself sat on a small piece of cardboard. In one corner was a small pile of clothes and a pair of shoes. The floor was littered with *khat* twigs. The green paint on the wall was gone, along with all the sentences written on it. Now, there was only soulless white paint bearing the inscription, in huge black letters: "www .mikiaszoom.com."

A few months later, after I had left Addis Ababa, Mikias was diagnosed with tuberculosis. I went to visit him when I returned nearly a year later in 2014. Many of his guests had gone. They came to visit him once in a while, but not having people around allowed him to rest. Mikias looked very tired and somehow older, but other than that he looked fine. There were now a few pieces of furniture: a bed, an old desk, a small cabinet, and some shelves, where Mikias had put some kitchenware. He had been in the hospital for several months and was on medication for his condition. Thugs like Getachew Bongar and Mamush Kuchere had been killed by this disease, but Mikias had survived it. We talked about his plans for the future. He had gone on a three-month training course offered by the local government office to learn how to prepare fast food. *You are a chef*, I teased him. "Of course I am, but there are no jobs. I am not doing much with it." He was planning to attend another training course, this time on producing ceramic items for construction. It would be more useful, he reckoned. This could be the opportunity he had been waiting for to get a proper job after years and years of hustling. "You know, *tesfa alkorettem*," literally, "I did not cut hope."

FIG. 8.1 Mikias's house © Marco Di Nunzio

Life Part Two

What is life about? When I posed this question to acquaintances and neighbors, sometimes to break the silence over coffee, I received standardized answers, perhaps triggered by the fact that I broke a very relaxing silence with such an awkward question. Among the answers I had received, one was particularly revealing: *rase taktaw m'alef*, "leaving, having given your place to another."

As I replaced my awkward questions about the meaning of life with a request to explain the sense of the phrase *rase taktaw m'alef*, my unfortunate interlocutors agreed that the expression could be used in different contexts, but mainly on a personal level. It meant to leave after having helped your offspring grow. Gizachew, the video house manager whom we met in chapter 3, agreed with this saying. He had a stable business that allowed him to support himself, his partner Fatima, and their young daughter.

Haile and Ibrahim also agreed with this idea, though their own personal lives were much more complicated. Ibrahim, for instance, had been in a long-term relationship with someone he described as the most wonderful woman he had ever met and confessed he believed he still loved. This relationship was during the years after the end of the *yemot midib* when Ibrahim attempted to change his life and opened his shoe shop. What happened afterward, with the failure of the shop and Ibrahim's return to street life full time, was made heavier by the gradual deterioration of the relationship between Ibrahim and his partner, who had by then bore him a son. Over the following years Ibrahim had been troubled both by the idea of having a child he was unable to care for and by the love he still felt for his ex. During the time I was in Addis Ababa, Ibrahim had tried a couple of times to mend his relationship, and his ex was often willing. But the fact that he could not prove himself to be on a track of social improvement still bothered Ibrahim and affected the relationship.

Haile's son was a year older than Ibrahim's son. Haile nurtured his sense of fatherhood through his ongoing attempts to care for his child and to make sure that the boy would not have the same life Haile had lived. His relationship with his wife, however, was not easy. The hardships they faced and the differences in their lifestyles eventually ended the relationship. Haile's son often spent time with Haile's mother, Wubit. When Haile moved into a small room that had space for only a single bed, his son moved permanently to Wubit's. Though he struggled to keep his promise to give his son a life that was significantly different from his own, Haile was determined to do so. As he told me, "This is my life part two, it is very different from before. You will see when you have a child."

Embracing Uncertainty

This chapter examines the grounds on which Haile and Ibrahim but also Mikias, Fasil, *Dr Dre*, Netsanet, Sara, and many others in the inner city established the possibility of action and hope in the face of the persistence of their condition of marginality, exclusion, and subjugation. In the previous chapter, we discussed how people in the inner city elaborated a harsh critique of the logics of power, success, and wealth that marginalized them. The moral indictment of greed, selfishness, the occult nature of the country's wealth, and the fakeness of politics enabled them to distance themselves from the sources of their predicament. However, such a critique can be potentially immobilizing or, rather, lead to a recognition of the inevitability of subjugation and oppression and the impossibility of action and hope. As Achille Mbembe famously wrote, the understanding of politics as a site of dissimulation and false compliance—or I might add, the understanding of wealth and success as a site of immoral and occult practice—results in a "mutual zombification" of the powerful and the weak: "this zombification meant that each robbed the other of their vitality and has left them both impotent" (1992, 4). On the streets of the inner city, the heaviness of the constraints imposed on my interlocutors' action and the sense of inevitability that pervaded experiences of subjugation and exclusion were often so overwhelming that immobility, self-destruction, or even death appeared inevitable or even desirable. Some tragically succumbed to this. Those who survived and endured did not have an easy life. The *act of living* remained a journey through pain and anxiety and a restless succession of experiences and possible lives that embodies the stubbornness of the search for something better, while, however, bearing the risk (as we saw in chapter 3) of one's efforts to achieve social improvement going nowhere.

The protagonists and coprotagonists of this book sought to navigate pain, anxiety, and the endurance of oppression and subjugation through their active search for being something other than their constraints. In previous chapters I discussed how street life and enjoyment constituted ways of living meaningfully through marginality and exclusion. However, enjoyment and street life were not concerned with delivering change or even transcending oppression. They consisted of ways of living *within* subjugation. In this chapter I show how an appreciation of the potentialities of the unknown and the uncertain constituted the grounds for seeing the possibility of change—namely, by crafting the *act of living* into a site of open-endedness and reversibility.

Expanding on the pragmatist philosopher John Dewey, the anthropologist Susan Reynolds Whyte argued that uncertainty is inherent in the ways people act and live through existence. Uncertainty pertains to our ability to know or even to "predict the outcome of events" (Whyte 2009, 213). Such a condition of being able to know what is going to be next has been described as a predicament and a condition of risk and vulnerability (Whyte 2009; Beck 1992). For my interlocutors, however, uncertainty was not a concern. What was known was often bleak and overwhelmingly distressing because it did not give them grounds for imagining a better life. Pain, anxiety, and madness were interpreted by my interlocutors as a result of people's potential obsession with making sense of what they saw, knew, and experienced. Instead, the fact that they could not know what was next and that life was uncertain, indeterminate, and unpredictable enabled them to think of their lives as open-ended and of their condition of marginality as neither final nor irreversible.

In other words, the uncertainty of living and existence yielded the possibility of change. As we will see, Haile, Ibrahim, Mikias, and many others among my informants and friends in the inner city not only valued uncertainty as a ground for social practice and hope; they embraced it. This certainly did not eradicate the logics of exclusion, oppression, and domination that framed their existence. Yet it provided a way of grounding actions and hopes in the face of all the challenges they encountered. Embracing uncertainty reinstated their ability to act and hope.

Haile and Ibrahim's appreciation of uncertainty resonates with what the philosophers Dewey (1930) and Bloch (1976) argued about the productivity of indeterminacy. That the future is unknown makes it indeterminate and potentially changeable. However, this by itself is often not enough to inspire a sense of possibility, especially in contexts of exclusion and marginality. Ethnographies on subjectivity and marginality on the continent and beyond have shown that, despite the enormous potentialities of an indeterminate future, deep anxieties and worries still arise (Weiss 2009; Scheper-Hughes 1993; Biehl 2013). As Miyazaki (2004) argued in his ethnographic study of knowledge in Fiji, this is fundamentally a matter of reversing philosophers' assumption that the indeterminate and uncertain intrinsically contain the seeds of possibility. The productivity of indeterminacy is not a given. Rather, it is seeing and appreciating the potentialities of indeterminacy that makes uncertainty productive, and this is an existential achievement that people pursue with the means available to them. My informants "embraced uncertainty" as an attempt to achieve indeterminacy. Yet they were not simply capitalizing on a generic belief that what has not been could yet come to be in an unknown future. They were tuning their social practice and daily life into a "mode" of existence that emphasized unlocking the potentialities of the present as a site of existence and action.

The rest of this chapter examines how and why marginalized young men embraced uncertainty in the different domains of their existence. I begin by making a distinction between a future imagined as the horizon of desired social goals and one that is conceptualized as open-ended. These initial methodological remarks set the scene for an exploration of how and why my informants embraced uncertainty. I trace how my informants came to embrace uncertainty as a mode of existence and social practice while dealing with cultural notions and moral and existential concerns revolving around time, age, and chance.

Present and Future

Uncertainty is about our inability to know what will be next, both immediately and in the long term. Thus, embracing uncertainty consists of a particular way of experiencing the present and imagining the future. In anthropology, there has been an increasing concern with the study of the future and its imagination. For Arjun Appadurai (2013), imaginations of the future are a platform for the elaboration of ideas of the good life. My informants nurtured particular visions of the good life, like the one typified by the high-rise steel-and-glass buildings dotting Addis Ababa's landscape. However, their search for grounds of action and hope in the face of marginality and subjugation was not linked to the imagination of the good life. They did dream about wealth and success, but they did not spend much time thinking about what their lives could be. In a context where abundance and wealth were unreachable and inexplicable (see chapter 7), visions of the good life were rarely imagined as actual plans to pursue in the present and the future. The possibility of achieving a better life in the future, the protagonists and coprotagonists of this book understood, was dependent on chances, not dreams. In Amharic, *idil* means "chance" or, better, a "stroke of luck." Before you get a chance, my interlocutors argued, you do not know what the future will look like. When you get one, you start to know where your life could be heading. Thus, my informants were not concerned with figuring out what the future would look like, but with exposing themselves to the possibility of getting a chance.

This focus on chances rather than dreams embodies a certain understanding of the relations between present and future as well as hope and expectation that are central to why the protagonists of this book embraced uncertainty. First, if we take the future as the embodiment of the good life, we inevitably find a disconnect between the present and the future, and a need to insert something in the middle: the steps needed to reach that imagined horizon of the good life. This is not an issue if one can rely on resources and connections to fulfill one's desires. However, if the imagined future does not materialize, the present becomes the site of a sense of failure and despair, the limbo of unfulfilled promises. This vision of the present is fundamentally immobilizing, yielding the impossibility of action and hope because it is doomed by the inevitable disjuncture between what could be in the future and what it is in the present. Instead, taking the future as open-ended, as my informants did, the present and the future are imagined as fundamentally interconnected, unleashing the possibility of action and hope. The future is seen as emerging from the present, shaped by the contingency and unpredictability of life because only by living in the present and navigating the ramifications of the immediate can one be in a position to shape a potential future (see also Bledsoe 2002; Cole 2010; Pedersen 2012; Vigh 2006; Whyte 2009).

Second, there is a fundamental difference between "hope" and "social expectation." The terms are related, but their precise meanings differ significantly. A social expectation is a prefigured vision of a future that implies a sense of entitlement: we feel we are owed something. For instance, educated young people in urban Ethiopia who prefer to stay unemployed instead of taking jobs in the informal sector not only desire to be employed in the public sector but feel entitled to it because of their educational backgrounds (Mains 2012a). Hope works differently. Crapanzano (2004) pointed out that hoping consists of recognizing that factors outside our control limit what we can do. Miyazaki (2004) went further, arguing that hope is a way through which we reorient our knowledge and, potentially, readjust our action while facing our limits vis-à-vis indeterminacy and unpredictability. In other words, hoping is both an expression of our limits and a method of dealing with them. In Addis Ababa's inner city, embracing uncertainty was the existential toolkit that enabled my informants to hope, or rather, see their lives through the lens of the possible—or as Whyte (1997, 2002) would put it, the "subjunctive." They did so because their condition of marginality did not give them much room to "expect" anything other than the continuation of their exclusion and subjugation—when you do not have much, my informants taught me, it does not make sense to wait for something to come up. "You have to move, go around," as Abiy, the physics graduate we met in chapter 3, said; you have to rework the fringes of the real with a restless sense of possibility.

Appreciating the present and the future as interconnected and pursuing hope as a way of reinstating the possibility of action vis-à-vis subjugation constituted the existential grounds for embracing uncertainty. In what follows I explore how embracing uncertainty became the method, the mode of existence, and the paradigm of social practice that the protagonists and coprotagonists of this book believed could put them in the position of benefiting from the workings of hope—namely, by getting a chance and achieving open-endedness both in the present and in the future. I begin by examining how my informants managed their fundamental worries about the irreversibility of their condition of poverty and exclusion. Next, I focus on the concept of "having time," key to my informants' ability to embrace uncertainty. Diverging from the broader literature on youth and marginality in Africa, I show how being young, or "still young," was not perceived as a serious concern. Indeed, claiming to be young allowed my informants to think they still had time to change their lives. I then examine how embracing uncertainty is embedded in a moral terrain. I show how my informants juggled with a crucial notion in their imagination of the unpredictable: *idil*, a "stroke of luck." *Idil* is a religious concept, meaning a gift of God. The centrality of this notion in the lives of my informants, both Muslim and Orthodox Christian, implied that they understood the indeterminacy of life in cosmological terms, linked to the inscrutable will of God. It also had another implication: *idil* gave a moral dimension to the ways my informants' social navigation of poverty and marginality affected their relations with God and thus the possibility of getting a chance through Him. Embracing uncertainty was a means of making sense, in moral terms, of the fact that getting by in Addis Ababa's inner city sometimes involved cheating and stealing—which, as my interlocutors were aware, would not have made God very happy.

Dealing with worries about one's inability to improve one's life, claiming to have time, and juggling with moral concerns constituted the major ways through which my informants embraced uncertainty as a mode of existence. Yet, as the last ethnographic section of this chapter shows, embracing uncertainty was also a paradigm of social practice, allowing my informants to expose themselves to the possibility of getting a chance. My informants were aware that being able to deal with existential, cultural, and moral concerns was not enough to get a chance. Only by actively inhabiting the contingency and unpredictability of life, or, as they said, by moving around, could they steer their lives toward a potential future away from marginality and exclusion.

"I Like My Brain"

Mikias described how he saw his own and his friends' lives: "Look at us. Our life is always the same, we chew [*khat*], we play, we drink, we are prisoners . . . legal prisoners." He did not mean that they had broken the law, of course, but that they were unable to have a life that was different from the past. The experience of living a life without potential for change was often a cause of distress. For instance, after a day of chasing tourists, looking for ways of getting by, Wolde, the street tourist guide, complained to me: "I got depression. All the days are always the same. . . . Marco, you are having a great opportunity. You are doing a research and I know that you will make it. I don't know about me, what I will do in the future. All days are always the same, I wish to get one opportunity, only one."

Stress, worry, concern, distress, pressure, anguish, and disturbance in Amharic is *č'inqet*, while *tečenneqe* means to "have anxiety, be in difficulty, be under stress, be in great straits, show concern, be solicitous, worry, feel uneasy, take great pains" (Leslau 2005, 239). In his ethnography of educated unemployed youth in Jimma, a city in southern Ethiopia, Mains (2012a) compared his informants' experience of *č'inqet* to what Weiss described as the "too much thinking" of marginalized young men in Arusha (2009). For these young men, these authors pointed out, stress and anxieties were active forms of thinking. By worrying and experiencing anxiety, young people work through the circumstances of their existence (Weiss 2009, 114). Ibrahim and Haile, like many others in Addis Ababa's inner city, worried. In doing so, they recognized that, despite the multiple engagements that constituted their lives, they had not managed to break from the oppressive routine represented by the everyday reproduction of their condition of marginality and exclusion: "You have *č'inqet* when you always do the same thing and you would do something different. For instance, I wake up, I have my breakfast and, then, I do my work, always the same. I have *č'inqet* for this reason."

At the same time, they were aware that living a life through stress and anxiety was an overwhelming existential experience that might have taken them toward self-destruction: the ultimate denial of their ability to act and hope. As Haile told me: "Ninety per cent of my friends, guys of my age have died. The reason why they died is because they did not survive the tension, they were not happy. . . . Some of them just started to drink too much and died because of this."

When I was in the field, people interpreted Abel's gradual descent into madness as a consequence of *č'inqet*. Abel was one of the youngest street tourist guides in my field site and a good friend of both Fasil and Wolde. He used to smoke marijuana (*ganja*), and some of his friends thought this was no help to him. You have to keep it real when things are difficult, and *ganja* is not good because it makes you think, said Fasil. Because of his stress and anxiety, Fasil said, Abel insulted a policeman on the street. He was taken to prison, where he was beaten for days. When he got out, he was a different person. He would not eat; he just smoked and behaved crazily. "Now everybody thinks he is crazy. Abel tries to say and show others that he is not crazy and tries to behave normally. This is the way you get crazier and crazier," Fasil told me. Things got worse day by day, until Fasil and his other friends managed to get him into the Maria Theresa hospital.

At the end of September 2010, the death of Fantahun came as a huge shock to many street tourist guides. Fantahun was in his mid-twenties and, unlike many other tourist guides, had grown up in Addis Ababa. He spoke very good French that he had learned at the Alliance Française in Addis. Many of his friends and acquaintances knew that he was a heavy drinker and that he should be careful, but he was not. He kept drinking *arakie* (a very strong local brandy), and, for this reason many thought, he died. His death was taken to be a consequence of *č'inqet*. Abebe, another street tourist guide, and *Dr Dre*, the part-time barber and hustler, made an appointment with me the day after Fantahun's death to go to his *lekso* (funeral). They did not show up. Abebe spent the whole day chewing *khat*, and *Dr Dre* told me he was busy working. When I met *Dr Dre* in the evening, we talked a bit about Fantahun. After a few minutes, he excused himself. "Marco, I have to go, I need a beer, I have *č'inqet*," he said, and went away.

Friends who had died or gone mad were the most dramatic reminder of the potential consequences of too much thinking. People created ways of living through anxiety about the irreversibility of their condition of poverty, and each had his own solution. Ibrahim, for instance, appealed to his ability to forget: "It is nice that you think about what you have to do, but don't do it much. People get crazy for much thinking. I like my brain, it is incredible, I can forget things, this makes things easier."

Haile emphasized the importance of being happy while dealing with hardship: "You know, when I was in prison, or running away to Kenya or fighting on the Eritrean border, it was hard, but I was happy."

Both relied on their ability to keep the noise of their thoughts low while tuning into the appreciation of what they could do with the materials that life in the here and now could offer. From this existential perspective, Ibrahim was ready to admit, worrying could be a good thing "because it pushes you to do something new." Or similarly: "Having *č'iggir* [problems] is good if you know how to deal with them."

Forgetting, being happy, exercising one's capacity to deal with problems, I argue, were components of a form of social reflexivity, or a discipline of the self that was grounded in the recognition that we are thrown into a world without control of the circumstances of our existence, as Michael Jackson (1989, 2005) reminded us in his anthropological writings, echoing Heidegger. For my informants, the existential choice was not "to be" or "not to be" but "to do something" or "to do nothing." Being in the world or slipping away from it through madness or death was perceived to be dependent on this dilemma. However, as we will see, this existential struggle was played out not by choosing whether to do something but by dealing with issues concerning time, morality, and the unpredictability of social life. These were terrains where embracing uncertainty became a viable mode of existence and social practice.

"Age Is Just a Number"

For my informants, the problem of "doing something" was concerned not only with how to approach the repetitiveness of everyday life but also with figuring out how this experience of the present could open up opportunities in the future. This was a problem of time, or rather, of having time. It involved how people conceptualized the unfolding of their life trajectories and, in particular, their age.

I was sitting in Mikias's house, talking about the past and trying to reconstruct the history of street groups and tough men. I wanted my informants to be more precise with chronologies, and asked Mikias, Ibrahim, and Haile to tell me their ages. I soon realized that telling me their ages in front of others in the room might cause embarrassment. To break the silence, I openly declared my own age at the time: twenty-six. Hakimu, a young engineer and Mikias's neighbor, followed: "Twenty-five!" To avoid doing the same, Ibrahim relied on my anthropological interest in the reasons why people do what they do. "I don't know why Ethiopians have a problem with saying their age," he observed. He continued: "There is a proverb in Ethiopia that says 'Never ask their age of women and their salary of men.'" *But you are not women!* I cried out. Ibrahim had his theory: "People don't want to retire, don't want their bosses to get rid of them. If they know that they are old, they would kick them out." Netsanet, the middle-aged woman living in Mikias's compound, had a similar theory: "If the government knew their age, they would not be able to enter into training or even do the jobs that they do!" Ibrahim replied to Netsanet: "What is age—it is just a number." Hakimu joined the conversation, "Age is not a factor here as it is for the *faranjii* [foreigner]." So I asked people in the room, *But are you afraid of being old?* "I don't like to be old, do you?" Mikias asked. Ibrahim retorted: "I don't want to be old. See, I am hanging out with all those kids, I am working with them. I hang out, I drink, I am still young. Then, look, when you are thirty, you want to have your own house, a good job, you want to marry a woman, have children and settle down. Then, the other stage is when you are fifty. You begin to worry about your health. Now, we are young, when we have something, we will say 'I don't care, tomorrow it will go away.' When you are fifty, you want to see the doctor straightaway!"

In saying that he did not want to be old, Ibrahim was comparing his potential life as an old man to that of his father and other old men in his neighborhood. Many among the interlocutors in my field site, in fact, thought that their fathers' jobs were far from desirable. One young man in a government employment program, for instance, said that the typical work of a father was that of a guard in a shop, earning no more than 300 birr (US$16) per month. This was considered insufficient to support a family, so other members, sometimes including children, would have to contribute to the household income. Others complained that their fathers did not work enough and that their lack of *yesera fikir* (dedication to work) was the reason for their poverty. As we saw in chapter 1, Ibrahim respected his father's social trajectory of rural-urban migration, but recognized that his old man's job did not advance his family. "He killed his age working there," Ibrahim said, referring to the pastry shop where his father had worked for more than forty years. "Some of his friends left the place and opened their own pastry shops. Now they are rich."

The comparison between their life trajectories and those of their parents and other older people in the neighborhood suggested to Ibrahim, Haile, and many others in the inner city that becoming an "adult" did not correspond to an improvement in their lives. For them, improvement, or even success, did not necessarily mean something specific. It was a generic and relative notion of success, and mainly consisted of being able to afford a better standard of life: "If you bought a car or a house"—something few of my informants could manage— "people will say that you are successful," Haile reckoned. By saying they did not want to be old, my informants were expressing their awareness of the fact that old people were not just poor; they were mired in irreversible poverty because their time had passed. Old age, not youth, as the literature on young people in the African continent has argued, was a condition of "social death" and crisis (cf. Vigh 2006; Cruise O'Brien 1996). Therefore, Ibrahim and his friends did not see "being young," or rather, "being still young," as a problem. What concerned them was the eventuality of becoming "poor old men." By hiding their real age, claiming to be "still young," Ibrahim and Mikias were engaging in a particular understanding of "youth" not as a stage of life but as the period of existence when individuals have time to change their lives and, more importantly, to push away the no-turning point of a predictable life in a condition of permanent poverty.

Having time and claiming to be "still young" were ways of living in the immediate while looking toward an unknown future that could still be realized. Things *could* change if one has time, my informants felt. While Ibrahim's father did not seize the opportunities to improve his life, the old man's friends somehow had managed to do so. Similarly, as Ibrahim and his friends were struggling with their inability to change their lives, the Ethiopian economy was booming and Addis Ababa was witnessing a dramatic transformation. The difference between these trajectories of change of others and the ones that they directly experienced revealed the constraints that the condition of exclusion imposed on their action. This was the very essence of their worries. The fact that things did change suggested to them that there were still opportunities out there, despite their inability to grasp them in the immediate term. Claiming to be "still young" enabled them to think of themselves as potential recipients of one of these opportunities: if one has time, the future may be shaped by how one lives the present. As Pedersen observes in his ethnography of dispossessed men in Mongolia, focusing on the present is not a denial of time but "involves an exalted awareness of the virtual potentials in the present" (2012, 145). In the next sections I show that such an awareness of the potentialities of time and the present gained further strength as my informants built meaningful relations with God, the ultimate dispenser of chances, and exposed themselves to the productivity of the unpredictable through their social practice.

The Morality of Chance

Not knowing what was going to be next, coupled with a belief that there was still time to steer the unpredictability of the future, was a reason to have hope. What my informants hoped for was a change, though how they wanted their lives to change was left unspecified. To appreciate how this could be, we need to go deeper into my informants' imagination of the unpredictable and, in particular, the way their understanding of chance (*idil*) informed their appreciation of uncertainty. For them, a chance, or rather, getting a chance, stood at the junction of the lives they had lived in the past, the contingency of the present, and the indeterminacy of the future. A chance is a "stroke of fortune": an event, or a series of events, that is unpredictable, but when it happens will take life in an unexpected direction. Holding this particular understanding of the unfolding of life, the protagonists of this book turned to the future, not looking for a specific and well-defined form of success but for a chance that might take them away from their condition of poverty and exclusion.

While the ideas of success and "change" are unspecified and vague, the notion of chance is grounded in a deep configuration of meanings, revolving around relations with God and morality. For many Ethiopians, a chance is a gift from God and dependent on his inscrutable will (Messay Kebedde 1999). Hence, the unpredictability of existence is an expression of the inscrutability of God and the fact that what will happen, "only God knows," as Ibrahim, Haile, and many others in inner city Addis Ababa often repeated. Yet this does not mean that individuals are powerless to change their lives. My informants believed that what they could do was to cultivate a good relationship with God: by signaling their loyalty to Him with prayers and religious acts and by showing, through good conduct, to be worthy of God's goodwill. In doing so, as the philosopher Messay Kebedde (1999) would suggest, they were not looking for evidence of predestination but to gain God's favor exactly because, they believed, God's will can change. In fact, the place that individuals occupy in His plans is never final, since arrogance (*tigab*), on the one hand, or a quest for God's forgiveness, on the other, could result in a change in God's favor and, hence, one's destiny.

Gaining God's favor, my informants knew, was not easy amid all the challenges of life. Haile, Ibrahim, and many others in their circle of friends and contemporaries had past and, sometimes, present involvement in the illegal street economy.

They had stolen, cheated, and hustled, and this, they were aware, was not something they could be proud of in front of God. How could they reconcile their bad conduct with their attempts to gain the favor of God, the dispenser of chances? One way was to cultivate a good relation with God through religious acts. Haile and Mikias, both Orthodox Christians, often went to church early in the morning, to ask for God's favor or just to start their day. Ibrahim was Muslim, or as he defined himself during one of our first meetings, a "plastic Muslim" who knew more about Orthodox Christianity than his own religion. Over the time I knew him, Ibrahim became increasingly committed to learning about Islam while continuing to read the Bible. When I returned to Addis Ababa in 2013, he had begun going to a religious school not far from his house to study the Koran a couple of times a week.

On top of their commitments to religious life, my informants also turned to an exercise of moral reflexivity to situate their acts in a more broadly based judgment on their conduct. The conversations I had with them about how they evaluated their deeds echoed what philosophers have debated about moral luck—whether or not what people do in situations outside their control can be an object of moral judgment (Williams 1993; Nagel 1993; Riescher 1993). For my informants, their bad acts were a result of the contingencies of their lives, and as such, they were not subject to clear moral judgment. They did not choose to be poor, and, as we saw in chapter 5, they believed that when you are poor you do what you need to do in order to get by.

Gabriel, a parking guy and a friend of Ibrahim's, helped me understand why, for example, stealing could be morally acceptable. *What did you feel when you did something bad, like stealing?* I asked. "People don't usually always think about God, it comes when you do something wrong. When you do something wrong, you feel something. It is called *şäşät.*"

Şäşät is "repentance, regret, remorse, qualm, sorrow" (Leslau 2005, 243), and, as Gabriel explained to me, it is different from a sin, *hatiat.*

> It is different. If you do *şäşät*, you would say sorry to God and He will forgive you. *Hatiat* is when you don't feel any *şäşät.* Then, it is *hatiat.*
>
> [I asked:] *What about if you, after the* şäşät, *keep on doing* čebu [robbery by hitting the victim on the neck] *and stealing, would God accept your* şäşät *again?*
>
> Yes, God is not merciless. He would understand and forgive you. It is life, if you don't have money and a job, what else can you do?

Stealing, Gabriel admitted, was wrong, but not necessarily morally condemnable because of the circumstances in which it was usually committed. In this context, if you are regretful, God might forgive you since, my informants reckoned, this kind of bad deed was driven by the contingencies of their lives. "I was stealing, doing things, but He [Allah] knew that it was not in my heart and He forgave me," Ibrahim said.

This belief in God's forgiveness for stealing, however, was not necessarily extended to what my informants judged more serious sins, such as killing someone or getting rich through the help of a *tanqway* (fortune-teller or spirit medium) or a *debtera* (expert in magic and spirits) (see chapter 7). Unlike stealing, murder was perceived to be very difficult to forgive on the basis of the circumstances in which the act was committed. Ibrahim argued: "Stealing small things to eat is not a big deal, whereas killing someone is a big one and God cares about this." Becoming rich through magic was even worse than killing because, Ibrahim reckoned, "going to the *tanqway* means going away from God." Relying on magic to get a chance is "big cheating," as Ibrahim put it—a fundamental betrayal of God's will, an arrogant offense to God. Being poor was not a choice, but becoming rich through magic, Ibrahim felt, certainly was: "God does not care if you are rich or poor. . . . Did God create the money? God does not care about these things of man, it is something among men, and God does not care about this. He gave us some law that we have to respect, but there is big cheating and small cheating."

Hence, he concluded, "the most important things is to be afraid of God."

In chapter 7 we saw how emphasizing the distinction between the small hustling of the poor and the big cheating of the rich was central to the way people in the inner city made sense of economic inequalities and questioned the moral authenticity and legitimacy of wealth, power, and success. Here, we see how such a distinction between big and small cheating was central to the ways they claimed a moral status as individuals who could exercise a clear judgment between what they could do and what they should not do in the face of marginality and oppression (Fassin 2012; Das 2012). This was a central matter that concerned the possibility of gaining God's favor and, importantly, as Mikias pointed out, the very fact of staying alive, the ultimate requirement of being able to enjoy a chance at some point in the future: "There is something wrong with rich people. Look we are poor, but we are healthy and we don't have health problems. The rich are always sick! . . . You know, we Ethiopians we can do everything, we all know about magic and how to get money. But we don't do it! Because we believe in God, we eat, we are healthy because of Him."

By recognizing the limits of their action, or rather, by arguing that they did not have control of the circumstances of their lives, my informants thought of themselves as moral subjects who could rightfully claim a chance from God. At the same time, they were aware that they still had work to do. On the religious side, feelings of regret and a certain level of commitment to religious life were considered central to cultivating a good relationship with God. On the level of their experience, thinking of themselves as good people in front of God opened up to them a sense of the possible; but, as we will see in the following section, being able to get that chance was fundamentally a matter of inhabiting the contingency of their lives.

"Everybody Is Moving out There"

People in my field site who were considered to have improved their lives expressed awareness of this disconnect between being a good person and finding a chance. For instance, when I asked Mimi, a young hotel manager living in my field site, about social opportunities and chance, she replied that young people should work and move around if they want to find opportunities. They should not fool themselves that *idil* will knock at their door and wake them up, she said.

As we have seen throughout this book, Haile and Ibrahim and many of their friends had already had a life of "moving around" (*inqisiqase*), engaging with a multiplicity of roles and careers from hustling to education, from construction work to migration, and from selling shoes to participating in the government's entrepreneurship schemes. As we saw in chapter 3, these multiple and possible lives had taken them nowhere. Yet my informants were determined to keep moving. Ibrahim, for instance, saw his business selling secondhand mobile phones (see chapter 5) as an opportunity for making a few extra bucks, but also continued to see whether other potential options would appear on the horizon of the here and now. Buying and selling secondhand mobile phones gave him the sense that he was "moving around," hustling for a chance. As he put it to me, describing how he combined his job at the cooperative of parking guys with his mobile phone business: "Marco, you know me, I cannot just be like this, just doing one thing."

Like him, many among my interlocutors were busy moving around. They did not do so because they had a clear vision of their future; indeed, their past and present experiences would suggest to them that they could not expect much from the future. Rather, their moving around was embedded in an understanding of the future through the lens of the possible. By moving around, my informants were not necessarily going somewhere. They were exposing themselves to the possibility that a chance might come. *Inqisiqase* was not just a practice; it was also a method: a way of relating what is here with what is not yet here.

The importance of moving around was often the theme of the many conversations I had at Mikias's. On a hot afternoon in September 2010, *Kebe* (literally, "butter") came to visit his old friend Mikias. He had just come back from Dubai, where he had been working as a guard. Like many guys back from Dubai, he wanted to show how successful he was. His sharp dress—a black shirt, a white jacket, and a pair of bright yellow shoes—surely made the point. He sat for a few minutes telling his old friends what his new home looked like. "Dubai is a very nice city," *Kebe* began, describing how modern it was and how you could find everything there. Then, he ended: "You guys, better you move around, you shouldn't stay here chewing *khat* all day. Everybody is moving out there."

As soon as he left, those in the room engaged in intense conversation. Brahanu, an old friend of Ibrahim's, cried out: "I don't want people to say what I am and what I have to be!" Abiy—in his mid-twenties and a graduate in physics from Addis Ababa University who was then a "parking guy" with Ibrahim and later became a gas station attendant working twenty-four-hour shifts (see chapter 3)—retorted: "I don't know how this guy was before, but he has changed his life. You don't think you will get your chance by just sitting around here do you? Where do you think your chance will come from if you don't work? How could you say this?"

Ibrahim looked crestfallen. Abiy turned to me: "Marco, everybody believes in *idil*. There are these guys having children, they just think that because of the *idil* God will feed them. It does not work like this. You have to work, taking any kind of job and little by little you can move up. You have to get experience of things, you learn how to do things. You have to keep on working, then you will get your *idil*. Maybe, after one year, two years, five years, when I will be around thirty, I know it will come, but you have to keep on working. You can't understand this by talking to them, Marco, they are done, they are already thirty or even forty, their time has passed."

Ibrahim took the stage and said, "Marco, I know how to sell things, I know how to find things. I even know how women choose their shoes. I had my opportunity to be rich, but I failed. But what else could I do? I don't have to be hopeless. I have to try to go on, thinking that I have a chance [*idil*]."

Abiy added: "You have to work in this life, you don't have to be hopeless. God is important if you are healthy and alive, but whether you are rich or poor does not depend on Him. It is about you, every second is running out, you have to move, go around. It is about your motivation! It is about your feelings inside you. If you don't have it, you don't move."

This discussion about the unpredictable nature of chance and the importance of moving around touched on many of the issues I have discussed in this chapter. With his performance of style, *Kebe* embodied the man who had achieved success because, as Abiy said, "he has changed his life"—even though *Kebe*'s success working as a guard in Dubai was most definitely relative. Brahanu's angry statement voiced the anxieties of everybody else in the room: the fear of being unable to change one's life. Abiy played the role of the young man. His university degree had not opened up opportunities, as he had been assigned to the Applied Physics

Department, which students called the "department of death" because its graduates never found jobs (see chapter 3). The fact that he was young, however, let him think that he would be able to change his life. He believed in God, and this made him think that he would stay healthy and alive. The rest was in his hands, in his ability to move around and expose himself to the possibility of a chance. Ibrahim took a different position: he had had his chance with his shoe shop in the early 2000s (see chapter 3). Unlike Abiy, he had less ground to say he had "time"—this was the heart of the argument between Ibrahim and Abiy—but still he knew he should not be hopeless.

Despite their differences, the two men agreed on the importance of moving around. In fact, both Abiy and Ibrahim grounded their action and hope in an embrace of uncertainty. Ibrahim hoped because hoping, as I have argued, echoing Miyazaki (2004), is not only a desire for something better. It is a way of readjusting one's action and social navigation in the present to open up for oneself the possibility of the unknown. Ibrahim and Abiy embraced uncertainty by articulating notions of present and future; by situating the idea of getting a chance at the junction of their past, the present, and the indeterminacy of the future; and by referring to an unspecified notion of success. Both Ibrahim and Abiy were convinced they could not be hopeless or indulge their worries, because by doing so, they would have denied themselves what really made their lives livable and worth living: the fact of being on the move, the fact of looking for a chance.

A Life Worth Living

This chapter has examined how people on the streets of Addis Ababa's inner city sought to transcend the circumstances of their living—namely, by translating their *act of living* from an experience of living through and within a condition of marginality to an attempt to imagine ways of being something other than one's constraints. I show how embracing uncertainty constituted the mode of existence for unlocking the potentialities of the unknown and indeterminate, crafting *the act of living* into a site of open-endedness and reversibility.

Embracing uncertainty, in this regard, is qualitatively different from what, for instance, street smartness had offered to generations of men and women in the inner city. Smartness held the promise of living meaningfully through a condition of marginality that could not be challenged and questioned. Instead, embracing uncertainty opened the possibility that things *could* change.

Life is unpredictable, the protagonists and coprotagonists of this book believed. Thus, it might be difficult to really assess whether embracing uncertainty would deliver on its promise. As I wrote in the introduction, we cannot elaborate a final judgment of what a life is about while still in the process of becoming. Only death can give a final and irreversible word to what it could have been and what it has not been (Glover 1990). In this regard, as we have seen in this chapter, embracing uncertainty was a fundamental way of pushing away the possibility of annihilation and self-disruption. As Haile, Ibrahim, and many others built an existential discipline of the self, turning to forgetting or controlling the power of their worries, they exposed the possibilities of that open-endedness that death and madness had denied to some of their friends and peers on the streets.

At the moment of writing, in July 2018, embracing uncertainty has not eradicated the logic of exclusion, oppression, and subjugation that has continued to pervade the existence of the protagonists and coprotagonists of this book. The effects of political authoritarianism and the strength of patterns of social differentiation in the inner city and in the city continue to weigh on the chances that Haile and Ibrahim have been given to imagine opportunities for social improvement. However, embracing uncertainty delivered on one of its promises: it has reinstated the possibility of action and hope in the face of subjugation, oppression, and marginality. It has made live worth living.

Judith Butler (1997) reminded us that the subject is both "the condition for and instrument of agency" and "at the same time the effect of subordination, understood as the deprivation of agency" (10). Embracing uncertainty was a way to recognize both the limits and the constraints of their actions and, at the same, tuned their actions and hope in the possibility that those same limits and constraints could be reconfigured and redrawn. This was possible, they were aware, only by being in the world, by trying to act on the reality we live in, by living in the contingency of life. As Butler puts it, the formulation of this predicament is "I would rather exist in subordination than not exist" (7). As Ibrahim said while making sense of his own limits, "I don't have to be hopeless, I have to try to go on thinking that I have a chance."

CONCLUSION

Haile and Ibrahim

Born into poor families and growing up through the economic stagnation that characterized the socialist regime of the 1970s and 1980s, the protagonists of this book experienced poverty as something that pervaded their existence and their society as a whole. Social inequality existed, but the limited amount of resources and goods circulating in the city made scarcity the overall background of their memories of their childhood and early youth. Amid generalized poverty and scarcity, the street economy offered generations of inner city youth a means of getting by as well as ways of living meaningfully through a persistent condition of marginality. By embodying valued notions of street smartness and toughness, Haile, Ibrahim, and many others in the inner city occupied its spaces and pursued a search for dignity and respect.

Living a tough life enabled action in the face of exclusion, poverty, and marginality, yet it had potential costs that Haile and Ibrahim soon became aware of: death, imprisonment, and self-destruction by various means. Caught in this predicament, Haile, Ibrahim, and many among their peers embarked on a search for a better life, away from the streets of the inner city. The circumstances of this search significantly affected how far they could actually go. At first, the economic growth that followed economic liberalization in the 1990s and early 2000s molded the horizons of their existence and their sense of the trajectory of their lives. It did this not through prefigured ideas of a "good life" but by triggering the idea that a quest for a better life (meaning the search for something preferable to their current existence or their parents' lives) could be effectively pursued. Unfortunately, this calculation turned out to be only partly true. Trying to take advantage of the expansion of the city's economies, my informants engaged with a multiplicity of careers and activities. However, these alternative careers took them nowhere. Either these careers failed to open up trajectories of social improvement in the face of the hardening patterns of social differentiation and exclusion that economic growth entailed, or they merely enabled the protagonists of this book to get by while continuing to live in poverty.

As alternative lives did not materialize, street life continued to characterize and define my informants' actual lives. Hustling enabled them to make a few extra bucks to add to their meager salaries. Embodying valued models of smartness and toughness continued to stand in as sources of self-worth and dignity, while street life offered opportunities of enjoyment and constituted the site of their sociality. On the other hand, the fact that street life endured as the only viable and meaningful way of living through marginality brought with it a deep sense of frustration that made the street economy a site of political struggle and confrontation. Ten years after the liberalization of the economy had promised a better future for all, the city's streets witnessed a new wave of street violence. The large number of young men who entered street life in the years immediately preceding and following the fall of the socialist regime were now competing and fighting each other for control of niches of street businesses. A few years later, the mounting frustration this generation felt toward the lack of social opportunities transformed street violence into tools of political contestation when, in 2005, they took to the streets in support of the opposition, asking for change.

This rising street violence and political disorder made securing the streets a key concern of the ruling party, especially in a context where the EPRDF's capacity to ensure political stability was an important factor in donors' and investors' engagement with development. To bring order, the government first responded with heavy-handed repression. Then, it implemented a range of development programs that aimed to rehabilitate and mobilize the "unemployed youth" and ultimately control the streets as a site of political disorder and unrest. The ruling party's intervention was successful in pacifying and politically mobilizing the streets. The implementation of development programs, with community policing schemes and small-scale entrepreneurship, integrated much of the street economy into a regulated, formalized, "developmental," politically loyal, and tax-paying service economy. At the same time, "integration" in this government-supported service economy did not provide a solution to the social exclusion that had long weighed on my informants' life trajectories and their quests for a better life. Instead, integration froze my informants into political compliance and economic marginality, and established a regime of oppression and subjugation embedded in the repressive exercise of power and a violent (and unprecedentedly effective) enforcement of social and political hierarchies.

Political authoritarianism and growing social inequality significantly constrained Haile's and Ibrahim's quests for a better life. However, aspirations of social improvement still populated minds and desires, as their willingness to keep moving, looking for a chance (*idil*), clearly suggests. This enduring expectation of a better life could be interpreted as a consequence of the current conjuncture of economic success: in spite of political authoritarianism and growing social inequality, economic growth and development enjoy a wider legitimacy because urban visions of abundance and success continue to shape the horizons of wants and desires of the marginalized. This interpretation may be true to an extent. There is no doubt that Haile and Ibrahim, like many others in this book, wanted to be rich. At the same time, if we consider how my informants related to wealth and the ruling party's development politics, we can appreciate how ambivalent the legitimacy of economic growth and development was for them. Attempts to reinstate hope and their desires for a better life in the face of marginality were imbued by a concern with emphasizing their distance from, and moral incommensurability with, the forces, powers, and attitudes that they regarded both as dominating the country's economy and as being directly responsible for their condition of exclusion: the immoral occult economies of the rich, the selfishness of the city and inner city businesspeople, and the fakeness of the ruling party's politics.

I read this ambivalence as a moral and existential tension. It is a tension between the legitimate desire of being something other than one's constraints—or more simply, for enjoying the benefits of living in a time of economic promise— and the recognition that the logics of power, success, and privilege that produce growth and development also contribute to the deepening of oppression, subjugation, and marginality. In these circumstances, embracing uncertainty and searching for open-endedness were my informants' attempts to reestablish grounds for action and hope in the face of the bleakness of the known, while seeing promise, potentiality, and possibility in what has not been yet and potentially could be.

The Act of Living

The title of the book, *The Act of Living*, gives a name to this moral and existential tension between people's attempts to be something other than one's constraints and the awareness of living an existence that is firmly embedded in experiences of subjugation and exclusion. I argue that this tension endures unresolved because while marginality and oppression persist through history, people's stubborn attempts to be "for somewhere else and for something else" (Fanon [1952] 2008: 170) remain untamed.

In portraying this moral and existential tension, I purposefully do not give in to the temptation to claim unilateral allegiance to either side in the long-term and unresolved debates about structure and agency, whether action and subjectivities are inevitably products of circumstances, or whether subjectivities have the intrinsic power to transcend circumstances. These debates remain unresolved because the tension within the structure-agency discussion does not have a historical final synthesis. As this book has shown, while the condition of marginality and exclusion endures, experiences of becoming and living are incommensurable with the ways living and action are governed, and projects of domination are rarely fully successful.

The final contention of this book is that we need to go beyond the assumptions dominating such a debate. Marginality and exclusion themselves are not excrescences of an underlying structure that transcends the subject, history, and the everyday. Nor, as the sociologist Pierre Bourdieu (1977) argued, are marginality and exclusion the results of the way structuring structures regulate actions, improvisations, and practices to be wittingly or unwittingly oriented to the reproduction of the conditions and circumstances of their making (79). The idea of underlying structures that regulate practices and produces a continuity transcending intentions, actions, and imaginations is, I argue, a product of the ways social science has come to objectify its own concepts, transforming analytical tools into social facts (Boudon 1986).

Moreover, as I hope this book has demonstrated, marginality and subjugation have a history that can be fruitfully witnessed, documented, and analyzed. Bringing in history is not to advocate a relativist analysis of social and political phenomena, as Michel Foucault reminds us (2008, 2–3). The analytical gain here is to understand marginality as a historical and political product, contingent on how policies, interventions, acts of government, and the making of regimes of relatedness and interconnectedness have shaped the terms of poor people's membership in society, and the limits of their action. As such, marginality is not a social condition produced by invisible hands, operating through invisible structures. Rather, it is the result of actions, responsibilities, and relationships of force that ethnography has the scholarly and political duty to assess, scrutinize, and document (I. Young 2011; Ferguson 2015; Gupta 2012).

By embracing these understandings of living as an unresolved tension and marginality as a contingent historical and political product I moved away from either celebrating the inherent capacity of the oppressed to resist (de Certeau 1984; Comaroff 1985) or, alternatively, closing the circle to state that attempts to live through the condition of oppression and subjugation simply end up reproducing the condition (Bourdieu 1977; Agamben 1998; Willis 1977; Bourgois 2003). Both analytical propositions and dispositions contain the risk of an "ethnographic refusal" (Ortner 1995).

Emphasizing resistance as an inherent dimension of the agency of the weak and the oppressed limits our capacity to understand how modes of existence, imaginations, and actions proliferate within limits and constraints (Jackson 2011). Subjugation and oppression constitute the overwhelming background of poor people's actions. Yet, experiences of living through marginality and exclusion are embedded in moral and existential concerns about being, living, and relating in the ordinary and the everyday, and not always about producing rupture and opposition. Documenting such concerns, as I have done in this book, does not mean dismissing the view that resistance, malcontent, and dissent occur. Conversely, it is an invitation to understand acts of resistance also through an ethnographic exploration of motivations, aspirations, and expectations.

Concomitantly, portraying actions and experiences of becoming as doomed by the weight of domination and the inevitability of reproduction entails a questioning of the ability of the subject to understand the implications of one's actions and own one's intentions and desires. There is a long tradition of sociological and philosophical thought that has either portrayed people's desires as an impediment to action or seen limited purpose in investigating how social actors understand the meanings of their action. For Pierre Bourdieu (1977), for instance, people's meanings, understandings, and intentions do not matter, since "actions and works are the product of a *modus operandi* of which [the subject] is not the producer and has no conscious mastery" (79). "Subjects," he wrote, "do not, strictly speaking, know what they are doing that what they do has more meaning that they know." For Freud ([1930] 1962), Foucault (1982), Deleuze and Guattari ([1972] 1983), and Agamben (1998), subjects desire, and, in doing so, they actively make the self. However, their desires are not their own, being embedded, arranged, and assembled by a social structure that produces and perpetuates their condition of exclusion and subjugation (Butler 1997, 6–14). Building on this tradition, the literary scholar Laurent Berlant (2011) wrote in her book *Cruel Optimism* that modes of existences, potentially comparable to the stubbornness of hope or the existential discipline my interlocutors embraced to seek open-endedness, are symptoms of an attachment to visions and desires of a better life that are "cruel" because, wittingly or unwittingly, they are obstacles to the actual ability to achieve one's dreams.

By focusing on the *act of living*, I recognized my interlocutors' ownership of their desires and documented how their understandings of their actions were grounded in a nuanced appreciation of the working of politics and the economy.

Though pervaded by moral ambiguities and engagement in illicit activities, their investment in street life was driven by a legitimate desire and concern with seeing the possibility of action in the face of exclusion, oppression, and subjugation. Likewise, embracing uncertainty was not just a fantasy, or worse, a form of false consciousness or a "cruel" impediment to the achievement of one's own desires. It was grounded in an understanding that what was known did not give them grounds for imagining and pursuing change. Embracing uncertainty voiced a refusal of what is known and, I argue, a powerful demand for new beginnings (Arendt 1958, 178).

My investigation of the *act of living* has been driven by a concern to bring such claims and demands to the fore and, ultimately, to help rethink anthropological approaches to the study of desires and actions in the midst of marginality and exclusion. While writing the book I committed to taking my interlocutors' desires and reckonings seriously. By describing the tensions in their living and recognizing the ownership of their desires, I aim to have given legitimacy to their ordinary struggles for living, action, and hope. I read their struggles as voicing a concern with crafting their lives into a site of open-endedness and possibility while continuing to inhabit the historical circumstances of their lives through claims, demands, and aspirations that belong not only to the domain of living and becoming but also to history, politics, and development.

A Success Story

Narratives on success and economic growth have shifted representations about Africa, from the continent of crisis, civil war, and famine to the continent of promise. African cities and countries are gradually moving up global indexes on quality of life and wealth (Knight Frank 2015). Increasingly, global consultancy firms, such as McKinsey (2012), Accenture (2011), and Knight Frank (2017), portray Africa as a potential destination for investments in manufacturing, infrastructure, real estate, and retail. This portrayal highlights the dreams of many and, importantly, has the power of mobilizing hope. However, replacing a stereotypical image of Africa as a continent of crisis, civil war, and famine with one of a continent of success and rising wealth remains problematic.

As Stuart Hall (1997) wrote, stereotypes select a few characteristics and traits to describe complex realities, *exaggerating* and *simplifying* these traits to *fix* heterogeneity into a totalizing portrayal of homogeneity (258). Stereotypes fix heterogeneous realities into solidly bounded concepts, expelling and excluding everything "which does not fit" the coherence of that image (258). They offer images that both simplify and exaggerate, turning realities into metaphors of something exceptional and potentially outside the norm and the expected. Portrayals of the continent as one of crisis and famine *fixed* "Africa" as a homogenous reality, doomed by abnormal levels of disorder and disaster (Ferguson 2006). Narratives of success operate in a similar way. They evoke imageries of success, expelling and excluding exclusion and subjugation from discourses and representations of Africa's economies and development. In doing this, they do not just fix "Africa" into an image of promise; they exaggerate traits of success and growth while perpetuating the image of Africa as thriving through exceptions. Imageries of success are powerful, not just because they narrate an existing moment of hope but because they play with imaginations of what is globally expected of "Africa" as a homogeneous geographical, historical, and economic entity.

This book calls for a more grounded and less stereotypical narration of trajectories of economic growth and development. Growth and development trigger imageries of a better future that the protagonists and coprotagonists of this book welcomed and hoped to fulfill through their search for open-endedness. However, what delivered growth and development—namely, political stability and the expansion of the city's economies—also made marginality the terms of poor people's membership into society. Growth has not resulted in a redistribution of opportunities for social improvement. Meanwhile, the pursuit of political stability has been grounded in a pervasive regime of control, surveillance, and repression, which enabled the leadership of the ruling party to pursue its developmental dreams while significantly constraining the ability of ordinary citizens to express dissent and affect policy.

Narratives of Africa's success stories have helped conceal how authoritarianism and social exclusion continue to shape experiences of ordinary citizens. By cherry-picking indicators, features, and correlations, most prominently the celebration of the nexus between the political centralism and growth in the literature on developmental patrimonialism (Kelsall 2013; Booth and Golooba-Mutebi 2012), discourses on Africa rising have provided only a partial account of economic growth and development (Jerven 2015). Such selective and stereotypical accounts of Africa's economies are not just a matter of representation. They have the power to effectively justify and impose a politics of exception and authoritarianism on ordinary citizens (Ong 2006; Agamben 2005; Mbembe 2001, 29). These narratives imply that "Africa" remains a land of exceptions—that both its development and growth are exceptional and require exceptional measures. Following this argument, authoritarianism and social inequality are not to be fought and challenged; instead they are necessary and inevitable steps for the achievement of economic growth and development. Government is not the exercise of mediating between demands and claims as a way of pursuing and imagining collective projects of emancipation. It is a "civilizing mission" (Mbembe 2001, 31–32) of progress, the fulfillment of which assumes a significance, a sense of finality and necessity that transcends the actual demands, experiences, and expectations of those on whom visions and missions of government and development are imposed.

The stories of Haile, Ibrahim, and many others in this book show us how teleologies of development and selective and stereotypical representations of growth have materialized into a politics of space that has carved out a place at the bottom of the urban society within which the marginalized and the urban poor are expected to live their lives and contribute to the making of an African success story with their compliance and obedience. Authoritarianism and social inequality, in this regard, are not features of a distinctively Ethiopian or African way to development and abundance. Arguing this would mean proposing a similarly stereotypical representation of the complex reality that I sought to capture and describe in this ethnography. Authoritarianism and social inequality are historical products and lived experience. They determine the balance of gains and benefits in urban society while shaping how people at its grassroots understand and relate to current trajectories, formulas, and narrations of development.

As I showed in the book, the benefits of living in a better-looking city were not considered a fair trade-off for the experiences of exclusion and subjugation that continued to pervade the ordinary and the everyday lives of many in Addis Ababa. Seeing high-rise buildings popping up in wealthier neighborhoods or recognizing wealth and abundance in the fancy cars passing by on the streets where Haile and Ibrahim slipped parking tickets in return for a meager salary did not give them a sense that they were citizens in a country of promise, progress, and development. Authoritarianism and social inequality have effectively turned the promise of economic growth and development into a wide experience of being cheated out of one's legitimate desires for a better life. Wealth, success, and, broadly, growth and development remain inexplicable, despicable, and unjust.

By reading Ethiopia's success story through the experiences of the marginalized, I have sought to not just give a view from below but also tease out how the making and narration of such stories through necessity, exceptionalism, and teleologies of change fail to fulfill their promises. However, an ethnography of development is not just an assessment of such a failure. It is an attempt to follow ordinary citizens in their efforts to question the logics of power, success, and wealth that marginalize them. The contention of this book is that appreciating the concerns pervading my interlocutors' existence does not just allow us to give complex "thick" descriptions beyond stereotypical and selective representations of the real. They urge us to reimagine the foundations of shared political and social projects for the future, the *success* of which does not depend on the sophistication of these projects but on our collective ability to turn claims and demands into indications of what could be, but has not been yet.

The Politics of Incommensurability

The sense of moral incommensurability that pervaded my interlocutors' understandings of growth and development has direct effects on current trajectories of economic growth and development in Africa. As Morten Jerven (2015) reminded us, economies are fundamentally volatile; conjunctures of economic growth can last for a while but are hardly eternal. In addition, even if economists claim otherwise, the literature has fallen short in proving relationships of causation between specific institutional arrangements and economic expansion in both the short and the long term. At the end of the day, Jerven contended, the feasibility and sustainability of economic growth ultimately depend on adopting and elaborating an "economic policy that reflects the desires of the population at large" (2015, 101). That my informants felt they needed to distance themselves from politics and denounce the occult nature of the city's wealth in order to guard their sense of self-worth and imagine trajectories of social improvement bears witness to how inadequate government policies were in addressing the predicaments of the urban poor during Ethiopia's period of economic growth. What was more alarming is that neither government institutions nor development organizations were making any particular effort to understand these predicaments and to take into account the range of claims, demands, and concerns expressed by the urban poor.

Throughout this book, I have provided an analysis of "politics" as comprising either inner city residents' tactics of opportunistic dissimulation or the strategies that the ruling party employed to expand its apparatus of control. During my time in the field, none of the claims, demands, and concerns that Haile, Ibrahim, and many others expressed at meetings with government officials and at NGO consultations to design new development projects were seriously discussed or considered. For the protagonists of this book, politics was simply not a site for debating and negotiating, even when they tried to initiate such a debate. For instance, while attending a youth conference organized by the local government's youth office in January 2010, about recent government initiatives, Ibrahim stood up and argued that the taxes paid by cooperatives of parking guys (such as the one he worked for) were too high and were a burden on already meager salaries. Later that year, Child Fund, an international NGO in the inner city, invited a select number of young people to gather feedback on a new project for entrepreneurship and youth empowerment. The conversation between the development worker leading the session and the people in the room became particularly animated when training, life skills, and employment opportunities were discussed. While the development worker tried to encourage a general debate about youth, employment, and income-generating activities without referring to individual cases, some participants kept talking about themselves and making explicit requests.

One young man, for instance, insisted that Child Fund should help him get a driver's license. Another emphasized what he saw as a contradiction in the NGO's development programs: he had attended an entrepreneurship training scheme through Child Fund but, after completing the scheme, had not been granted a loan to start his small-scale enterprise. He complained: "How could I work by just taking an entrepreneurship course without having money to start my enterprise?"

When I was in Addis Ababa in December 2014, Haile was troubled by a similar set of concerns, which he had promptly expressed to the local government's youth office. He had been working as a parking guy for the past four years. As he and his colleagues understood it, the local government office was planning to dissolve their enterprise. This had been a possibility since the beginning: the cooperative was supposed to enable Haile, Ibrahim, and their colleagues to build the capital to move from a small-scale enterprise to a medium-scale one. Haile and Ibrahim did not know what kind of business they would be assigned to, but were worried that it would require more labor but without a significantly better salary. Haile was willing to change his life, yet he understood that this would not come by working hard and earning low pay in a medium-scale enterprise as the government envisioned him doing. He was not alone in believing so, and backed by his colleagues' approval, he went to the local government office and proposed a solution. The cooperative had saved a certain amount of money that had been initially intended to help the cooperative grow into a medium-scale enterprise. Haile suggested that the funds be redistributed among the workers so that they could individually initiate their own businesses. "*Imbi alu*"—"they said no"—Haile told me.

Ibrahim and the people at the Child Fund consultation received similar responses. Local government officials told Ibrahim that taxation was not a problem that concerned them; it could be addressed only by the city government. The development worker leading the consultation left the invitees' requests unaddressed and urged them to think in wider terms and not just about themselves. We could argue that local government officials and the development worker did so because they were concerned with keeping the conversation focused. Yet they did not make a particular effort to follow up on these requests, leaving the complaints—and hence the concerns of these young people in the inner city— fundamentally unheard and unaccounted.

I went to Ethiopia in 2015, 2016, and again in 2017 and 2018. Haile and Ibrahim continued to face similar challenges and impediments. "Nothing has changed since you left," Ibrahim told me on a rainy day in the summer of 2016. The cooperative of parking guys was still there, but many of its members were trying to find a way out of it, either by finding replacements for their own work and continuing to receive a share of the profit, or by asking the government to give them their part of the capital the cooperative had saved. Ibrahim found a replacement to work for him at the cooperative, handing him two-thirds of his salary at the end of the month, and keeping the difference. This gave him more time and enabled him to combine his one-third salary with his secondhand mobile phone business. In the end his income was not much different from the one he would have made if he had kept working full time in the cooperative, but the arrangement made him feel free to consider other options. Haile eventually quit the cooperative without getting a share of the capital it had saved over the years. He decided to pool resources with his sister to open a little container shop within the government scheme for small-scale commercial activities. In 2015, Haile was talking about his family shop with pride and excitement. He was selling small items, from chewing gum to bottles of water. By 2016, his mood had radically changed. He realized that the family shop had simply replaced one meager income with another. The prospects of achieving that "life part two" of social and economic improvement for himself and his young son were still out of reach.

The disengagement of government institutions, NGOs, and development organizations from the predicaments that the protagonists and coprotagonists of this book faced is not a matter concerning individual government officials or development workers. It is systemic and emerged from the political project of command underpinning the implementation of development programs at the bottom of urban society and the wider discourse that both government officials and NGO workers shared about the place that "lazy" and indecisive unemployed youth should occupy in society. These views, and the approval that the country's trajectories of economic growth and political stability enjoyed among donors, business correspondents, and policy commentators, strengthened the ruling party's political and developmental machine. At the same time, however, when the world of policy becomes more distant from and less responsive to poor people's predicaments, concerns, and claims, incommensurability not only can harden but can produce an incoherent, harmful, and disruptive politics of incivility (Holston 2008, 274–275). This is a form of "politics from below" (Bayart 1981) that expresses itself through ordinary acts of disorder and crime and has erupted into public space, in South Africa and Brazil, for instance, where the failure of promises of democracy and emancipation has created "new estrangements" (Holston 2009, 271; see also Steinberg 2004; Comaroff and Comaroff 1999).

Ethiopia is still far from these horizons of ordinary violence and incivility. However, the country in 2018 found itself at a critical juncture. In 2014, and more dramatically between 2015 and 2016, demonstrations occurred in the peripheries of Addis Ababa against the attempts of the city government to include the outskirts of the neighboring Oromia region in its planned expansion. Protesters feared that the expansion of the city would result in a wave of evictions and dispossession at the expense of Oromo farmers and to the advantage of the national and international investors demanding land near the capital. Demonstrations soon snowballed, triggering a countrywide wave of protests demanding fairer redistribution of the benefits of economic growth.[1] The government responded with brutal repression before declaring a state of emergency.[2] Between 2015 and 2016, five hundred people died and tens of thousands were detained. The state of emergency was finally lifted in August 2017,[3] and it was soon evident that the government's response to protests had created fractures within the ranks of the ruling party. In January 2018, the then Prime Minister Hailemariam Desalegn—the man who replaced EPRDF ideologue Meles Zenawi after his death in 2012—made an unprecedented move. He released thousands of political prisoners. His resignation just a month later led to a moment of political uncertainty[4] and was followed by a proclamation of a second state of emergency.[5]

After two months of negotiations behind closed doors, at the end of March 2018, Abiy Ahmed was chosen by the EPRDF coalition as the next prime minister.[6] The first Oromo in Ethiopian history to lead the Ethiopian state, dubbed as a reformer and appreciated for his eloquence and openness about the challenges ahead, Abiy Ahmed was viewed as a politician who could address demands for political opening and greater inclusion, not only by party supporters but also critical members of local media and the diaspora. By July 2018, Abiy Ahmed had fulfilled some of his promises. He lifted the ban on those opposition parties that until then had been listed as "terrorist groups," signed a historical peace agreement with Eritrea, revoked the state of the emergency, and stated he was eager to amend Ethiopia's restrictive laws on media and civil society.

While optimism and hope dominated narratives on social media, skepticism still populated the streets in inner city Addis Ababa. When I talked to Ibrahim in May 2018, he, like many others in my field site, remained dubious about the actual possibility for change. "He is a good speaker. But, if you ask me, it is like when

---

1. "What Is behind Ethiopia's Wave of Protests?," BBC News, August 22, 2016, accessed July 18, 2018, http://www.bbc.com/news/world-africa-36940906.

2. "Seven Things Banned under Ethiopia's State of Emergency," BBC News, October 17, 2016, accessed July18 2018, http://www.bbc.com/news/world-africa-37679165.

3. "Ethiopia Lifts State of Emergency after Ten Months," Addis Fortune, August 4, 2017, accessed July 18, 2018, https://addisfortune.net/articles/parliament-ends-extened-state-of-emergency.

4. "Ethiopian Prime Minister Resigns after Mass Protests," *Guardian*, February 15, 2018, accessed July 18, 2018, https://www.theguardian.com/world/2018/feb/15/ethiopia-prime-minister -hailemariam-desalegn-resigns-after-mass-protests.

5. "Ethiopian Lawmakers Approve State of Emergency," *Washington Post*, March 2, 2018, accessed July 18, 2018, https://www.washingtonpost.com/world/africa/ethiopian-lawmakers-approve -state-of-emergency/2018/03/02/.

6. "Ethiopia Seeks Calm with a New Leader," *New York Times*, March 28 2018, accessed July 18, 2019, https://www.nytimes.com/2018/03/28/world/africa/ethiopia-prime-minister-oromo.html.

you move your teapot from one fire to another." It is unclear whether Abiy Ahmed will be able to translate this momentum of political change into a commitment to challenge those regimes of subjugation and oppression that continue to frame the existence of the protagonists of this book. As this book goes to press, the apparatus of political mobilization and control that characterized my interlocutors' experience of politics is very much in place. Dismantling the bureaucracy of surveillance and political mobilization inherited from the previous administration is without a doubt a daunting task, yet essential if greater enjoyment of political rights is to trickle down to those at the bottom of urban and rural societies. An unequal distribution of political and civil rights could potentially further experiences of abjection and exclusion.

The long-term closure of political spaces for making demands and influencing policy, an increasing tendency in the country's wealthy to lock themselves into secured gated communities in the suburbs, and the wider sense of inexplicability and immorality that my informants expressed when they looked at both the ruling party's politics and the wealthy bear witness to a deep fracture between elites and ordinary citizens and show a need for measures to enhance integration across the fence of incommensurability. Incommensurability is not a given, however. It is not embedded in some form of ontological difference, yielding different modes of existence, as a new turn in anthropology is now suggesting. Incommensurability can be bridged through a greater responsiveness by governments, NGOs, and scholars to the claims and demands that the marginalized continue to express. Doing so requires tuning the design of policy and intervention through broader experimentation. And it entails opening the political and civic space for the marginalized to not simply "assess" but also effectively elaborate, affect, and negotiate the terms, objectives, and conditions of the multiplicity of interventions needed to address social problems.

Responsiveness and Open-Endedness

The protagonists of this book turned their search for a better life into an existential appreciation of open-endedness. This rested on an attempt to keep things open in the face of the predictable destiny of poverty and exclusion toward which they felt their lives were heading. This quest for open-endedness pervaded my informants' demands to be granted opportunities to experiment and pursue the trajectories they felt would deliver the change they yearned for. Ibrahim's refusal of work, as Antonio Negri (1978) might describe it, was an attempt to claim time to look for options beyond the condition of marginality he felt relegated to. Haile's request for the small pot of money he felt entitled to after working as a low-paid parking guy for four years was a straightforward demand for open-endedness and an attempt to break the normativity of the notions of development and poverty reduction imposed on him. Being responsive to such requests would entail recognizing the knowledge of social trajectories and economies held by those who express these demands. It follows that entrepreneurship schemes and microfinance cannot be the only options offered, especially when they fail to bring about change. While asking for his pot of money, Haile was already screening the range of business opportunities he felt he could go for. Ibrahim's refusal of work was an attempt to challenge the ways his position in society had been defined through low-wage labor and political compliance. In a similar way, asking to be supported to obtain a driver's license was a demand for training tailored to the city's labor market and the growing transport economy.

Responding to these claims and demands entails a commitment to transform the search for open-endedness into a trajectory of social improvement. This is not possible when development is conceptualized exclusively as a venture concerned with enabling the poor to help themselves and take advantage of the expansion of the economy via life skills training. Amartya Sen's (1999) capabilities approach, as embodied in entrepreneurship schemes, has failed the poor. Instead, we need to tune interventions into a commitment to provide opportunities of continuous and predictable improvement. My interlocutors' understandings of the *act of living* are central here. Life and living are not the denial of politics, contrary to Hannah Arendt's (1958) argument that the will to survive has hijacked politics through the biological, ultimately serving the capitalist concern with reproducing life for feeding the cycle of production. As I have sought to show in this book, life is not the mere experience of letting oneself breathe, and it remains incommensurable with projects of domination and control. Living is a fertile terrain for the elaboration of concerns, aspirations, and expectations that are central to the imagination of the political (Das 2011) as the pursuit of justice, and as a collective project to achieve a fair redistribution of opportunities for economic, political, social, and cultural self-determination (Harvey 1973; Fainstein 2010; Rancière [1983] 2003; I. Young 2011).

As I discussed in chapter 1, Haile, Ibrahim, and many others learned to understand their living in the city as revolving around their efforts to achieve a form of relative yet significant improvement. They expected to be better placed than their parents, and they hoped to enable their children to live a better life than they did. Their search for open-endedness was an attempt to fulfill this generational duty of incremental improvement. Pursuing responsiveness to these claims for open-endedness and demands for continuous improvement would imply questioning the long-held idea that the main objectives of social policy are to change poor people's minds, penalize the unworthy and the lazy, and help the deserving poor help themselves out of poverty (Foucault 2008; Wacquant 2009). Responsiveness rests on the idea that tackling poverty and exclusion requires a collective effort to question the political and social hierarchies that produce subjugation and exclusion. It is a straightforward call for a politics of redistribution that targets poor people as members of society and not as bearers of some form of either commendable or reprehensible morality.

Responsiveness is thus less a vision of an ideal future and more a method of achieving an open-ended future. As my informants understood with their quests for open-endedness, there is not much point in prefiguring a vision of the future. It did not work for them, and it did not work when visions of the future functioned as justifications for political authoritarianism and growing social inequality. Instead, what is required is the elaboration of a method that can get us closer to the realization of something better—moving us away from normative understandings of development (Englund 2006), policies of integration that exclude (Levitas 1996), and politics of empowerment and participation that subjugate (Cooke and Kothari 2001). And when that *better* is not just a trade-off but something imagined, discussed, debated, and pursued openly and collectively, we reach the moment when a better world is coming to be.

Works Cited

Aalen, Lovise, and Kjetil Tronvoll. 2009. "The 2008 Ethiopian Local Elections: The Return of Electoral Authoritarianism." *African Affairs* 108 (430): 111–120.

Abbink, Jon. 2006. "Discomfiture or Democracy? The 2005 Election Crisis in Ethiopia and Its Aftermath." *African Affairs* 105 (419): 173–199.

Abbink, Jon, and Ineke van Kessel. 2005. *Vanguard or Vandals: Youth, Politics, and Conflict in Africa*. Leiden: Brill.

Accenture. 2011. *The Dynamic African Consumer Market: Exploring Growth Opportunities in Sub-Saharan Africa*. Johannesburg: Accenture.

Agamben, Giorgio. 1998. *Homo Sacer: Sovereign Power and Bare Life*. Stanford, CA: Stanford University Press.

———. 2005. *States of Exception*. Chicago: University of Chicago Press.

Akyeampong, Emmanuel, and Charles Ambler. 2002. "Leisure in African History: An Introduction." *International Journal of African Historical Studies* 35 (1): 1–16.

Amit-Talai Vered, and Helena Wulff, eds. 1995. *Youth Cultures: A Cross-Cultural Perspective*. London: Routledge.

Andargatchew Tesfaye. 1988. "Patterns and Trends in Ethiopia: A Comparative Analysis of the Crime Problem in the Pre- and Post-revolution Periods." In *Proceedings of the Eighth International Conference of Ethiopian Studies*, edited by Taddesse Beyene, 431–450. Addis Ababa: Institute of Ethiopian Studies.

———. 2004. *The Crime Problem and Its Correction*. Addis Ababa: Addis Ababa University Press.

Andrews, Edmund L. 1997. "Behind the Scams: Desperate People, Easily Duped." *New York Times*, January 29, 3.

Appadurai, Arjun. 2004. "The Capacity to Aspire: Culture and the Terms of Recognition." In *Culture and Public Action*, edited by Vijayendra Rao and Michael Walton, 59–84. Washington, D.C.: International Bank for Reconstruction and Development / World Bank.

———. 2013. *The Future as Cultural Fact: Essays on the Global Condition*. London: Verso Books.

Arendt, Hannah. 1958. *The Human Condition*. Chicago: University of Chicago Press.

Aspen, Harald. 2001. *Amhara Traditions of Knowledge: Spirit Mediums and Their Clients*. Wiesbaden: Harrassowitz Verlag.

Assefa Damte. 1993. "Urbanization in Ethiopia: Pre and Post Revolution Experience." PhD diss., University of Wisconsin.

Austen, Ralph A. 1986. "Social Bandits and Other Heroic Criminals: Western Models or Resistance and Their Relevance in Africa." In *Banditry, Rebellion, and Social Protest in Africa*, edited by Donald Crummey, 89–108. Oxford: James Currey.

Awol Allo. 2017. "Protests, Terrorism, and Development: On Ethiopia's Perpetual State of Emergency." *Yale Human Rights & Development Law Journal* 19: 133–177.

Bach, Jean Nicholas. 2011. "Abyotawi Democracy: Neither Revolutionary nor Democratic, a Critical Review of EPDRF's Conception of Revolutionary Democracy in Post-1991 Ethiopia." *Journal of Eastern African Studies* 5 (4): 641–663.

Bahru Zewde. 2005. "The City Centre: A Shifting Concept in the History of Addis Ababa." In *Urban Africa: Changing Contours of Survival in the City*, edited by Abdou Maliq Simone and Abdelghani Abouhani, 121–137. London: Zed Books.

———. 2009. "The History of the Red Terror: Contexts & Consequences." In *The Ethiopian Red Terror Trials*, edited by Kjetil Tronvoll, Charles Schaefer, and Girmachew Alemu Aneme, 17–32. Oxford: James Currey.

———, ed. 2010. *Documenting the Ethiopian Student Movement: An Exercise in Oral History*. Addis Ababa: Forum for Social Studies.

Bakhtin, Mikhail. 1984. *Rabelais and His World*. Bloomington: Indiana University Press.

Balsivik, Randi R. 2007. *The Quest for Expression: State and the University in Ethiopia under Three Regimes, 1952–2005*. Addis Ababa: Addis Ababa University Press.

Barber, Karin. 1997. Introduction to *Readings in African Popular Culture*, ed. Karin Barber, 1–12. Bloomington: Indiana University Press.

Bateman, Milford. 2010. *Confronting Microfinance: Undermining Sustainable Development*. Bloomfield, CT: Kumarian Press.

Bayart, Jean François. 1981. "Le politique par le bas en Afrique noire." *Politique Africaine* 1: 53–82.

Bayat, Asef. 1997. *Street Politics: Poor People's Movements in Iran*. New York: Columbia University Press.

Beck, Ulrich. 1992. *Risk Society: Towards a New Modernity*. London: Sage Publications.

Behrend, Heike. 2002. "I Am Like a Movie Star in My Street": Photographic Self-Creation in Postcolonial Kenya." In *Postcolonial Subjectivities in Africa*, edited by Richard Werbner, 44–62. London: Zed Books.

Benjamin, Walter. (1982) 1999. *The Arcades Project*. Cambridge, MA: Belknap Press of Harvard University Press.

Berhanu Lameso. 1983. "Eri Bekentu Sefer." BA thesis, Addis Ababa University.

Berlant, Lauren. 2011. *Cruel Optimism*. Durham, NC: Duke University Press.

Bethlehem Tekola. 2005. *Poverty and the Social Context of Sex Work in Addis Ababa: An Anthropological Perspective*. Addis Ababa: Forum for Social Studies.

Biehl, Joao. 2013. *Vita: Life in a Zone of Social Abandonment*. Berkeley: University of California Press.

Biehl, Joao, Byron Good, and Arthur Kleinman. 2007. "Rethinking Subjectivity." In *Subjectivity: Ethnographic Investigations?*, edited by Biehl Joao, Byron Good, and Arthur Kleinman, 1–23. Berkeley: University of California Press.

Bigsten, Arne, and Negatu Makonnen. 1999. "The Anatomy of Income Distribution in Urban Ethiopia." *African Development Review* 11 (1): 1–30.

Bledsoe, Caroline H. 2002. *Contingent Lives: Fertility, Time, and Aging in West Africa*. Chicago: University of Chicago Press.

Bloch, Ernst. 1976. "Dialectics and Hope," *New German Critique* 9: 3–10.

Boddy, Janice. 1989. *Wombs and Alien Spirits: Women, Men, and the Zar Cult in Northern Sudan*. Madison: University of Wisconsin Press.

Boltanski, Luc, and Eve Chiapello. 2005. *The New Spirit of Capitalism*. London: Verso Books.

Booth, David, and Frederick Golooba-Mutebi. 2012. "Developmental Patrimonialism? The Case of Rwanda." *African Affairs* 111 (444): 379–403.

Boudon, Raymond. 1986. *Theories of Social Change: A Critical Appraisal*. Cambridge: Polity Press.

Bourdieu, Pierre. 1977. *Outline of a Theory of Practice*. Cambridge: Cambridge University Press.

———. 1984. *Distinction: A Social Critique of the Judgement of Taste*. Cambridge, MA: Harvard University Press.

Bourgois, Philippe. 2003. *In Search of Respect: Selling Crack in el Barrio*. Cambridge: Cambridge University Press.

Brennan, Denise. 2004. *What's Love Got to Do with It? Transnational Desires and Sex Tourism in the Dominican Republic*. Durham, NC: Duke University Press.

Brown, Robert L. 1971. "Juvenile Delinquency in Ethiopia." *Ethiopian Observer* 14 (2): 99–114.

———. 1973. "Comparative Statistics on Crime: Ethiopia and the United States." *African Studies Review* 16 (3): 365–403.

Burawoy, Michael. 2012. "The Roots of Domination: Beyond Gramsci and Bourdieu." *Sociology* 46 (2): 187–206.

Butler, Judith. 1997. *The Psychic Life of Power: Theories in Subjection*. Stanford, CA: Stanford University Press.

Butler, Judith, and Athena Athanasiou. 2013. *Dispossession: The Performative in the Political*. London: Polity Press.

Carrier, Neil. 2007. *Kenyan Khat: The Social Life of a Stimulant*. Leiden: Brill.

Chapple, David. 1987. "Some Remarks on the Addis Ababa Food Market up to 1935." In *Proceedings of the International Symposium on the Centenary of Addis Ababa. November 24–25 1986*, edited by Ahmed Zekaria, Bahru Zewde, and Taddesse Beyene, 143–160. Addis Ababa: Addis Ababa University.

Chernoff, John M. 2003. *Hustling Is Not Stealing: Stories of an African Bar Girl*. Chicago: University of Chicago Press.

Chinigò, Davide. 2014. "Decentralization and Agrarian Transformation in Ethiopia: Extending the Power of the Federal State." *Critical African Studies* 6 (1): 40–56.

Clapham, Christopher. 1988. *Transformation and Continuity in Revolutionary Ethiopia*. Cambridge: Cambridge University Press.

Cole, Jennifer. 2010. *Sex and Salvation: Imagining the Future in Magadascar*. Chicago: University of Chicago Press.

Collier, Stephen J. 2012. "Neoliberalism as Big Leviathan, or . . . ? A Response to Wacquant and Hilgers." *Social Anthropology* 20 (2): 186–195.

Comaroff, Jean. 1985. *Body of Power, Spirit of Resistance: The Culture and History of a South African People*. Chicago: University of Chicago Press.

Comaroff, Jean, and John L. Comaroff. 1999. "Occult Economies and the Violence of Abstraction: Notes from the South African Postcolony." *American Ethnologist* 26 (2): 279–303.

———. 2006. "Figuring Crime: Quantifacts and the Production of the Un/Real." *Public Culture* 18 (1): 209–246.

Cooke, Bill, and Uma Kothari. 2001. "The Case for Participation as Tyranny." In *Participation: The New Tyranny?*, edited by Bill Cooke and Uma Kothari, 1–15. London: Zed Books.

Cornwall, Andrea, and Nancy Lindisfarne, eds. 1994. *Disclocating Masculinity: Comparative Ethnographies*. London: Routledge.

Cornwall, Andrea, Frank G. Karioris, and Nancy Lindisfarne, eds. 2016. *Masculinities under Neoliberalism*. London: Zed Books.

Crapanzano, Vincent. 2004. *Imaginative Horizons: An Essay in Literary-Philosophical Anthropology*. Chicago: University of Chicago Press.

Cruise O'Brien, Donal B. 1996. "A Lost Generation? Youth Identity and State Decay in West Africa." In *Postcolonial Identities in Africa*, edited by Richard Werbner and Terence Ranger, 55–74. London: Zed Books.

Daniel Tesfaye. 1991. "The History of Seretegna Sefer." BA thesis, Addis Ababa University.

Daniel Wondimu. 2004. "Crime Incidence in Addis Ababa with an Emphasis on the Nature, Spatial Pattern, Causes, Consequences and Possible Remedies." MA thesis, Addis Ababa University.

Das, Veena. 2007. *Life and Words: Violence and the Descent into the Ordinary*. Berkeley: University of California Press.

——. 2011. "State, Citizenship, and the Urban Poor." *Citizenship Studies* 15 (3–4): 319–333.

——. 2012. "Ordinary Ethics." In *A Companion to Moral Anthropology*, edited by Didier Fassin, 133–149. Malden, MA: Wiley-Blackwell.

Davis, Mike. 2006. *Planet of Slums*. London: Verso Books.

De Certau, Michel. 1984. *The Practice of the Everyday Life*. Berkeley: University of California Press.

Decoudras, Pierre-Marie, and Annie Lenoble-Bart. 1996. "Introduction au thème. La rue: Le décor et l'envers." *Politique Africaine* 63: 3–12.

Deleuze, Gilles. 1990. "Control and Becoming: Gilles Deleuze in Conversation with Antonio Negri." *Futur Anterieur* 1. Translated by Martin Joughin.

Deleuze, Gilles, and Felix Guattari. (1972) 1983. *Anti-Oedipus: Capitalism and Schizophrenia*. Minneapolis: University of Minnesota Press.

De Martino, Ernesto. 2002. *La fine del mondo: Contributo all'analisi delle apocalissi culturali*. Torino: Einaudi.

Dereje Feyissa. 2006. "The Experience of Gambella Regional State." In *Ethnic Federalism: The Ethiopian Experience in Comparative Perspective*, edited by David Turton, 208–230. Oxford: James Currey.

——. 2011. "Aid Negotiation: The Uneasy 'Partnership' between EPRDF and the Donors." *Journal of Eastern African Studies* 5 (4): 788–817.

De Soto, Hernando. 1989. *The Other Path: The Economic Answer to Terrorism*. New York: Basic Books.

——. 2002. *The Mystery of Capital: Why Capitalism Triumphs in the West and Fails Everywhere Else*. New York: Basic Books.

Devereux, Stephen, and Philip Whyte. 2010. "Social Protection in Africa: Evidence, Politics, and Rights." *Poverty & Public Policy* 2 (3): 53–77.

De Waal, Alex. 2013. "The Theory and Practice of Meles Zenawi." *African Affairs* 112 (446): 148–155.

Dewey, John. 1930. *The Quest for Certainty: A Study of the Relation of Knowledge and Action*. London: Allen & Unwin.

Diamantini, Corrado, and Domenico Patassini. 1993. *Addis Ababa: Villaggio e Capitale di un continente*. Milan: Franco Angeli.

Di Nunzio, Marco. 2014a. "'Do Not Cross the Red Line': The 2010 General Election, Dissent, and Political Mobilization in Urban Ethiopia." *African Affairs* 113 (452): 409–430.

——. 2014b. "Thugs, Spies and Vigilantes: Community Policing and Street Politics in Inner City Addis Ababa." *Africa* 84 (3): 444–465.

——. 2015a. "What Is the Alternative? Youth, Entrepreneurship and the Developmental State in Urban Ethiopia." *Development and Change* 46 (5): 1179–1200.

——. 2015b. "'Capitalism Is an Old Word': Labour, the State and Construction Companies in Addis Ababa." Paper presented at the 19th International Conference of Ethiopian Studies, Warsaw, August 24–28, 2015.

——. 2017. "Marginality as a Politics of Limited Entitlements. Street life and the Dilemma of Inclusion in Urban Ethiopia." *American Ethnologist* 44 (1): 91–103.

Donham, Donald. 1986. "Old Abyssinia and the New Ethiopian Empire: Themes in Social History." In *The Southern Marches of Imperial Ethiopia*, edited by Donald Donham and Wendy James, 3–48. Cambridge: Cambridge University Press.

——. 1999. *Marxist Modern: An Ethnographic History of the Ethiopian Revolution*. Berkeley: University of California Press.

Durham, Deborah. 2000. "Youth and the Social Imagination in Africa: Introduction to Part 1 and 2." *Anthropological Quarterly* 73 (3): 113–120.

——. 2004. "Disappearing Youth: Youth as a Social Shifter in Botswana." *American Ethnologist* 31 (4): 589–605.

Elyachar, Julia. 2002. "Empowerment Money: The World Bank, Non-Governmental Organizations, and the Value of Culture in Egypt." *Public Culture* 14 (3): 493–513.

Emmenegger, Rony, Sibilo Keno, and Tobias Hagmann. 2011. "Decentralisation to the Household: Expansion and Limits of State Power in Rural Oromia." *Journal of Eastern African Studies* 5 (4): 733–754.

Emrakeb Assefa. 2005. "An Investigation into the Popularity of American Action Movies Shown in Informal Video Houses in Addis Ababa, Ethiopia." MA diss., Rhodes University.

Englund, Harri. 2006. *Prisoners of Freedom: Human Rights and the African Poor*. Berkeley: University of California Press.

EPRDF (Ethiopian People's Revolutionary Democratic Front). 2006. "Development, Democracy and Revolutionary Democracy." Statute adopted at the 4th General Assembly of the EPRDF. Addis Ababa: EPRDF (internal document).

Evans-Pritchard, Edward E. 1937. *Witchcraft, Oracles and Magic among the Azande*. Oxford: Clarendon Press.

——. 1940. *The Nuer*. Oxford: Oxford University Press.

Ezekiel, Gebissa. 2003. *Leaf of Allah: Khat & Agricultural Transformation in Harerge, Ethiopia 1875–1991*. Oxford: James Currey.

——. 2010. "Khat in the Horn of Africa: Historical Perspective and Current Trends." *Journal of Ethnopharmacology* 132 (1): 607–614.

Fabian, Johannes. 1978. "Popular Culture in Africa." *Africa* 48 (4): 315–334.

Fainstein, Susan. 2010. *The Just City*. Ithaca, NY: Cornell University Press.

Falceto, Francis. 2001. *Abyssinie Swing: A Pictorial History of Modern Ethiopian Music*. Addis Ababa: Shama Books.

Fanon, Frantz. (1952) 2008. *Black Skin, White Masks*. London: Pluto Press.

Fassin, Didier. 2009. "Another Politics of Life Is Possible." *Theory, Culture & Society* 26 (5): 44–60.

——. 2010. "Ethics of Survival: A Democratic Approach to the Politics of Life." *Humanity: An International Journal of Human Rights* 1 (1): 81–95.

——. 2012. "Towards a Critical Moral Anthropology." In *A Companion to Moral Anthropology*, edited by Didier Fassin, 1–17. Malden, MA: Wiley-Blackwell.

——. 2013. *Enforcing Order: An Ethnography of Urban Policing*. London: Polity Press.

Federal Negaritgazeta of the Federal Democratic Republic of Ethiopia. 2004. "Proclamation No. 384/2004 Vagrancy Control Proclamation." *Federal Negaritgazeta of the Federal Democratic Republic of Ethiopia* 10 (19): 2533.

Federal TVET Agency. 2014. *Country Report on Policies and Mechanisms for Labor Market Oriented Technical and Vocational Education & Training (TVET) Provision and Employment Creation*. Addis Ababa: Federal TVET Agency.

Ferguson, James. 1994. *The Anti-Politics Machine: "Development," Depoliticization, and Bureaucratic Power in Lesotho*. Minneapolis: University of Minnesota Press.

——. 1999. *Expectations of Modernity: Myths and Meaning of Urban Life on the Zambian Copperbelt*. Berkeley: University of California Press.

——. 2006. *Global Shadows: Africa in the Neoliberal World Order*. Durham, NC: Duke University Press.

——. 2009. "The Uses of Neoliberalism." *Antipode* 41 (1): 166–184.

———. 2015. *Give a Man a Fish: Reflections on the New Politics of Distribution*. Durham, NC: Duke University Press.

Foucault, Michel. 1979. *Discipline and Punish: The Birth of the Prison*. London: Penguin Books.

———. 1982. "The Subject and Power." *Critical Inquiry* 8 (4): 777–795.

———. 2008. *The Birth of Biopolitics: Lectures at the College de France 1978–1979*. Basingstoke: Palgrave Macmillan.

Fourchard, Laurent. 2005. "Urban Poverty, Urban Crime and Crime Control. The Lagos and Ibadan Cases, 1929–45." In *African Urban Spaces in Historical Perspective*, edited by Steven J. Salm and Toyin Falola, 291–319. Rochester: University of Rochester Press.

Fraser, Nancy. 1992. "Rethinking the Public Sphere: A Contribution to the Critique of Actually Existing Democracy." In *Habermas and the Public Sphere*, edited by Craig Calhoun, 109–142. Cambridge, MA: MIT Press.

Freud, Sigmund. (1930) 1962. *Civilization and Its Discontents*. New York: W. W. Norton.

Friedman, Jonathan. 1994. "The Political Economy of Elegance: An African Cult of Beauty." In *Consumption and Identity*, edited by Jonathan Friedman, 120–134. London: Routledge.

Fukuyama, Francis. 1992. *The End of History and the Last Man*. London: Penguin.

Garland, David. 2001. *The Culture of Control: Crime and Social Order in Contemporary Society*. Chicago: University of Chicago Press.

Garretson, Peter. 2000. *A History of Addis Ababa from Its Foundation in 1886 to 1910*. Wiesbaden: Harrassowitz Verlag.

Geertz, Clifford. 1973. *The Interpretation of Cultures*. New York: Basic Books.

Getahun Benti. 2007. *Addis Ababa: Migration and the Making of a Multi-ethnic Metropolis, 1941–1974*. Trenton, NJ: Red Sea Press.

Glaser, Clive. 2000. *Bo-Tsotsi: The Youth Gangs of Soweto, 1935–1976*. Oxford: James Currey.

Glover, Jonathan. 1990. *Causing Death and Saving Lives*. London: Penguin Books.

Goffman, Alice. 2014. *On the Run: Fugitive Life in an American City*. Chicago: University of Chicago Press.

Goffman, Erving. 1961. *Encounters: Two Studies in the Sociology of Interaction*. Indianapolis: Bobbs-Merrill.

Gondola, Didier. 1999. "Dream and Drama: The Search for Elegance among Congolese Youth." *African Studies Review* 42 (1): 23–48.

Graeber, David. 2001. *Toward an Anthropological Theory of Value: The False Coin of Our Dream*. New York: Palgrave.

Gupta, Akhil. 2012. *Red Tape: Bureaucracy, Structural Violence, and Poverty in India*. Durham, NC: Duke University Press.

Hagmann, Tobias. 2007. "Bringing the Sultan Back In: Elders as Peacemakers in Ethiopia's Somali Region." In *State Recognition and the Democratization of Sub-Saharan Africa: A New Dawn for Traditional Authorities*, edited by Laars Buur and Helene Maria Kyed, 31–51. Basingstoke: Palgrave Macmillan.

Hall, Stuart, 1997. "The Spectacle of the Other." In *Representations: Cultural Representations and Signifying Practices*, edited by Stuart Hall, 223–278. Sage: London.

Hall, Stuart, and Tony Jefferson. 2006. *Resistance through Rituals: Youth Sub-cultures in Post-War Britain*. London: Routledge.

Hansen, Karen Tranberg. 2005. "Getting Stuck in the Compound: Some Odds against Social Adulthood in Lusaka, Zambia." *Africa Today* 51 (4): 3–16.

Harvey, David. 1973. *Social Justice and the City*. Athens: University of Georgia Press.

Harvey, Penny, and Hannah Knox. 2015. *Roads: An Anthropology of Infrastructure and Expertise*. Ithaca, NY: Cornell University Press.

Heap, Simon. 1997. "'Jaguda Boys': Pickpocketing in Ibadan 1930–60." *Urban History* 24 (3): 324–343.

Heidegger, Martin. (1953) 1996. *Being and Time.* Albany: State University of New York Press.

Heinonen, Paula. 2011. *Youth Gangs and Street Children: Culture, Nurture and Masculinity in Ethiopia.* Oxford: Berghahn Books.

Henkle, Heiko, and Roderick Stirrat. 2001. "Participation as Spiritual Duty: Empowerment as Secular Subjection." In *Participation: The New Tyranny?,* edited by Bill Cooke and Kothari Uma, 168–84. London: Zed Books.

Henze, Paul. 2007. *Ethiopia in Mengistu's Final Year: Until the Last Bullet.* Addis Ababa: Shama Books.

Hilgers, Mathieu. 2012. "The Historicity of the Neoliberal State." *Social Anthropology* 20 (1): 80–94.

Himmelreich, Jorg. 2010. "Suburbing Addis: Marketing an African Suburbia." In *Cities of Change, Addis Ababa: Transformation Strategies for Urban Territories in the 21st Century,* edited by Marc Angélil and Dirk Hebel, 133–138. Basel: Birkahuser.

Holston, James. 2008. *Insurgent Citizenship: Disjunctions of Democracy and Modernity in Brazil.* Princeton, NJ: Princeton University Press.

Honwana, Alcinda. 2012. *The Time of Youth: Work, Social Change, and Politics in Africa.* Sterling, VA: Kumarian Press.

Honwana, Alcinda, and Filip de Boeck, eds. 2005. *Makers & Breakers: Children & Youth in Postcolonial Africa.* Oxford: James Currey.

Horvath, Ronald. 1970. "The process of Urban Agglomeration in Ethiopia." *Journal of Ethiopian Studies* 8 (2): 81–88.

Human Rights Watch. 2010a. *"One Hundred Ways of Putting Pressure": Violations of Freedom of Expression and Association in Ethiopia.* New York: Human Rights Watch.

——. 2010b. *Development without Freedom: How Aid Underwrites Repression in Ethiopia.* New York: Human Rights Watch.

Iliffe, John. 1987. *The African Poor: A History.* Cambridge: Cambridge University Press.

——. 2005. *Honour in African History.* Cambridge: Cambridge University Press.

Jackson, Michael. 1989. *Paths toward a Clearing: Radical Empiricism and Ethnographic Inquiry.* Bloomington: Indiana University Press.

——. 2005. *Existential Anthropology: Events, Exigencies and Effects.* Oxford: Berghahn Books.

——. 2011. *Life within Limits: Well-Being in a World of Want.* Durham, NC: Duke University Press.

James, Wendy, Donald Donham, Eisei Kurimoto, and Alessandro Triulzi, eds. 2002. *Remapping Ethiopia: Socialism & After.* Oxford: James Currey.

Jeffrey, Craig. 2010. *Timepass: Youth, Class, and the Politics of Waiting in India.* Stanford, CA: Stanford University Press.

Jensen, Steffen. 2008. *Gangs, Politics & Dignity in Cape Town.* Chicago: University of Chicago Press.

Jerven, Morten. 2015. *Africa: Why Economists Get It Wrong.* London: Zed Books.

Johnson-Hanks, Jennifer. 2002. "On the Limits of the Life Stages in Ethnography: Toward a Theory of Vital Conjunctures." *American Anthropologist* 104 (3): 865–880.

——. 2006. *Uncertain Honor: Modern Motherhood in an African Crisis.* Chicago: University of Chicago Press.

Jones, William, Ricardo Soares de Oliveira, and Harry Verhoeven. 2013. "Africa's Illiberal State Builders." Working Papers No. 89, Refugees Studies Centre, Oxford Department of International Development, University of Oxford.

Kelsall, Tim. 2013. *Business, Politics and the State in Africa: Challenging the Orthodoxies on Growth and Transformation.* London: Zed Books.

Kennedy, Elizabeth. 1995. "Telling Tales: Oral History and the Construction of Pre-Stonewall Lesbian History." *Radical History Review* 62: 59–79.

Knight Frank. 2015. *The Wealth Report 2015.* London: Knight Frank.

———. 2017. *Africa Report 2017: Real Estate Markets in a Continent of Growth and Opportunity.* London: Knight Frank.

Krishnan, Pramila, Tesfaye Gebre Selassie, and Stefan Dercon. 1998. "The Urban Labour Market during Structural Adjustment: Ethiopia 1990–1997." CSAE Working Paper Series 1998-09, Centre for the Study of African Economies, University of Oxford.

Laketch Dirasse. 1991. *The Commoditization of Female Sexuality: Prostitution and Socio-Economic Relations in Addis Ababa, Ethiopia.* New York: AMS Press.

Lambek, Michael. 2010. "Toward an Ethics of the Act." In *Ordinary Ethics: Anthropology, Language and Action,* edited by Michael Lambek, 1–39. New York: Fordham University Press.

Lefort, René. 1983. *Ethiopia: An Heretical Revolution?* London: Zed Press.

———. 2010. "Powers—Mengist—and Peasants in Rural Ethiopia: The Post-2005 Interlude." *Journal of Modern African Studies* 48 (3): 435–460.

———. 2012. "Free Market Economy, 'Developmental State' and Party-State Hegemony in Ethiopia: The Case of the 'Model Farmers.'" *Journal of Modern African Studies* 50 (4): 681–706.

Leiris, Michel. 1958. *La possession et ses aspects théatraux chez les Ethiopiens de Gondar.* Paris: Plon.

Leslau, Wolf. 2005. *Concise Amharic Dictionary.* Addis Ababa: Shama Books.

Levine, Donald. 1965. *Wax and Gold: Tradition and Innovation in Ethiopia.* Chicago: University of Chicago Press.

Levitas, Ruth. 1996. "The Concept of Social Exclusion and the New Durkheimian Hegemony." *Critical Social Policy* 46 (16): 5–20.

Lund, Christian. 1998. "Struggles for Land and Political Power." *Journal of Legal Pluralism and Unofficial Law* 30 (40): 1–22.

MacGaffey, Janet, and Rémy Bazenguissa-Ganga. 2000. *Congo-Paris: Transnational Traders on the Margins of the Law.* Oxford: James Currey.

Mains, Daniel. 2007. "Neoliberal Times: Progress, Boredom, and Shame among Young Men in Urban Ethiopia." *American Ethnologist* 34 (4): 659–673.

———. 2012a. *Hope Is Cut: Youth, Unemployment, and the Future in Urban Ethiopia.* Philadelphia: Temple University Press.

———. 2012b. "Cynicism and Hope: Urban Youth and Relations of Power during the 2005 Ethiopian Elections." In *Contested Power in Ethiopia: Traditional Authorities and Multi-party Elections,* edited by Kjetil Tronvoll and Tobias Hagmann, 137–163. Leiden: Brill.

Maira, Sunaina, and Elisabeth Soep, eds. 2005. *Youthscapes: The Popular, the National, the Global.* Philadelphia: University of Pennsylvania Press.

Markakis, John. 1974. *Ethiopia: Anatomy of a Traditional Polity.* Addis Ababa: Berhanena Selam Printing Press.

Markakis, John, and Nega Ayele. 1986. *Class and Revolution in Ethiopia.* Trenton, NJ: Red Sea Press.

Martin, Phyllis. 1995. *Leisure and Society in Colonial Brazzaville.* Cambridge: Cambridge University Press.

Mauss, Marcel. 1990. *The Gift: The Form and Reason for Exchange in Archaic Societies.* London: Routledge.

Mbembe, Achille. 1992. "Provisional Notes on the Postcolony." *Africa* 62 (1): 3–37.

———. 2001. *On the Postcolony.* Berkeley: University of California Press.

Mbembe, Achille, and Sarah Nuttall. 2004. "Writing the World from an African Metropolis." *Public Culture* 16 (3): 347–372.

McKinsey Global Institute. 2012. *Africa at Work: Job Creation and Inclusive Growth.* New York: McKinsey Global Institute.

McNay, Lois. 2009. "Self as Enterprise: Dilemmas of Control and Resistance in Foucault's The Birth of Biopolitics." *Theory, Culture & Society* 26 (6): 55–77.

Meles Zenawi. 2006. "African Development: Dead Ends and New Beginnings." Unpublished dissertation. Accessed July 30, 2018. http://www.meleszenawi.com/african-development-dead-ends-and-new-biginnings-by-meles-zenawi/african_development-dead_ends_and_new_beginnings_by_meles_zenawi/.

Mercier, Jacques. 1997. *Art That Heals: The Image as Medicine in Ethiopia.* New York: Museum for African Art.

Messay Kebedde. 1999. *Survival and Modernization—Ethiopia's Enigmatic Present: A Philosophical Discourse.* Lawrenceville, NJ: Red Sea Press.

——— 2008. "The Civilian Left and the Radicalization of the Dergue." *Journal of Developing Societies* 24: 159–182.

Miescher, Stephan, and Lisa A. Lindsay. 2003. "Men and Masculinities in Modern African History." In *Men and Masculinities in Modern Africa,* edited by Lisa A. Lindsay and Stephan Miescher, 1–29. Portsmouth, NH: Heinemann.

Ministry of Finance and Economic Development. 2010. *Growth and Transformation Plan (GTP) 2010/11–2014/15.* Addis Ababa: Ministry of Finance and Economic Development.

Ministry of Works and Urban Development (MWUD). 2006. *Industry & Urban Development and Package.* Unofficial translation. Addis Ababa: Ministry of Works and Urban Development.

Ministry of Youth, Sports and Culture. 2004. *National Youth Policy.* Addis Ababa: Ministry of Youth, Sports and Culture.

Mitchell, Timothy. 2008. "Rethinking Economy." *Geoforum* 39: 1116–1121.

———. 2010. "Fixing the Economy." *Cultural Studies* 12 (1): 82–101.

Miyazaki, Hirokazu. 2004. *The Method of Hope: Anthropology, Philosophy, and Fijan Knowledge.* Stanford, CA: Stanford University Press.

Molvaer, Reidulf Knut. 1995. *Socialization and Social Control in Ethiopia.* Wiesbaden: Harrassowitz Verlag.

Myers, Gareth. 2011. *African Cities: Alternative Visions of Urban Theory and Practice.* London: Zed Books.

Nader, Laura. 1972. "Up the Anthropologist: Perspectives Gained from Studying Up." In *Reinventing Anthropology,* edited by Dell Hymes, 284–31. New York: Pantheon.

Nagel, Thomas. 1993. "Moral Luck." In *Moral Luck,* edited by Daniel Statman, 57–72. Albany: State University of New York Press.

Negri, Antonio. 1978. *Il dominio e il sabotaggio. Sul metodo marxista della transformazione sociale.* Milan: Feltrinelli.

Newell, Sasha. 2012. *The Modernity Bluff: Crime, Consumption, and Citizenship in Côte d'Ivoire.* Chicago: University of Chicago Press.

Nieuwenhuys, Olga. 2001. "By the Sweat of Their Brow? 'Street Children', NGOs and Children's Rights in Addis Ababa." *Africa* 71 (4): 539–557.

Nilan, Pam, and Carles Feixa. 2006. *Global Youth? Hybrid Identities, Plural worlds.* London: Routledge.

Nino-Zarazua Miguel, Armando Barrientos, Samuel Hickey and David Hulme. 2011. "Social Protection in Sub-Saharan Africa: Getting the Politics Right." *World Development* 40 (1): 163–176.

Ong, Aihwa. 2006. *Neoliberalism as Exception: Mutations in Citizenship and Sovereignty.* Durham, NC: Duke University Press.

Ortner, Sherry. 1995. "Resistance and the Problem of Ethnographical Refusal." *Comparative Studies in Society and History* 37 (1): 173–193.

Pankhurst, Richard. 1961. "Menelik and the Foundation of Addis Ababa." *Journal of African History* 11 (1): 103–117.

——. 1968. *Economic History of Ethiopia, 1800–1935.* Addis Ababa: Haile Selassie I University Press.

——. 1974. "The History of Prostitution in Ethiopia." *Journal of Ethiopian Studies* 12 (2): 159–178.

——. 1985. *History of Ethiopian Towns: From the Mid-nineteenth Century to 1935.* Stuttgart: Frank Steiner Verlag Wiesbaden GMBH.

Paulos, Milkias. 2003. "Ethiopia, the TPLF, and Roots of the 2001 Political Tremor." *Northeast African Studies* 10 (2): 13–66.

Passerini, Luisa. 1987. *Fascism in Popular Memory: The Cultural Experience of the Turin Working Class.* Cambridge: Cambridge University Press.

Pedersen, Morten A. 2012. "A Day in the Cadillac: The Work of Hope in Urban Mongolia." *Social Analysis* 56 (2): 136–151.

Perks, Robert, and Alistair Thomson, eds. 1998. *The Oral History Reader.* London: Routledge.

Perlman, Janet. 1976. *The Myth of Marginality: Urban Poverty and Politics in Rio de Janeiro.* Berkeley: University of California Press.

——. 2004. "Marginality: From Myth to Reality in the Favelas of Rio de Janeiro, 1969–2002." In *Urban Informality: Transnational Perspectives from the Middle East, Latin America and South Asia,* edited by Roy Ananya and Nezar AlSayyad, 105–146. Lanham, MD: Lexington Books.

Pieterse, Edgar. 2010. "Cityness and African Urban Development." *Urban Forum* 21 (3): 205–219.

Piot, Charles. 1999. *Remotely Global: Village Modernity in West Africa.* Chicago: University of Chicago Press.

——. 2010. *Nostalgia for the Future: West Africa after the Cold War.* Chicago: University of Chicago Press.

Poluha, Eva. 2004. *The Power of Continuity: Ethiopia through the Eyes of Its Children.* Uppsala: Nordiska Afrikainstitutet.

Population Census Commission. 2008. *Summary and Statistical Report of the 2007 Population and Housing Census. Population Size by Age and Sex.* Addis Ababa: Population Census Commission.

Portelli, Alessandro. 1991. *The Death of Luigi Trastulli and Other Stories: Form and Meaning in Oral History.* Albany: State University of New York Press.

Povinelli, Elizabeth. 2011. *Economies of Abandonment: Social Belonging and Endurance in Late Liberalism.* Durham, NC: Duke University Press.

Prahalad, Coimbatore K. 2006. *The Fortune at the Bottom of the Pyramid.* Upper Saddle River, NJ: Wharton School Publishing.

Pype, Katrien. 2007. "Fighting Boys, Strong Men and Gorillas: Notes on the Imagination of Masculinities in Kinshasa." *Africa* 77 (2): 250–271.

Rajak, Dinah, and Catherine Dolan. 2016. "Remaking Africa's Informal Economies: Youth, Entrepreneurship and the Promise of Inclusion at the Bottom of the Pyramid." *Journal of Development Studies* 52 (4): 514–529.

Ralph, Laurence. 2014. *Renegade Dreams: Living through Injury in Gangland Chicago.* Chicago: University of Chicago Press.

Ralph, Michael. 2008. "Killing Time." *Social Text* 97 (4): 1–29.

Rancière, Jacques. (1983) 2003. *The Philosopher and His Poor*. Durham, NC: Duke University Press.

Rankin, Katharine N. 2001. "Governing Development: Neoliberalism, Microcredit, and Rational Economic Woman." *Economy and Society* 30 (1): 18–37.

Riescher, Nicholas. 1993. "Moral Luck." In *Moral Luck*, edited by Daniel Statman, 141–166. Albany: State University of New York Press.

Rogaly, Ben. 1996. "Micro-finance Evangelism, 'Destitute Women', and the Hard Selling of a New Anti-poverty Formula." *Development in Practice* 6 (2): 100–112.

Rorty, Richard. 1989. *Contingency, Irony and Solidarity*. Cambridge: Cambridge University Press.

Rose, Nikolas. 1999. *Powers of Freedom: Reframing Political Thought*. Cambridge: Cambridge University Press.

Rose, Nikolas, Pat O'Malley, and Mariana Valverde. 2006. "Governmentality." *Annual Review of Law and Social Science* 2: 83–104.

Roy, Ananya. 2010. *Poverty Capital. Microfinance and the Making of Development*. London: Routledge.

—— 2011. "Slumdog Cities: Rethinking Subaltern Urbanism." *International Journal of Urban and Regional Research* 35 (2): 223–238.

Sassen, Saskia. 2014. *Expulsions*. Cambridge, MA: Harvard University Press.

Scheper-Hughes, Nancy. 1993. *Death without Weeping: The Violence of Everyday Life in Brazil*. Berkeley: University of California Press.

Schwittay, Anke. 2011. "The Marketization of Poverty." *Current Anthropology* 52 (3): 571–582.

Scott, James C. 1979. *The Moral Economy of the Peasant: Rebellion and Subsistence in Southeast Asia*. New Haven, CT: Yale University Press.

——. 1985. *Weapons of the Weak: Everyday Forms of Peasant Resistance*. New Haven, CT: Yale University Press.

Sen, Amartya. 1999. *Development as Freedom*. New York: Knopf.

Sewell, William H., Jr. 2005. *Logics of History: Social Theory and Social Transformation*. Chicago: University of Chicago Press.

Shiferaw Bekele. 2006. "State and Society (1930's to 1970's): Contextualizing Gebre Kristos Desta." In *Gebre Kristos Desta: The Painter Poet*, edited by Elizabeth Giorghis, Yonas Admassu, and Birhanu Teferra, 21–37. Addis Ababa: Institute of Ethiopian Studies.

Simeneh Betreyohannes. 2008. "Music and Politics in Twentieth Century Ethiopia: Empire, Modernization and Revolution." MA thesis, Addis Ababa University.

Simmel, Georg. (1908) 1971. *On Individuality and Social Forms*. Chicago: University of Chicago Press.

Simone, Abdoumaliq. 2004a. *For the City yet to Come: Changing African Life in Four Cities*. Durham, NC: Duke University Press.

——. 2004b. "People as Infrastructure: Intersecting Fragments in Johannesburg." *Public Culture* 16 (3): 407–429.

Skleton, Tracey, and Gill Valentine, eds. 1998. *Cool Places: Geographies of Youth Cultures*. London: Routledge.

Solomon Mulugeta. 2006. "Market-Oriented Reforms and Changes in Urban Household Income: A Study in Selected Small Towns of Ethiopia." *Eastern Africa Social Science Research Review* 22 (2): 1–30.

Spivak, Gayatri Chakravorty. 1999. *A Critique of Postcolonial Reason: Toward a History of the Vanishing Present*. Cambridge, MA: Harvard University Press.

Steinberg, Jonny. 2004. *The Number: One Man's Search for Identity in the Cape Underworld and Prison Gangs*. Cape Town: Jonathan Ball Publishers.

Stewart, Frank H. 1994. *Honor*. Chicago: University of Chicago Press.

Strathern, Marilyn. 1988. *The Gender of the Gift: Problems with Women and Problems with Society in Melanesia*. Berkeley: University of California Press.

Stroll, Katrina. 2010. "Dubai Fever: The Dream of an Urban Model in Ethiopia." In *Cities of Change, Addis Ababa: Transformation Strategies for Urban Territories in the 21st Century*, edited by Marc Angélil and Dirk Hebel, 150–155. Basel: Birkahuser.

Suriano, Maria. 2009. "Popular Music, Identity and Politics in a Colonial Urban Space: The Case of Mwanza, Tanzania (1945–1961)." In *African Cities: Competing Claims on Urban Spaces*, edited by Francesca Locatelli and Paul Nugent, 261–289. Leiden: Brill.

Tatek Abebe. 2008. "Earning a Living on the Margins: Begging, Street Work and the Socio-spatial Experiences of Children in Addis Ababa." *Geografiska Annaler: Series B. Human Geography* 90 (3): 271–284.

Tegegne Gebre Egziahbier, and Meheret Ayenew. 2010. *Micro and Small Enterprises as Vehicles for Poverty Reduction, Employment Creation and Business Development: The Ethiopian Experience*. FSS Research Report No. 6. Addis Ababa: Forum for Social Studies.

Tekeste Negash, and Kjetil Tronvoll. 2000. *Brothers at War: Making Sense of the Eritrean-Ethiopian War*. Oxford: James Currey.

Thompson, Edward P. 1971. "The Moral Economy of the Crowd in the Eighteenth Century." *Past and Present* 50: 76–136.

Toggia, Pietro S. 2008. "The State of Emergency: Police and Carceral Regimes in Modern Ethiopia." *Journal of Developing Societies* 24 (2): 107–124.

Tronvoll, Kjetil. 2011. "The Ethiopian 2010 Federal and Regional Elections: Re-establishing the One-Party State." *African Affairs* 110 (438): 121–136.

———. 2012. "The 'New' Ethiopia: Changing Discourses of Democracy." In *Contested Power in Ethiopia: Traditional Authorities and Multi-party Elections*, edited by Kjetil Tronvoll and Tobias Hagmann, 269–287. Leiden: Brill.

Tronvoll, Kjetil, Charles Schaefer, and Girmachew Alemu Aneme, eds. 2009. *The Ethiopian Red Terror Trials*. Oxford: James Currey.

UN-Habitat. 2008a. *The State of African Cities 2008: A Framework for Addressing Urban Challenges in Africa*. Nairobi: UN-Habitat.

———. 2008b. *Ethiopia: Addis Ababa Urban Profile*. Nairobi: UN-Habitat.

———. 2010. *The State of African Cities 2010: Governance, Inequality and Urban Land Markets*. Nairobi: UN-Habitat.

———. 2017. *The State of Addis Ababa 2017: The Addis Ababa We Want*. Nairobi: UN-Habitat.

Van De Walle, Nicolas. 2016. "Democracy Fatigue and the Ghost of Modernization Theory." In *Aid and Authoritarianism: Development without Democracy*, edited by Tobias Hagmann and Filip Reyntjens, 161–178. London: Zed Books.

Vaughan, Sarah. 2006. "Responses to Ethnic Federalism in Ethiopia's Southern Region." In *Ethnic Federalism: The Ethiopian Experience in Comparative Perspective*, edited by David Turton, 181–207. Oxford: James Currey.

———. 2011. "Revolutionary Democratic State-Building: Party, State and People in the EPRDF's Ethiopia." *Journal of Eastern African Studies* 5 (4): 619–640.

Vaughan, Sarah, and Mesfin Gebremichael. 2011. *Rethinking Business and Politics in Ethiopia: The Role of EFFORT, the Endowment Fund for the Rehabilitation of Tigray*. Research Report 02/2011. London: Africa Power and Politics Programme.

Vaughan, Sarah, and Kjetil Tronvoll. 2003. *The Culture of Power in Contemporary Ethiopian Political Life*. Stockholm: Sida.

Venkatesh, Sudhir. 2006. *Off the Books: The Underground Economy of the Urban Poor.* Cambridge, MA: Harvard University Press.

Vigh, Henrik. 2006. *Navigating Terrains of War: Youth and Soldiering in Guinea Bissau.* Oxford: Berghahn Books.

Vigil, James Diego. 2003. "Urban Violence and Street Gangs." *Annual Review of Anthropology* 32: 225–242.

Wacquant, Loïc. 1998. "Inside the Zone: The Social Art of the Hustler in the Black American Ghetto." *Theory, Culture & Society* 15 (2): 1–36.

———. 2009. *Punishing the Poor: The Neoliberal Government of Social Insecurity.* Durham, NC: Duke University Press.

———. 2010. "Crafting the Neoliberal State: Workfare, Prisonfare, and Social Insecurity." *Sociological Forum* 25 (2): 197–219.

Waller, Richard. 2006. "Rebellious Youth in Colonial Africa." *Journal of African History* 47 (1): 77–92.

Warner, Michael. 2002. "Publics and Counterpublics." *Public Culture* 14 (1): 49–90.

Watson, Elizabeth. 2002. "Capturing a Local Elite: The Konso Honeymoon." In *Remapping Ethiopia: Socialism & After*, edited by James Wendy, Donald Donham, Eisei Kurimoto, and Alessandro Triulzi, 198–218. Oxford: James Currey.

Weidner, Jason R. 2009. "Governmentality, Capitalism, and Subjectivity." *Global Society* 23 (4): 387–411.

Weiss, Brad. 2002. "Thug Realism: Inhabiting Fantasy in Urban Tanzania." *Cultural Anthropology* 17 (1): 93–124.

———. 2005. "The Barber in Pain: Consciousness, Affliction & Alterity in Urban East Africa." In *Makers & Breakers: Children & Youth in Postcolonial Africa*, edited by Alcida Honwana and Filip De Boeck, 102–120. Oxford: James Currey.

———. 2009. *Street Dreams and Hip Hop Barbershops: Global Fantasy in Urban Tanzania.* Bloomington: Indiana University Press.

Wenger, Etienne. 1998. *Communities of Practice: Learning, Meaning, and Identity.* Cambridge: Cambridge University Press.

Werbner, Richard. 2002. "Postcolonial Subjectivities: The Personal, the Political and the Moral." In *Postcolonial Subjectivities in Africa*, edited by Richard Werbner, 2–21. London: Zed Books.

Werotaw Bezabih Assefa. 2010. *Entrepreneurship: An Engine for Sustainable Growth, Development, Prosperity and Good Governance. Book 1.* Addis Ababa: Werotaw Bezabih Assefa / Genius Training and Consultancy Service.

West, Harry, and Todd Sanders, eds. 2003. *Transparency and Conspiracy: Ethnographies of Suspicion in the New World Order.* Durham, NC: Duke University Press.

White, Geoffrey. 2000. "Emotional Remembering: The Pragmatics of National Memory." *Ethos* 27 (4): 505–529.

White, Luise. 2000. *Speaking with Vampires: Rumor and History in Colonial Africa.* Berkeley: University of California Press.

Whyte, Susan. 1997. *Questioning Misfortune: The Pragmatic of Uncertainty in Eastern Uganda.* Cambridge: Cambridge University Press.

———. 2002. "Subjectivity and Subjunctivity: Hoping for Health in Eastern Uganda." In *Postcolonial Subjectivities in Africa*, edited by Richard Werbner, 171–188. London: Zed Books.

———. 2009. "Epilogue." In *Dealing with Uncertainty in Contemporary African Lives*, edited by Haram Liv and Bawa Yamba, 213–216. Uppsala: Nordiska Afrikainstitutet.

Williams, Bernard. 1993. "Moral Luck." In *Moral Luck*, edited by Daniel Statman, 35–36. Albany: State University of New York Press.

Willis, Paul. 1977. *Learning to Labour: How Working Class Kids Get Working Class Jobs*. Farnborough: Saxon House.

World Bank. 2011. *Yes Africa Can: Success Stories from a Dynamic Continent*. World Bank.

Yeraswork Admassie. 2008. "The Gated Communities of Inner-City Addis Ababa." *Journal of Ethiopian Studies* 41 (1–2): 111–141.

Yisak Tafere and Laura Camfield. 2009. "Community Understandings of Children Transitions in Ethiopia: Possible Implications for Life Course Poverty." Working paper no. 41. Young Lives Project, Department of International Development, University of Oxford.

Yonas Alem, Gunnar Köhlin, and Jesper Stage. 2014. "The Persistence of Subjective Poverty in Urban Ethiopia." *World Development* 56: 51–61.

Young, Iris M. 2011. *Responsibility for Justice*. Oxford: Oxford University Press.

Young, John. 1997. *Peasant Revolution in Ethiopia: The Tigray People's Liberation Front*. Cambridge: Cambridge University Press.

Zewdu Temtime Asrat. 1995. "A Social History of Arada c. 1890–1935: A Survey." MA thesis, Addis Ababa University.

Žižek, Slavoj. 1997. *The Plague of Fantasies*. London: Verso Books.

Index

Page numbers in italics indicate illustrations. Ethiopians use a given name plus a patronymic and are indexed in that order.

CPSIA information can be obtained
at www.ICGtesting.com
Printed in the USA
LVHW111833310319
612461LV00001B/100/P